Hello...

...and welcome to the fourth edition of the *Independent Guide to the Mac*, your one-stop guide to buying and using an Apple computer.

Since the last edition, the world of Apple has undergone a series of enormous changes. The iPad has established itself as the world's best-selling and most desirable tablet device, the Mac has seen growth that has outstripped PCs to an almost unprecedented degree, and a revolutionary new operating system – Lion – has arrived, making our Macs not only more fun to use, but better performers, too, as Apple brings together the best of iOS and OS X in one tidy package.

More and more of us are now using the Mac App Store to buy software in a simple, secure one-click operation. Developers have welcomed it with open arms, leading to an explosion of new software for us to buy and try, heralding an age of discovery that, for Mac users at least, rivals that last seen at the birth of the Internet.

There's never been a better time to own a Mac, and this guide is a celebration of the best that the platform has to offer. We'll show you how to choose and buy your first model, and then set it up when you get it back home. We'll walk you through OS X Lion, explaining key concepts so you can get the most out of your new purchase and be productive from the very first day.

We've taken an in-depth look at Lion's core applications, including Mail, Safari and iCal, as well as those tools that are installed alongside the operating system – specifically the various applications that go to make up iLife, including GarageBand, iMovie and iPhoto.

And, when you're ready to move on from those apps that arrive with your Mac, we've highlighted the best applications from the Mac App Store

Whether you're new to the Mac, or an old hand, thanks for picking us up. Turn the page and enjoy the ride...

Nik Rawlinson

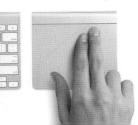

CONTENTS

■ MAC OS X LION

The complete beginner's guide to using the Mac.

■ OS X APPLICATIONS

The Independent Guide to the Mac

EDITOR Nik Rawlinson

ADVERTISING

020 7907 6000 Fax 020 7907 6600 *alex_skinner@dennis.co.uk*
ACCOUNT MANAGER Alexandra Skinner 020 7907 6623
MAGBOOK ACCOUNT MANAGER Katie Wood 07971 937162
MAGBOOK ACCOUNT EXECUTIVE Matt Wakefield 020 7907 6617
AD PRODUCTION EXEC Michael Hills 020 7907 6129
DIGITAL PRODUCTION MANAGER Nicky Baker 020 8907 6056
US ADVERTISING MANAGER Matthew Sullivan-Pond +1 646 717 9555 *matthew_sullivan@dennis.co.uk*

PUBLISHING AND MARKETING

020 7907 6000 Fax 020 7636 6122
MANAGING DIRECTOR Ian Westwood 020 7907 6355
PUBLISHER Paul Rayner 020 7907 6663
MAGBOOKS MANAGER Dharmesh Mistry 020 7907 6100
MARKETING MANAGER Emily Hodges 020 7907 6270

DENNIS PUBLISHING LTD

GROUP MANAGING DIRECTOR Ian Westwood
MANAGING DIRECTOR John Garewal
MANAGING DIRECTOR OF ADVERTISING Julian Lloyd-Evans
NEWSTRADE DIRECTOR David Barker
CHIEF OPERATING OFFICER Brett Reynolds
GROUP FINANCE DIRECTOR Ian Leggett
CHIEF EXECUTIVE James Tye
CHAIRMAN Felix Dennis

HOW TO CONTACT US

MAIL 30 Cleveland Street, London, W1T 4JD
EMAIL mailbox@macuser.co.uk
WEB *www.macuser.co.uk*
PHONE 020 7907 6000

LICENSING AND SYNDICATION

Material in The Independent Guide to the Mac may not be reproduced in any form without the publisher's written permission.
Licensing: Hannah Heagney; +44 (0)20 7907 6134; *hannah_headney@dennis.co.uk*
Syndication: Anjum Dosaj; +44 (0)20 7907 6132; *anj_dosaj-halai@dennis.co.uk*

MAGBOOK

The 'MagBook' brand is a trademark of Dennis Publishing Ltd, 30 Cleveland Street, London W1T 4JD. Company registered in England. All material © Dennis Publishing Ltd, licensed by Felden 2011, and may not be reproduced in whole or part without the consent of the publishers. The Independent Guide to the Mac is an independent journal, not affiliated with Apple Inc. 'Apple' and the Apple logo, 'Macintosh', 'Mac' and the Mac logo are all trademarks of Apple Inc.

Printed in England by BGP Print Ltd, Chaucer International Estate, Launton Road, Bicester OX6 7QZ

LIABILITY

While every care was taken during the production of this MagBook, the publishers cannot be held responsible for the accuracy of the information or any consequences arising from it. Dennis Publishing takes no responsibility for the companies advertising in this MagBook.

The paper used in this magazine is produced from sustainable fibre, manufactured with a valid chain of custody.

Keys and pointers

Not everything on the Mac keyboard is quite as it seems, and if you're using a Windows alternative plugged in to a Mac mini, things can get confusing. This one page guide will keep you on track.

. . . .

■ KEYBOARD

Throughout this book, we assume that you're using a regular Mac keyboard – and an up-to-date one at that. All of Apple's current keyboards feature an 'alt' button, but some older versions have this marked as 'opt'. We call this 'alt'.

Two further important buttons on Mac keyboards are command and control. Command is found immediately to the left and right of the space bar and is marked with 'cmd', an Apple logo or a square with a circle on each corner. This is sometimes referred to as the 'Apple key', although Apple never uses this name. Control is usually found in the bottom left of a full-length keyboard (with a numeric keypad) or beside the

'fn' key in the lower-left on a MacBook keyboard or a Bluetooth wireless keyboard. The key is usually marked with the letters 'ctrl'.

■ CURSOR KEYS

The keys arranged in an upside-down T, with triangles on them, are sometimes referred to as the arrow keys. Throughout this book we will refer to them by their official name, cursor keys.

■ MOUSE AND TRACKPAD

Most Mac mice have only one button. You can click anywhere on their surface to make selections. Current Apple trackpads no longer have any buttons. They can be clicked, though, and if you've enabled tapping through system preferences you can also lightly tap them to select items.

However, the Mac will also work perfectly well with a two-buttoned mouse, like the ones used on Windows-based PCs. Clicking the right mouse button will usually call up a context-sensitive menu for making changes.

On a one-button mouse or a trackpad, holding control while clicking or tapping emulates clicking the right-hand button on a two-button mouse and calls up the same context-sensitive menu. Throughout this book, where we refer to right-clicking, you can use control and your mouse or trackpad to perform an equivalent task.

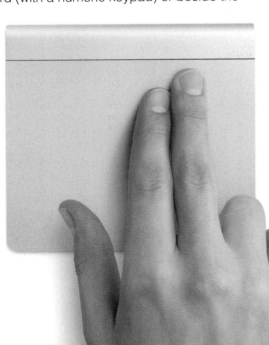

The Mac range

Despite having only five models in its range, with differing specs on each, Apple really has built a Mac for everyone. Starting over the page we'll look at each model in detail, but for the confused shopper, here's a handy overview.

. . . .

■ MacBook Air

The most slender portable in Apple's whole range is also the most affordable, starting at just £849. For that you get an 11in screen (there's a 13in model, too), and a super slim body, which is just 1.7cm deep at its fattest part when closed. Perhaps the most appealing feature, though, is the flash memory storage that replaces conventional hard drives, making this machine not only super fast when it comes to writing and accessing data, but also super quiet, as it has no moving parts. The only compromise is the slim selection of ports and connectors, but if you need them take a look at the bulkier MacBook Pro.

■ MacBook Pro

Apple's high-end portable computers can hold their own against their desktop equivalents, running the most demanding apps without breaking a sweat. Although not as svelte as the Air range, they're far from hefty, but they do boast a full complement of ports, and a slot for digital camera memory cards. With Intel Core i7 processors and powerful graphics processors they are designed for the most demanding users, gamers included. The most recently upgraded models also feature Thunderbolt, the super fast port for external devices, including drives and Apple's latest Cinema Display monitors.

■ MAC MINI

You'll have to look a long way to find a computer more deserving of the name 'mini', for this tiny wonder is just 3.6cm deep and less than 20cm along each side. Despite that it packs a hard drive of at least 320GB, Intel Core i5 and Core i7 processors and a neat memory card slot tucked away around the back. Since the demise of the Xserve server line, the mini has become an even more important player in the enterprise market, with one model eschewing the optical drive in favour of double the hard drives and an installation of OS X Server.

■ iMAC

This graceful fusion of aluminium and glass is a descendent of the machine that revived Apple's fortunes. By packing the workings of a powerful desktop computer into the back of the screen, Apple has given us back our desks, and in the process given us something nice to look at. The LED display, perched on a graceful single-foot stand is as easy on the eye as it is on your electricity bill. The company has even managed to keep the starting price of this most desirable of all desktop computers below £1000. There's an iMac for every user, but if you need a machine that's easy to upgrade, check out the Mac Pro.

■ MAC PRO

It doesn't come with a monitor like the iMac, but the Mac Pro does come with a heap of upgrade options thanks to that smart drilled aluminium case. Inside you'll find four drive bays, up to 12 processor cores and enough memory slots to ensure your apps simply fly. It is, as Apple declares, 'the fastest Mac ever'. Apart from the bragging rights it earns you, one of the best reasons to buy a Mac Pro is its expansion slots, which let you add new graphics or Raid cards, making this an ideal platform for the most demanding of tasks, including movie editing. Just make sure you have at least £2000 to spend.

MacBook Pro

The MacBook Pro is Apple's line of high-end portable computers. There are three to choose from, with screens ranging in size from 13in to 17in, each cut with care from a single piece of smart aluminium.

· ·

Don't be fooled by the current crop of MacBook Pros, which look exactly the same – on the outside, at least – as those that preceded them. Every model has been updates and the insides replaced with faster parts, including new Core i5 and Core i7 processors, which are based on Intel's Sandy Bridge architecture. That's good news as it means big boosts in performance across the range, especially for the new quad-core 15in and 17in models.

The feature that everybody is talking about, though, is the new Thunderbolt port. This offers remarkable opportunities for expansion further down the line once peripherals and adapters hit the market. It also doubles as the display port.

Apple has waved goodbye to Nvidia's graphics support in this range in favour of AMD, the processor giant into which graphics chipmaker ATI was absorbed. The result is blazingly

fast performance to suit graphics professionals, who will be working in applications such as Adobe AfterEffects, Maya and Motion. Choose your MacBook Pro with care and you can even enjoy screen sizes that rival some desktop.

There is considerable variation in price and performance across the range, with prices to suit every budget, so we've looked at each of the five standard configurations to find out how they compare and help you choose the machine that best suits your needs.

Apple has made no changes on this occasion to its aluminium unibody design – a good thing, in our opinion. All models are the same size and weight as before. Milled from a single piece of metal, the shell gives a sturdy feel, while the tapered edges round off the minimalist lines.

The glass trackpad remains a highlight of the modern MacBook Pro. Gestures make it easier to control common features, and they play an even bigger role in Mac OS X 10.7 Lion than they have done in previous releases.

The backlit keyboard helps in photo studios, press conferences and wherever light is dim, too. Its intensity can be adjusted through the keyboard itself. This lets you cut down on the glare that can become problematic as the ambient lighting dims. It can also be turned right down to conserve the battery life.

The MacBook Pro is available as a 13in, 15in or 17in laptop. All display sizes are widescreen, with a 16:10 aspect ratio, and the resolutions are the same as those of previous models. The 13in screen resolution is 1280 x 1050 pixels; the 15in is 1440 x 900 (upgradable to 1680 x 1050 of the time of ordering when buying direct through Apple); and the 17in is 1920 x 1200, making this the only model that can display full 1080p HD.

Like Apple's other current machines, the MacBook Pro has a glossy screen. This improves crispness and looks great when switched off, but

if you find reflections distracting an antiglare option can be chosen at the point of ordering. This is available only on the 17in model at its regular resolution and on the 15in when upgrading to the high-resolution option. It's not available on the 13in model. Some Apple Stores and resellers will also have display stock of the antiglare variant.

The online Apple Store allows you to tweak the configuration of your MacBook Pro before you buy it, but some options here cost a lot more than you'd pay to add the same components yourself. Your friendly local Mac reseller may be able to offer better deals, or you can easily shop around and do it yourself. The manual shows how to get the user upgradable parts but fails to say which size of Phillips screwdriver you'll need. pgrade and repair website iFixit.com has full details.

The standard allocation of Ram in all MacBook Pros is 4GB, but if you're paying for a high-end CPU and GPU it would be foolish not to install a full 8GB, either at the point of purchase or as a self-performed upgrade at a later point.

Solid-state drive options, meanwhile, offer a significant performance boost, but remain disproportionately expensive. Fitting a third-party internal hard disk isn't too hard, and so this remains a more affordable option for those who want to upgrade their machines on a budget. Drives with an equivalent to Apple's Sudden Motion Sensor may cause your Mac to become unstable, in which case try turning the feature off.

One area where these MacBook Pros haven't improved is in their battery life. Apple quotes seven hours for all models, down from the eight to 10 measurement on the outgoing range. We

The MacBook Pro, seen here running Aperture, is a powerful machine, whatever its size. Its more ambitious configurations are sufficiently well-specced to act as a mobile studio or editing suite, comfortably running Apple's professional-grade applications, including Final Cut X and Logic Studio. Pairing it with an external monitor, plugged in to the Mini DisplayPort socket, it works just as well as a full-scale desktop replacement.

carried out our own tests, replicating Apple's Wi-Fi and brightness conditions and updating them with playback of the 30-second 720p YouTube trailer. The model we tested was the 15in Core i7. Although battery life was down, it exceeded Apple's estimate at seven hours and 49 minutes. We suspect differences in the content on webpages are an influence, especially those with Flash, which will explain some of the difference, but unfortunately, Apple doesn't disclose the sites used in its revised tests, so they are impossible to exactly replicate.

The battery should last 1000 charging cycles before needing to be replaced, which, annoyingly, can only be done by Apple.

This latest MacBook Pro line-up represents a significant boost when compared directly to its predecessor. The new processors alone will do much to keep the hardware in step with advancing and ever more demanding software.

The MacBook Pro has always been a viable alternative to a desktop Mac, and with the greater use of gestures in Mac OS X 10.7 Lion the integrated trackpad will be an ever-greater asset which, unless you've invested in a Magic Trackpad, you won't have with a desktop.

It was once true that buying a laptop machine limited your upgrade options when compared to a desktop, but that's no longer the case. Apple offers a generous range of build-to-order options, which should be considered before you place your order. Items like non-reflective screens can't be upgraded at a later date, and although you could conceivably perform end-user upgrades yourself, the uninitiated may well prefer to leave this task to Apple.

. . . .

THUNDERBOLT

▨ WHAT IS THUNDERBOLT?

It's a connection for peripherals derived from an Intel project known as Light Peak. One port provides two channels for 10Gbit/sec of bandwidth in both directions simultaneously. It also provides 10 Watts of power for low-power devices.

▨ WHERE'S THE MINI DISPLAYPORT?

Thunderbolt carries DisplayPort video (with audio) and uses the Mini DisplayPort cinnector, so recent Cinema Displays and existing adaptors work directly with it.

▨ HOW WILL MY WORK BENEFIT?

Low latency and huge bandwidth allows smooth communications between devices; multiple HD video streams can play without stuttering, and files transfer super-fast. Intel says it's trivial to make adaptors for other sorts of interfaces, including USB and FireWire. You might finally use an eSata-equipped drive to its full potential with a MacBook, getting the kind of performance from an external drive that you'd expect from your Mac's hard disk.

▨ WHY IS THERE JUST ONE PORT?

Up to six devices can be daisy-chained from one port. Check that the devices you choose have a second port to allow it. Displays must be at the end of the chain.

MacBook Air

As the slimmest, most attractive computers in Apple's line-up, the two MacBook Airs are light, highly portable and very desirable. They're the perfect companion to a desktop Mac, but could equally hold their own as your only Mac.

. . . .

Apple has spent the last few years working out how to make things smaller. First was the Mac mini, then the ever more powerful iPhone, iPhone 3, iPhone 3G and iPhone 4 and the superslim iPad 2. By its own admission, it has applied many of the lessons learned in developing those products to its notebook line and come up with the latest revision of the MacBook Air. Just 17mm thick as its fattest, taperint to almost a point, it really is a marvel of engineering genius.

There are two MacBook Airs in the range, with 11in and 13in displays. The smaller of the two is almost small enough to rival the satchel-friendly size of a netbook, yet far exceeds that class of device in terms of power and ability. Both

MacBook Airs feature an Intel Core i5 processor, with 2GB of memory in the lower-end 11in machine (upgradable to 4GB) and 4GB as standard in the 13in. Graphics are handled by an Intel HD Graphics 3000 processor with either 256MB or 384MB of shared memory, which is borrowed from the main system memory.

Beyond the screen sizes, the biggest difference between the two is in the amount of storage they pack inside their sleek bodies. The 11in model has a choice of either 64GB or 128GB, while the 13in model has 128GB and 256GB options. Neither comes close to rivalling the hard drives in any other Mac in terms of sheer size, but that's because neither is actually a hard drive.

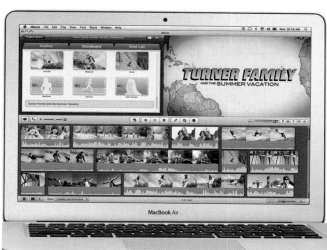

In order to reduce the overall weight of each notebook, increase their speed and improve robustness by doing away with as many moving parts as possible, Apple has chosen to use flash storage instead instead of magnetic hard drives. This has two primary benefits.

First, it's extremely fast, so when you open the lid of your MacBook Air it really is ready for action right away. Applications launch faster and files open and save more quickly.

The second benefit is one of more conservative power consumption. Because there are no moving parts, no platters to spin and no heads to position, flash storage doesn't drain your battery as quickly as a hard drive would, which helps Apple achieve a seven hour battery life in the 13in model and five hours for the 11in Air, despite having had to squeeze the battery cells into such a slim case. They each boast 30 days' standby.

The 11in Air is built around 1.6 GHz processor and the 13in model the more powerful 1.7GHz chip. You can't change the 1.4GHz processor in the 64GB 11in model, but if you upgrade your storage to 128GB you can also opt for a faster processor, running at 1.8GHz. Likewise, while the 128GB 13in model can't be tweaked as far as the processor is concerned, you can upgrade the 256GB Air, again to a 1.8GHz chip. It's worth considering these upgrades if you can afford them as they will likely extend the useful life of your notebook, saving you money in the long run.

The 11in MacBook Air has a native resolution of 1366 x 768 pixels, while the 13in model runs out 1440 x 900. Each has a FaceTime camera.

Of course, Apple has had to make some compromises to achieve this feat of miniaturisation. While there is 802.11n wireless networking and Bluetooth built-in, there's no wired Ethernet port, which would simply be too big to accommodate within the case, so if you need to connect physically, you'll have two use an adapter plugged into one of two USB ports. Bear this in mind if you foresee travelling to a hotel that provides only wired internet access in its rooms, and be sure to pack the adaptor before you leave.

There is, however, a headphone jack and microphone – both useful for FaceTime – a MagSafe connector for power and a Mini DisplayPort for connecting an external monitor. The 13in model also has an SD card slot in the side, which is perfect for digital camera media.

There's no optical drive in any MacBook Air – even the 13in model – but Apple does sell an external SuperDrive, as it does for the server version of the Mac mini, for those who still need to use optical media.

Whichever MacBook Air you choose, it is sure to turn heads wherever you use it in public. Both the 11in and 13in models are among the most attractive notebooks yet created by any manufacturer, and despite their sizes their well suited to both business and creative use.

iMac

The iMac was the computer that rebooted Apple's fortunes. Originally a translucent, madly-coloured squat machine, it's matured to become a sleek, smart, metal and glass device you'd be proud to have on your desk.

. . . .

The iconic all in one desktop Mac features a new range of processors, much faster AMD graphics cards than their predecessors, a tweaked internal design, enhanced storage options and a Thunderbolt port, which not only lets you connect external hard disks at similar speeds to the internal drive, but also promises to make it possible for the first time to add third-party expansion cards. Whatever anyone might say about Apple's real interest lying in the world of iPads and iPhones these days, you only need look at this line-up to see that it's still very interested in traditional desktop computing indeed.

This is a set of machines that runs the gamut from consumer to professional, and whether you're looking at the surprisingly robust entry-level model for less than £1000 for a top end system at around two and a half times that amount, your money is going to be well spent.

Apple is sometimes criticised for producing uncompetitive hardware, in which the lowest-end model comes nowhere close to matching the price of a low-end PC. That's true here: you could get a PC for around half the price of the cheapest iMac. In the long run, though, the iMac is likely to win out. Apple puts a lot of thought into the internal components of all of its machines, and if you were to spec up a PC to the same degree, it's likely the Mac would soon look cheap.

As far as the iMac is concerned, then, dual core processors are no more. Every model now has a brand-new Core i5 at its centre, with four cores to chew through the most demanding of tasks. Unlike the Core i5s at the top end of the previous iMac range, these particular processors are based on Intel's latest Sandy Bridge architecture, with optimisations that have a big impact on performance. For even more oomph, higher models can be upgraded to i7 processors, which feature hyper threading to run supported simultaneous tasks more efficiently.

Apple has a history of choosing processors that match the top end of contemporary PCs, but pairing them with graphics processors regarded in the Windows world is a little off the pace, at least unless you shelled out for optimal upgrades. Not so with these machines: the latest AMD chips give them real pizazz, making them ready both to display and to create state-of-the-art motion graphics. With more top end games such as Portal 2 appearing on the Mac, it's great to see Apple's mid-range machines ready to do them justice. Just to make sure, you can even specify a massive 2GB of graphics memory to keep the data pumping.

As before, the iMac comes with a choice of two screen sizes, 21.5in and 27in. We tested all four of the standard Apple Store configurations, two in each case design, plus a special build to order 27in model that sits at the very top of the range. Read on to find out which will be the specification for you, whatever your budget.

The aluminium case introduced in 2009 hasn't changed, with its edge to edge glass front masking the black bezel that surrounds the screen. The rear panel is sensuously curbed, rather like a scaled up version of the iPad, and the overall impression is of extreme solidity and nanometre-precise engineering. The internal standard provides a useful range of tilt, but no height adjustment. With the mouse and, by default, the keyboard using Bluetooth, the only cable required for the whole system is the mains power lead. This plugs in at the bottom centre of the rear panel, with the cable exiting through a circular cutout in the stand, which can also be used to support any peripheral cables to keep things tidy.

There's a built-in infrared sensor for the optional Apple Remote which controls iTunes, Front Row and other apps; or you can use the free Remote app for iOS, and similar apps for other Mac software, to use your iPad, iPod Touch or iPhone as a remote.

Apple's iSight camera has been looking a bit basic for awhile and now the iMac gets the same upgrade as the MacBook Pro, with the ability to make FaceTime video calls or record footage at 720p resolution. Its widescreen aspect ratio helps you fit more of the family into the frame, says Apple, glossing over the fact that for one-person FaceTime calls, it only makes sense if you're lying down. Of more definite benefit is the camera's improved performance in low light.

Also new is an ambient light sensor to the left of the camera, as on iOS devices, which is supposed to adjust the screen brightness (starting from the level you set manually) in response to the amount of background light in the room. The excellent displays are unchanged; the still no antiglare matte screen option, so to avoid reflections rendering the display illegible, you'll need to avoid sunny windows.

The SuperDrive lets you read and write DVDs and CDs, but there is still no Blu-ray option. Below it, a built-in SD card reader saves you connecting your digital camera via USB; it can handle all current capacities.

Although the new high-speed peripheral connection port, Thunderbolt, first saw light of day when Apple updated its MacBook Pro, we've yet to lay hands on any actual Thunderbolt peripherals to test, although companies including LaCie, Promise and Sonnet have announced a variety of products that will be available by the time you read this.

They include storage that can play 5K video or as many as six 10-bit HD video files simultaneously at full resolution, thanks to Thunderbolt's impressive bandwidth. It isn't just about high-end storage, though. Other products will bring unprecedented expansion possibilities to the iMac.

Sonnet announced a FireWire 800 adapter at the NAB show in April, and Thunderbolt's direct access to the Mac's PCI Express bus means adapters for all interfaces are a possibility. It might be possible to reap the speed benefits of an eSata port on an existing external hard drive, for example. Even more interestingly, Sonnet's external PCIe card enclosures will allow conventional expansion cards to be added. These will be installed in a box of the end of a Thunderbolt cable instead of inside the computer, which is impossible with the iMac's case design.

Thunderbolt isn't exclusive to Apple. It's a joint-venture with Intel, and the specification is available to PC manufacturers, too. Apple's Boot Camp drivers include support for Thunderbolt, so you can make use of Windows-specific hardware as well if you run Windows on your iMac.

Thunderbolt provides a connection for external peripherals. Each port allows two channels of 10Gbits/sec in both directions at the same time, and up to 10 Watts of power for devices.

Up to six devices can be connected to a single port. Do check the devices you buy have a second port to allow for this, though, especially with the 21.5in iMac, otherwise will have to choose between peripherals and a second display.

Thunderbolt uses the same physical connector as Mini DisplayPort, the monitor output on all recent Macs, and it can carry DisplayPort video (with audio) at the same time as sending data back and forth to peripherals. The display must be connected to the end of the chain.

Recent Apple Cinema Displays can be connected directly to the port and the iMac can drive even the massive 30in model at its full resolution of 2560 x 1600. Monitors with a VGA or DVI ports can be hooked up using one of Apple's existing Mini DisplayPort adaptors.

The 27in iMacs allow you to connect two additional displays, enabling an even larger

workspace in creative apps. Although some very demanding tasks will still require a Mac Pro, only a small minority of users won't be satisfied.

Every Mac comes with iLife 11. When you order from the Apple Store, there's a choice of seven further apps that you can have pre-installed. In the past, this was a handy option, but the prices haven't been updated to match the better deals you'll be able to get directly from the online Mac App Store after you set up your machine.

Aperture is the worst offender, charged at the boxed price even though you don't get the box. It is also cheaper to buy the constituent applications within iWork individually from the App Store that it is to buy iWork pre-installed. A further advantage of buying later is that Mac App Store purchases can be installed on multiple Macs as long as they're authorised using the same Apple ID; this makes the iWork Family Pack option redundant.

No all-in-one computer is going to be easy to get inside to replace parts, and adding extra components is generally prevented by lack of space. The iMac does provide some small

exceptions to these rules, though. Independent repair website iFixit.com found it was relatively easy, by service engineer standards, to remove the glass display panel, which is held in place with magnets, and then to go on and remove the LCD screen itself, revealing the iMac's internals. We wouldn't try it at home, though.

Memory is the only component counted by Apple as user serviceable and is very easy to fit: lie the iMac down, remove the central panel from the grill under the front edge using an ordinary crosshead screwdriver, pull some rather stiff tabs to eject the existing Ram. Apart from the entry-level model, the new iMacs have a 1TB drive as standard, upgradable to 2TB. The hard drive can be swapped later, but with no easy DIY way to get at it it'll be an engineer job. Since Apple has started using a non-standard pinout for its drive connectors, you won't appeal to choose just any replacement hard disk, either: fitting a unit that hasn't been specially adapted will result in the iMac's cooling fans whirring at maximum speed non-stop.

Mac Pro

Apple may be best known for the iPad, iPod and iPhone, but it's by no means a lightweight when it comes to desktop computing. The Mac Pro line can hold its own against even the most powerful competitors.

· ·

The Mac Pro is Apple's high end workstation computer. Since the demise of the Xserve, it is also one of the company's two suggested options for users who want to run Mac OS X Server, the other being the Mac mini, which includes Mac OS X Server as one of its default installation options.

The Mac Pro is one of only two Apple lines to ship without a monitor. Inside the box you'll find only the computer itself, plus a keyboard and mouse, cables, documentation and installation media. All of the machines in the range are built around Intel Xeon processors, and they are the fastest and most capable computers Apple sells.

They are also the most flexible, being the only ones to feature internal expansion slots. The introduction of Thunderbolt ports on the new iMac and MacBook Pro have, however, gone some way to addressing this issue, as the port will be able to accommodate expansion cards housed in connected external boxes.

The Mac Pro dispenses with the need for such boxes, with three full length slots left open. Each provides support for 16-lane cards, with a maximum power of 300 Watts available, divided between the three slots.

Apple has two standard configurations for the Mac Pro. At the time of writing, the 8-core line featured two 2.4GHz Xeon E5620 processors with 12MB of cache per processor. The quad-core line featured one 2.8GHz Xeon W350 processors with 8MB of cache.

Memory is banded, with the 2.4GHz dual processor and 2.8GHz and 3.2GHz single processor systems each shipping with 1066MHz DDR3 ECC SDRam, while the 2.66GHz and 2.93GHz dual processor and 3.33GHz single processor machines sport 1333MHz modules. Each model can support four memory modules per processor, which means it's possible to install a maximum of eight in a dual-processor machine. With 1GB, 2GB, 4GB and 8GB modules to choose from, that gives the single and dual processor machines a maximum 32GB and 64GB of memory to call on respectively. On arrival, unless you've chosen to upgrade the standard configuration, the single-processor machines arrive with 3GB of memory in the form of three 1GB modules, while dual-processor machines arrive with 6GB, again in the form of six 1GB modules.

The Mac Pro really delivers in terms of storage. Drives are accommodated on carriers, making them easy to install, remove and swap. Each machine is supplied with four carriers, with the ability to address a maximum internal storage of 8TB in the form of hard drives or solid state drives. Raid is available as an optional upgrade.

Although the front of the case would suggest that the Mac Pro ships with two optical drives in place, this isn't the case. Behind one of the drive face plates is an 18-speed SuperDrive with double-layer support; the other is left vacant for future upgrades which can, unlike those for the

iMac and other consumer devices, be installed by the end user.

The Mac Pro is far from a slouch when it comes to graphics. Whereas all of Apple's other machines use a graphics chip seated directly in the logic board, the Mac Pro uses a double-wide, 16-lane PCI Express 2.0 graphics card, with a choice of either the ATI Radeon HD 5770 or HD 5870, each with 1GB of GDDR5 memory, two Mini DisplayPort outlets and one dual-link DVI port. Optionally, either can be upgraded at the point of purchase to dual ATI Radeon HD 5770 cards with support for six displays and digital resolutions up to 2560 x 1600 pixels (2048 x 1536 pixels for analogue signals).

The Mac Pro ships with Mac OS X pre-installed, alongside iLife, and Apple offers the choice of a number of point-of-sale installs for those who would rather have their machine ready to run on arrival. These include Final Cut, Aperture, Logic Studio or Express, and iWork.

Dedicated power users, though, should look beyond Apple's default options to the extreme build-to-order model that is available only when ordering direct from Apple.

This 12-core monster features two 6-core processors, each running at 2.66GHz, and as standard ships with 6GB of memory. This is a machine built with the future in mind, and while commanding a high price should nonetheless run and run. If you can afford it, and if you can justify it, it's the ultimate Mac available to date.

Mac mini

The cheapest desktop Mac you can buy is also one of the smallest computers made by any tech firm. The sleek, beautiful Mac mini is a triumph of engineering, and the ideal starting point for first-time Mac users.

. . . .

Smaller than ever before, the Mac mini is nonetheless a more powerful device now than it ever has been in its history. Without even an optical drive slot at the front, you'd be forgiven for thinking it had very limited abilities, but Apple is so confident in this machine's talents that it sells two variations: one regular consumer computer, and a server variation for use as the hub of an office network.

■ UNDER THE HOOD

The standard Mac mini has a 2.3GHz Core i5 processor and 500GB hard drive. Internal memory runs to 2GB and the graphics are driven by an Intel HD Graphics 3000 chip. The server variation keeps the same graphics processor, and hard drive but ups the processor to a 2.5GHz chip. It also has 4GB of memory installed as standard and, obviously, ships with the server variation of OS X Lion.

Around the back, there is a plethora of ports, including one FireWire 800 port and four USB 2.0 ports. There is also an SD card slot like one found on the side of the MacBook Pro for directly downloading photos from a digital camera memory card. However, while this slot is easily accessible on the MacBook Pro, it feels poorly positioned here on the Mac mini, as it is difficult to see without turning the device around. Further, if you have taken advantage of one of the major

Mac mini is a bring-your-own machine; you'll need to provide the keyboard, mouse and monitor, each of which can be bought as an upgrade at the time of purchase. Apple's suggested monitor is the 27in LED Cinema Display, which is a fine choice, and would look great on any desk. However, it's a pricey option, costing more than the Mac mini itself, and needs a large area to accommodate, so not helpful if you bought a Mac mini to save space.

benefits of its small size – the option to tuck it away somewhere discreet – you may find yourself clambering about on or under your desk to find it. It's a shame Apple didn't see fit to position the slot centrally on the front of the case. This would have been a practical solution to the problem, yet not have spoiled the Mac mini's good looks.

The Mac mini leads a double life, for while there is a regular Thunderbolt socket on the rear plate for connecting a monitor (among other things), there is also an HDMI port, which allows you to connect it to a television, and which supports resolutions up to 1920 x 1200 pixels.

This makes the Mac mini a viable alternative to Apple TV, allowing you to play back your media directly rather than streaming to your network. Buyers beware, though, that as of OS X Lion, the bundled Front Row appliation has been removed.

As an added benefit, now that Apple has integrated the power adapter within the case, the cabling is more discreet and will cause less of a mess at the back of your TV unit than was the case with the first Mac mini, which used an external adapter brick.

Apple sells the Mac mini as a standalone product. Unlike the iMac, it doesn't have an integrated display, and unlike the Mac Pro, it doesn't ship with a keyboard and mouse. You can use existing keyboards, mice and displays if they have compatible connections or, in the case of the keyboard and mouse, use Bluetooth, but if not then you should factor in the cost of buying these additional pieces of hardware when working out how much you can afford to spend.

■ MINI UPGRADES

The case design of the original Mac mini came in for some criticism in its early days for not being easy to crack open. However, it wasn't long before enterprising fiddlers worked out that you could gain access to the insides by slipping a palette knife down between the base and side walls to undo the clips that held everything together. This would allow you to replace the hard drive with a more capacious model. Apple has improved access in this case design, with a removable base plate that gives direct access to the memory

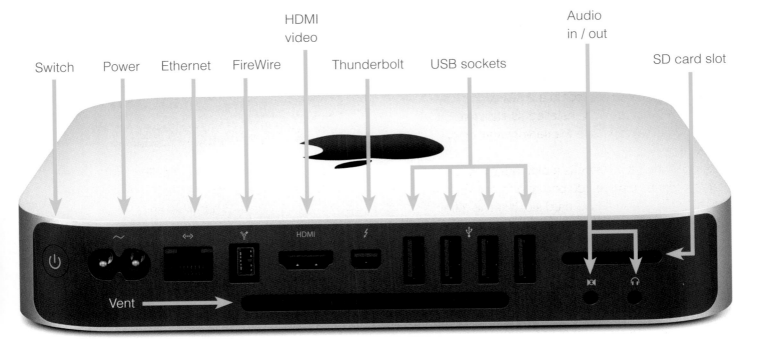

Switch   Power   Ethernet   FireWire   HDMI video   Thunderbolt   USB sockets   Audio in / out   SD card slot

Vent →

slots, allowing you to buy third-party modules and perform upgrades yourself. This will enable you to make significant savings.

If you prefer to order a fully configured machine rather than tweak it yourself at a later date, then there is a variety of options available through the Apple Store. The consumer device can have its memory increased to either 4GB or 8GB, and the hard drive hiked by 50% to an impressive 750GB. You should also consider whether you want to order a keyboard, mouse and monitor at the same time, with Apple offering the choice of either Magic Mouse or a regular mouse, and wired or wireless keyboards, as well as the Apple Remote. At the time of writing, the only display offered as a bundle deal with the Mac mini is the 27in LED Cinema Display. This is a beautiful piece of kit, but costs more than the Mac mini itself.

The server grade Mac mini can have the same 750GB drive upgrade, as well as the option of a 256GB solid state drive. The processor can be upgraded to a 2.7GHz Intel Core i7 and the memory to 8GB.

■ LEAN, GREEN MACHINE

Apple is rightly proud of the fact that the Mac mini is more friendly to the environment than many other computers. In this latest revision, it has kept the machine's power consumption at just 85 W, down from over 100 W in earlier models, and in making it smaller has been able to reduce the amount of packaging needed to transport the product. Even the casing can be recycled.

■ IN CONCLUSION

If you already have a keyboard, mouse and display the Mac mini represents the cheapest rung on the Mac ladder. If, on the other hand, you need to buy these them, then you risk spending almost as much as an entry-level iMac.

Think carefully about your needs before making a purchase, and consider the Mac mini's position within Apple's overall lineup, rather than making it the first and last Mac you consider simply on account of its price.

The beauty of the Mac mini is its simplicity. The unibody case is smarter and sleeker than the first Mac minis, yet Apple has still managed to make the user-serviceable parts easier to access thanks to a removable plate in the base. One single slot – an SD card slot for digital camera media – is housed in the back plate where it doesn't spoil the unit's clean lines.

AirPort

Every Mac is equipped with the necessary hardware for connecting to a wireless network, and while they can use any third-party base station it makes sense to pay Apple's own networking kit some serious attention.

. . . .

AirPort is the name Apple gives to its networking products – the full-sized AirPort Extreme base station and the portable AirPort Express. Allied to these is Time Capsule, a combined base station and networked hard drive used not only to share network connections but also to remotely back up wirelessly connected Macs using Time Machine.

■ AirPort Extreme

AirPort Extreme is the hub of the whole AirPort system. It's a powerful, business-grade base station that works as well in an office as it does the home, allowing up to 50 uses to connect simultaneously and share a single Internet connection.

Thanks to the integrated Ethernet and USB sockets in its backplate, it can share printers and attached drives with all connected users, bringing NAS (network-attached storage) features to

regular drives, and turning regular stand-alone printers into fully networked-devices that don't require a host Mac to piggy-back.

In Mac OS X 10.6 and later, connected drives appear as network volumes in the Finder sidebar, and it's possible to 20create individual password-protected accounts so that users can keep their files and folders secure and away from prying eyes elsewhere on the network. Windows users, and those running an earlier version of Mac OS X, can install a helper application, which will let them access the same resources.

Each AirPort Extreme base station has one USB port and three Ethernet ports on the back, alongside a single Wan port, used for connecting it to your existing network, or to a broadband router whose connection you want to share with other computers in your organisation.

It offers the best compatibility possible for current and legacy devices by broadcasting on

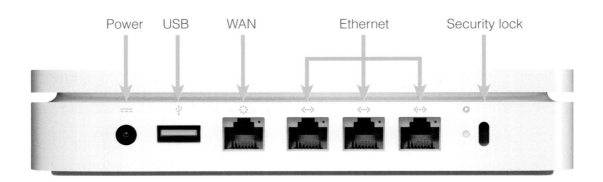

Power   USB   WAN   Ethernet   Security lock

both the 2.4GHz and higher-speed 5GHz band, allowing devices to connect to whichever they can. Apple's own tests reveal it to do this at up to five times the speed of a regular 802.11g base station without MIMO (multiple in, multiple out).

■ AIRPORT EXPRESS

AirPort Express is a more affordable, lightweight network sharing hub. It can connect to a router in the same way as AirPort Express to give a group of up to 10 users wireless Internet access, but its real benefits are its size and additional features.

An AirPort Express device is slightly larger than a pack of cards. It plugs directly into the wall socket using an integrated plug, so doesn't require any trailing leads. This makes it highly portable, and well suited to use when travelling. If you check in to a hotel that offers wired Internet access in your room, you can connect this to an AirPort Express and share the connection without having to pay for multiple users.

There are just three connections on the bottom – a wired Ethernet port for connecting to the rest of your network or the router whose Internet access you want to share, a USB port for connecting a printer to be shared among connected users, and a 3.5mm headphone jack, which is used to connect the AirPort Express to a set of external speakers. Do this and you can stream music from your iTunes library by selecting the AirPort Express at the bottom iTunes window.

AirPort Express is a discreet, portable networking device that lets you share not only your Internet connection, but also your music, by connecting speakers to the 3.5mm jack on the base.

Connect remote speakers to your AirPort Express and use the AirTunes feature in iTunes to play your music library throughout your house.

As well as having a lower maximum user limit than AirPort Extreme, AirPort Express has some other limitations. It lacks the three wired Ethernet ports for connecting local hardware devices such as VoIP phones. It also lacks the AirDisk utility; despite having a built-in USB port this can't be used to share a connected hard drive. This port is used solely for printer sharing.

Like AirPort Extreme, it is configured through Mac OS X using AirPort Utility, with the only physical indicator of its system health being a single light on the front that glows or flashes to indicate its current state. A recessed button on the bottom of the device is used to reboot it should it become unresponsive.

■ TIME CAPSULE

While you can connect an external drive to an AirPort Extreme base station, Apple has come up with a simpler solution for those who know from day one that they want to share a storage device on their network: Time Capsule.

Visually similar to AirPort Extreme, this sleek box has a 2TB or 3TB Serial ATA hard drive hidden inside it. Apple claims that this is a server-grade device, which means it should be well up to the task of backing up several users' data.

Any Mac running Mac OS X 10.5 or later can be set to use a visible Time Capsule as the destination for its Time Machine backups. This means that they don't need to use up a valuable USB port to connect a drive locally, and system administrators can make sure that the data backed up on the Time Machine is looked after and, optionally, physically protected.

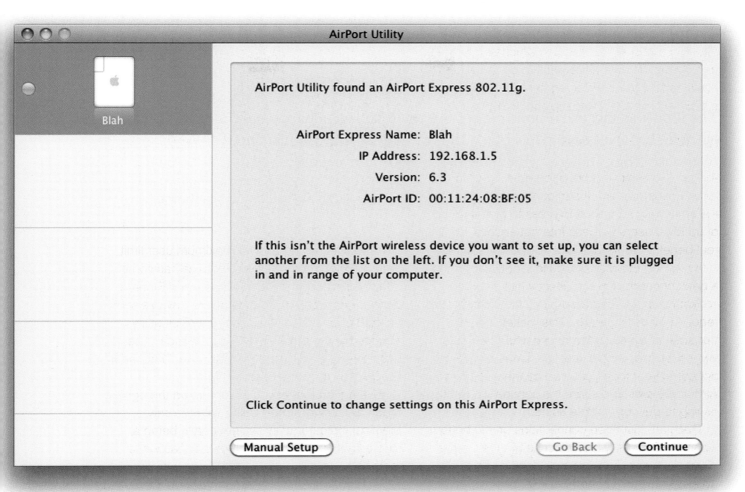

AirPort Utility simplifies the task of setting up and administering your network. It presents each of the AirPort devices on your network in one place with indicator lights copying those on the devices themselves to give you an at-a-glance overview up of the health of your network.

As well as performing backup duties, Time Capsule copies many of AirPort Extreme's abilities, sharing connected printers and external hard drives with up to 50 connected users on the network. It also sports the same collection of ports on the back plate, thus allowing devices that can only use a wired connection, such as VoIP telephones, to access the Internet without Wi-Fi.

It looks like AirPort Extreme, but Time Capsule is more featured, with an internal hard drive.

■ CONFIGURATION

All of Apple's networking products are configured using the AirPort Utility that ships as part of Mac OS X (see grab, above). This allows you to set passwords, change network names and configure how each device connects to the rest of your network remotely, and for any authorised user on the network to act as administrator.

AirPort Utility can update a base station's firmware and reboot it remotely, set up a guest network or change the security settings without having to gain physical access to the device. Each AirPort device is presented in the sidebar, with coloured indicators beside them replicating the condition of the lights on the devices themselves, so you can see at a glance whether any devices on your network need attention.

iPad

The iPod was big, the iPhone bigger, but the iPad is a phenomenon. This sleek, light tablet device has taken the world by storm. With six models to choose from, though, which one best meets your needs?

. . . .

The iPad is Apple's tablet computer. Far more than an oversized iPhone, it works more like this shrunken Mac, with the browser and e-mail client bolstered by downloads from the App Store.

The current iPad is the second-generation model. It has the same 1024 x 768 resolution of the original, but is now thinner and runs faster thanks to the Apple A5 chip at its heart. With two cores and faster graphics processing, it makes the iPad a viable gaming device as well as a legitimate business tool.

The iPad comes in two colours: white and black. Each features a camera in the front and back of the case, allowing you to make video calls using the integrated FaceTime application to anyone else with an iPad 2, Mac or recent generation iPod touch. The camera is also used for the Photo Booth application, which is found on the Mac and used to take amusing photos of anyone sitting in front of the camera.

With the arrival of iOS 5, the latest generation of Apple's portable operating system (which also runs on the iPhone and iPod touch) the iPad is a more standalone product than ever before. It's no longer necessary to use a Mac to set up an iPad from scratch, and thanks to iCloud it's also possible to synchronise a lot of your data without connecting the iPad to a Mac or PC. Previously, if you wanted to transfer tracks from iTunes on your Mac to the iPod application on an iPad, you had no choice but to connect the two together and

perform a physical synchronisation. Now, though, the iCloud service keeps an eye on much of what you do with your iPad and any Mac or iPhone registered to the same Apple ID and synchronises data passively over the air. So, buy a track on your Mac and it will immediately appear on your iPad and iPhone. Buy an app on your iPhone and, if it's compatible, it will be simultaneously installed on your iPad and backed up on your Mac.

There are six iPads to choose from in each colour. The differences are their capacities – 16GB, 32GB and 64GB – and their connectivity options. Each of those capacities comes with a choice of Wi-Fi and Bluetooth connectivity, or Wi-Fi, Bluetooth and cellphone network connections. The former options share data over your home network, while the other extends these features when you're out and about.

If you have a Wi-Fi network at home and at work, you might still want to buy one of the 3G-enabled models, but rather than signing up to an ongoing data plan, you could choose to pay-as-you-go, sourcing a Sim that allows a limited amount of data on a specified number of days each month for use only in emergencies. Although each day would work out individually more expensive, over the course of the month you would have made a significant saving by not paying for those days when you didn't need to use it. This can reduce the cost of running your iPad over its total life.

The iPad is smaller than a sheet of A4, and 8.8mm deep. The Wi-Fi and Bluetooth model weighs just 601g; the 3G enabled device weighs between 607g and 613g depending on model.

In all cases, the screen is a respectable 9.7 inches across the diagonal, and apart from the home button, volume rocker, mute or rotation switch and power button, is driven entirely by touching the glass surface with your finger.

Under the hood, there's a 25W battery, which Apple says will run for 10 hours on Wi-Fi and nine on 3G. It has a stereo headphone jack, and a built-in speaker and mic to enable voice features. All models can triangulate your position using Wi-Fi and a built-in digital compass to accurately plot your position on maps and append geotagging data to photos, but if this kind of data is of particular importance to you, consider upgrading to the 3G model, which supplements those features with assisted GPS and cellular triangulation using features built into the 3G chip.

The iPad ships with a wide range of applications already installed. Mobile editions of iCal, Address Book, Mail and Safari will be immediately familiar to anyone who has used the equivalents on a Mac, and the built-in App Store looks very similar to the Mac App Store in OS X. Some apps aren't what they might seem. ITunes isn't used to play back music and videos, as it is on the Mac, but instead used to buy media that is then played in the music and video applications.

The iPad also features an ebook application called iBooks, which is tied to Apple's own bookstore. This works in much the same way as the Kindle from Amazon, allowing you to buy books directly and have them delivered to your device. If you're reading the same book on multiple devices-say, then your position on each one will be synchronised with the other so that they are always on the same page. Although you can browse books using iTunes on the Mac, you can't, sadly, buy books to read in OS X.

When choosing an iPad, therefore, you need to consider not so much what software it's running, as that is the same across all devices, but how you think you will end up using it. The iPad is such a first-class media playback device that it's likely downloaded media will consume the majority of the space on your device. Capacity, therefore, should be your prime consideration, as you will likely know already whether or not you should opt for a 3G enabled device. So what do each of the three iPad capacities mean in the real world?

Obviously the amount you have available will be determined in part by the number of third-party applications you install, the size of your Address Book, how many documents you have created in the various iWork applications and so on, but even the smallest 16GB device will be enough to keep you entertained for hours.

Using Apple's figures for the iPod, 16GB gives you space for up to 4000 songs or 16 hours of video, which will outlast the battery life of 10 hours. Double this to 32GB and you more or less double the capacity: 7000 songs and 40 hours of video. Not surprisingly the capacity of 64GB allows for 14,000 songs and 80 hours of video.

It is up to you how much storage you want to invest in, but the highest capacity device is the best value, as you have already invested in the base specification, so are only paying for a marginal increase in memory. But does that mean is right for you? 64GB is an awful lot of space. If you assume that every track in your collection is around four minutes long, as Apple does, 14,000 of them would run for 39 days back-to-back and that's without allowing for a short gap between each one. And 80 hours of video is almost enough to watch the entire James Bond series from Dr No to Quantum of Solace twice over.

iPhone

The iPhone was so highly anticipated that it's no wonder it has proved to be such a success. More than a simple mobile handset, it's a fully-fledged portable computer that fits in your pocket.

· ·

The iPhone has been a runaway success for Apple. No other phone manufacturer has managed to capture such a large chunk of the market with, essentially, just one handset on sale at any one time. It may now come in a choice of white or black, and boast various different capacities, but in essence every iPhone is the same... and every iPhone is wildly different, as we each tailor them to our own needs by downloading and installing apps.

The App Store is Apple's ace card, putting the company well ahead of its competitors in terms of range and choice. After all, you only buy a smartphone because you want to run apps, so why would you buy one for which only a narrow range is available? You wouldn't. By offering the best-stocked app store in the market, Apple has simultaneously offered its users access to the most versatile mobile phone yet invented, and with every new model enabling more exciting features in third-party apps, it just gets better.

Apple's modus operandi has been to update its handset every 12 to 18 months, and to retain the previous top-end unit as a fallback for those who want a cheaper way onto the iOS platform while benefitting from the kind of wireless out-and-about versatility that even the iPod touch can't rival. So, if you're happy to buy last year's model you can make a considerable saving while still enjoying almost all of the benefits that the current, must-have device can offer.

■ SHORT BACK AND SIDES

The iPhone's almost featureless case has the absolute minimum of switches, buttons and ports dotted around its edges. The most obvious among them is the Home button on the front of the case, which quickly takes you back to the iPhone app menu from which you select the application you want to launch next.

Beneath this, on the underside, is the Dock connector through which you sync it with your computer using iTunes. With the introduction of iCloud this is becoming less important by the day as it enables full over-the-air syncing of your data, photos and applications. Whenever you buy an app on your iPhone it is also downloaded by your Mac and any other iOS devices logged in to the Store using the same Apple ID. Likewise, whenever you take a photo it's added to the list of your most recently captured shots stored in the cloud. Soon it's likely we'll only ever use this connector for charging the iPhone and as an interface with third-party peripherals such as speakers and charging docks.

You'll find the power switch at the top of the unit, alongside a 3.5mm jack connector. This is smarter than the connectors found in the iPod and most other portable media players, and it accepts input as well as providing output. This lets you connect a headset with a built in microphone with which you'd make hands-free calls.

Finally, there's the switch and buttons on the side. The two buttons are volume controls, which affect both the level of the ringer and any media playing through your speakers. The switch mutes your phone entirely, so is an essential feature for anyone taking their iPhone into a cinema. On the iPad this switch is also optionally used to lock the screen in either portrait or landscape orientation.

Everything else is controlled through software by tapping and swiping on the screen which is, of course, the biggest, smartest and most versatile control of them all.

■ UNDER THE HOOD

The iPhone runs on Apple's own A4 processor, making it one of the fastest smartphones available. It has a high resolution 960 x 640 pixel display in which the pixels are literally too small for the human eye to discern. Don't believe us? Pop down to your nearest retailer and take a look.

It has two cameras – one in the front, facing you, and a higher resolution model around the back, facing away – for use with the FaceTime video conferencing software and for taking photos like you would with a regular camera.

The operating system that underpins everything is iOS, the most recent version of which is 5. If you buy an earlier model of the phone second-hand you may find that it's running a previous version, as it will likely have been returned to its factory settings to wipe all of its data. It's well worth updating this to the most recent version compatible with your phone, as some applications downloaded from the store will only run on more recent versions. Bear in mind, though, that as the hardware specification changes, so will the phone's ability ro be updated. Thus, the oldest iPhones are unable to run iOS 5. The current and previous generation, though, are a safe bet.

■ CHOOSING AN IPHONE

So which iPhone is the right one for you? Fortunately choosing is a lot less complicated than it is for iPad shoppers, who have to decide whether they want a 3G model or can manage with a wifi-only device. Anyone investing in an iPhone need only consider capacity.

Any colour you like, so long as it's black or white. The iPhone, for so long available in only one finish, is now available in a choice of two colours. However, there's nothing to stop you tailoring this with your own choice of cover or bumper.

There are two capacities to choose from, with one running to 16GB and the other stretching to 32GB, both provided in the form of flash storage. If you frequently synchronise your media, even the most music-fanatical user could probably manage with the smaller of those two, so shoppers on a budget needn't feel disappointed that they can't afford the top-end model.

Should you buy an earlier model? That largely depends on the kind of demands you'll make of your phone and how often you'll upgrade it.

The last-but-one model always shares around 90% of the features of the latest handset, so will run pretty much anything you should care to download from the App Store. However, it will obviously go out of date more quickly than the newer model, and so your choice of available apps will become narrower more quickly.

However, if you're happy with what the phone does today and don't envisage installing too many new apps on it, then it represents a sensible purchase on account of the cost savings.

That's not to say that app-monsters should always automatically opt for the most recently released iPhone. If you plan on upgrading to the best iPhone currently available as soon as its successor knocks it off its perch – thus always being only one step behind cutting-edge – then that cost saving comes in to play again.

You'll always be able to run pretty much the full range of software available to the bleeding-edge users, but because you're paying so much less for your phone by staying one step behind them all the way, the chances are you'll be able to upgrade more frequently.

Thus, when the iPhone 6 – or whatever Apple chooses to call it – knocks the iPhone 5 off its perch and you upgrade to iPhone 5, you'll have caught up with the one-time tech leaders. Unless they're dedicated followers of fashion, there's a good chance that a lot of them will stick with the handset that they already have, perhaps for the next couple of upgrade cycles (they paid much more than you, remember). You, on the other hand, always buying just less than the latest must-have handset, will able you to leapfrog them to that desirable iPhone 6 before they get there themselves.

In short, then, it can pay to consider not what is the most advanced specification you can afford, but perhaps what is the least advanced specification that will see you through, without buying anything less than one step behind the current headline device.

■ CHOOSING A NETWORK PROVIDER

Finally, before buying your iPhone, it's worth thinking about which network you want to use (and, if you don't plan on using its 3G features, consider instead buying an iPod touch).

If you plan on running your phone on an ongoing contract, it's worth checking out the prices of the device through the networks rather than buying direct from Apple, as signing up to a fairly premium tariff often attracts a discount on the price of the phone. If, however, you plan on using a pay-as-you-go contract, there is unlikely to be any difference in price between buying from Apple and buying from the network.

It's important to factor in the price of the cellphone network contract when buying your iPhone, and remembering that it will considerably increase the overall cost of buying and maintaining your handset over its useable life.

Check for low-cost non-contract deals from the major networks, some of which will bundle texts, calls and up to 1GB of 3G data use for as little as £10 a month, with unused credit rolling over to the next month.

Apple TV

Not a television per se, Apple TV is a neat box that streams your iTunes assets from a drive on your network, and movies and TV shows direct from the iTunes Store with the help of Apple Remote.

Steve Jobs famously described Apple TV as a hobby. It's a monicker that has unfortunately stuck, despite the product being far more powerful and exciting than earlier editions.

The new Apple TV is a small, neat black box. It's far smaller than previous editions – 80% smaller, in fact – having lost the earlier Apple TV's internal hard drive. It has no moving parts, and thus no fan, so it's entirely silent and perfect for sitting in the living room below your television.

Apple TV is, in effect, the ultimate iTunes add-on. It connects to your shared media library to stream your movies, TV shows and music.

Under the hood you'll find an Apple A4 processor – the same as was found in the original iPad and the iPhone 4 – while around the back there's a power socket, HDMI port for connecting to your television, optical output and an Ethernet port for wired networking. A sensor at the front works with the Apple Remote so you can control it from the comfort of your favourite armchair.

Apple TV works even better if you have an iPhone, iPad or iPod touch. For starters, you can swap the sleek Apple Remote for the iOS Remote application, which lets you use a full keyboard to search for media by name, rather than using the hunt and peck menus.

Better yet, because Apple TV uses Apple's AirPlay technology, you can play any media downloaded to your iOS device on your TV without connecting it directly, simply by tapping

the icon on the transport control and selecting the appropriate destination.

Apple TV doesn't have a tuner or any built in storage. Instead it relies on streaming media from a hard drive somewhere on your local network, or direct from the iTunes Store. It doesn't need a keyboard or mouse, so to watch a movie through the Store you search it on your TV screen using the Apple Remote, watch the preview and, when you're sure it's the film you want, start streaming it right away. You can choose from SD and HD versions of each film and, whichever you chose, have 48 hours in which to finish viewing it.

If you don't have an iTunes Store account, or prefer not to stream your entertainment from the net, then you can also use Apple TV to stream your local media. The simple menus let you quickly navigate your iTunes library, picking out films and tracks.

You can also use it to show off your photos, making it the equivalent of an old-school projector and slides.

Apple accessories

The Mac itself is only one part of Apple's complete computer line-up, which also includes a wide variety of stylish, minimalist accessories. Whatever your machine needs, check out these official add-ons.

■ APPLE WIRELESS KEYBOARD

When you buy a new Mac you have a choice of keyboards: wired or wireless. The most obvious difference is that the wired keyboard includes a numeric keypad on the right hand end where the wireless one does not, but the differences are more than skin deep.

The wireless keyboard uses Bluetooth, which means you can use it with a lot more than just your Mac. Enable Bluetooth on your iPhone or iPad and you can type directly into iOS apps. It's a lot more comfortable than typing onto a glass surface – particularly on the iPhone.

The most recent version of the wireless keyboard uses just two batteries, not three like the previous version. This sounds like a minor consideration, but if you are using rechargeable cells and have bought Apple's own charger and batteries then you'll know that it can charge only two at a time. Using the old version of the keyboard, then, you'll have to go through two charging cycles just to juice up sufficient batteries to carry on typing.

Like the wired keyboard, it has a full complement of function keys, each with supplementary features to change screen brightness, open the Dashboard, invoke Exposé, control media playback in iTunes and change the volume.It works with any Mac with Bluetooth and Mac OS X 10.5.8 or later.

APPLE KEYBOARD

The standard Apple keyboard is quite simply called Apple Keyboard with numeric keypad. It has none of the wireless trickery of its shorter sibling, but features the same comfortable keys, with their short travel and quiet action. It's great for use in a shared office as it doesn't draw attention to itself by making undue levels of noise.

As well as the numeric keypad on the right-hand end, it has one other trick up its sleeve that has been denied the wireless version: two USB sockets cleverly hidden in the shallow stand at the back. This lets you keep your USB accessories close at hand, but beware of the fact that some memory keys will be too thick to fit in it, while the power draw of other devices will be too high to allow them to be charged through the keyboard. The iPad is a notable example here. The keyboard sockets, then, are not a universally acceptable replacement for a good quality powered USB hub.

Neither is two ports quite so generous as it might sound. Certainly putting any more into it would have spoiled its sleek lines, so we wouldn't have wanted to see more than two in place, but bear in mind that as you lose one port when you plug in your keyboard in the first place, you're really only gaining one extra port on the keyboard.

BATTERY CHARGER

With so many of Apple's peripherals running on AA batteries, it was only natural that the company would want to get into the batteries and chargers market. What it came up with was a beautiful, tiny device that perfect complements the existing plug-based chargers for the iPad and iPhone.

Free of Apple branding, this small white box is a part of the plug itself, so sits neatly on the wall, suspended from the outlet. A single pinhead-sized LED on the top of the body glows amber to indicate charging and green to show when it has finished. It takes two batteries at a time, but works just as well with only one in place.

When it's finished charging it automatically reduces the amount of power to 30mW, which Apple claims is more than ten times better than the industry average.

It's supplied with six batteries that, again, are minimalist and tasteful in their design, despite the fact that most of the time they'll be hidden away inside your kit. Sadly you can't buy these on their own – they're only available with the charger.

It's not cheap, but the savings it could make you over several years' use mean it should more than pay for itself in the long run, both financially and ecologically.

MAGIC TRACKPAD

Apple is clearly set on putting multitouch features onto every desk. It's become such an important part of OS X, particularly with Lion, that the company has had to produce some external hardware for those desktop Mac users – with iMacs, Mac minis and Mac Pros – who would otherwise be missing the notebooks' integrated trackpads. The answer was the Magic Trackpad.

This connects to your Mac using Bluetooth, so can be positioned wherever is most comfortable, whether that's to the side of you keyboard or in front of it, like it is on a MacBook. This is important, as unlike a mouse the Trackpad won't be moved as you use it, so you need to ensure it can be positioned in the most comfortable spot on your desk for day-long work. Dragging your fingers moves the on-screen pointer, and it supports the full range of multitouch gestures. A pane in System Preferences lets you tweak how it works and you can also set whether you need only tap its surface or click it (the whole thing is one large button) to make a selection.

Apple's smartest move was in designing the Magic Trackpad to precisely complement the Wireless Keyboard. From front to back it's exactly the same depth and the battery holder that props it up does so at exactly the same angle, so you can push them up against one another, end to end, and they look like two halves of the same piece of kit. Even the curved edges turn at the same angle on both devices.

Like the Magic Mouse and Wireless Keyboard, it takes two AA batteries.

MAGIC MOUSE

Apple's eye for design extends even as far as the mouse. You might think that there wasn't much it could do to smarten up such a simple device, but you'd be wrong.

The Magic Mouse is more than just a pointing device; it's also a fully-fledged multitouch surface, performing many of the same functions as the trackpad on a notebook Mac, or the stand-alone Magic Trackpad. You don't need much space to perform these touch and swipe gestures, and it really does make sense to have a surface you can stroke to scroll a document or web page rather than relying on clicking or dragging a scroll bar.

Unlike some rival mice that are clearly designed to fit in either the left or the right hand, Magic Mouse looks the same from all directions, with only the Apple logo on its tail telling you which is the back end. You can therefore use System Preferences to customise it for either hand, so that that left-handed users can perform a 'right' click for context-sensitive menus using the left-hand side of the mouse.

The Magic Mouse is shipped as standard along with the iMac, but works just as well with any other Bluetooth-enabled Mac, making it the perfect companion to the wireless keyboard. It even takes the same batteries, and with two of them taking up a good portion of the inside of the mouse body they give it a satisfying, weighty feel.

It's the most feature-packed, and most comfortable mouse we've used in years.

OS X Lion

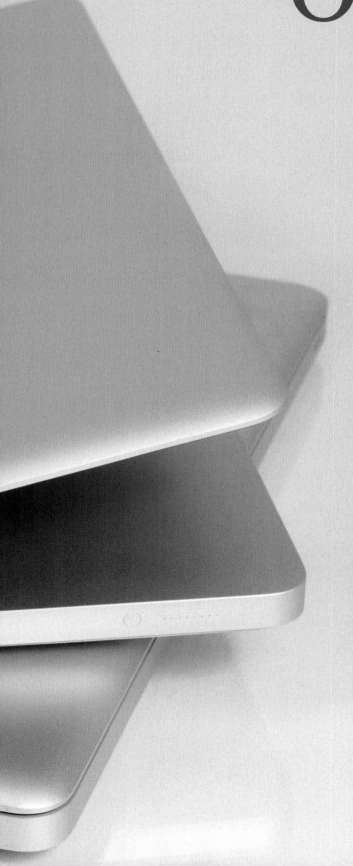

Mac OS X Lion

Mac OS X has a distinct look and feel all of its own. It's smart, fluid and understated, and although it may bear only a passing resemblance to Windows, once you get under its skin you'll find it reassuringly familiar.

Mac OS X and Windows may look different but they have many common features. Both are controlled by the mouse and keyboard, and each uses discrete application windows to display your files and what you're working on.

Where Windows has the Task Bar at the bottom of the screen, the Mac has the Dock, and it also has a menubar at the top of the screen, which doesn't feature in Windows.

Many Mac mice only have one button, and the trackpad on a portable Mac such as the MacBook, MacBook Pro and MacBook Air has no buttons at all. To right click, therefore, you'll need to hold down the control key while clicking. We will use this convention throughout this book, but if you have a mouse with two buttons then you should be able to use the right hand button to right click without pressing anything on your keyboard.

THE DOCK

The Dock is the most distinctive feature in OS X, and sets it apart from Windows and Linux. It is a bar that runs across the bottom of your screen, on which you can organise your most commonly used applications. To the very left are the Finder and Launchpad, and to the very right is the Trash. What sits in between is up to you.

You'll notice that the Dock is split into two unequal halves. The larger half, to the left, is where you organise your applications and where running applications appear while active. Applications bounce in this area while they're launching or when in need attention. To the right of the divider sit those elements that you always want to remain visible. By default, besides the Trash, this is where you will find a link to your Documents folder and your Downloads. Click either one of them and you will see that its

■ FIND YOUR WAY AROUND THE DOCK

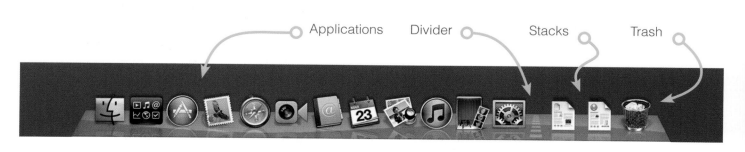

Applications   Divider   Stacks   Trash

Stacks pop up from the Dock when clicked, exposing their contents so that you can quickly access your most-used files, folders and applications. Right-click on a Stack to change the way it works.

contents the pop up in a fan formation. You can then click on one of the items in the fan to open or execute it. If you have too many items to display in the fan before it reaches the top of the screen, click the ringed arrow at the top of the list to open the relevant folder in a regular window.

■ STACKS

These are called stacks. You can change the way that they behave by holding control and clicking. This gives you the option to change the way the icons in each stack are sorted. You can also choose whether stacks should open as a fan, organised like files in a regular window or as a list, which can be scrolled if it's too long to fit on your screen. You can also allow your Mac to switch between them as appropriate depending on the number of files in each stack by choosing automatic under 'view content as'. When you switch on your Mac for the first time, stacks will be displayed as a pile of documents in a view appropriately called 'stack'. This can make your stacks difficult to differentiate, so you may want to change this to 'folder' under the 'Display as' section of this menu. This way, if you change the way your folders icons look, they will each look distinct when displayed in the Dock.

■ CREATING NEW STACKS

You can add new folders as stacks very easily. Open a new window by clicking the Finder icon on the far left hand side of the Dock. Let's imagine we want to create a stack for our Applications folder so that we can find them quickly even if they don't have icons of their own on the Dock.

Click on your hard drive in the Devices section of the sidebar and the Applications folder will appear in the pane to the right. Drag this down to the Dock and position it to the left of the Trash. Notice how the Documents and Downloads stacks shuffle along to make space for it. Don't let go of the folder until you've positioned it where it should live. When you do, it will move smartly into place. Now try clicking the applications stack on the Dock and see how it opens as a grid, because there are too many icons to display as a fan.

■ ADDING APPLICATIONS TO THE DOCK

You can add your most commonly used applications to the Dock in just the same way. Again, click the Finder icon to open a new window, and then click Applications in the sidebar. Let's add the Dictionary application to the Dock to make it more accessible.

Add your Applications folder to the Dock and you can open it as a Stack for immediate access to every item installed on your Mac. Stacks can be created simply by dragging folders onto the Dock.

Click and hold on the Dictionary icon and drag it down to the Dock, positioning it immediately to the left of the divide that splits the left and right hand side is of the Dock. Again, notice how the icons shuffle themselves around to make space for it. If you now want to move it to a new position in the Dock, drag it to your desired location.

REMOVING APPS FROM THE DOCK

You can remove apps just as easily. Only three icons are permanent residents of the Dock: the Trash, the Finder and Launch Pad. All the rest can be removed to slim it down.

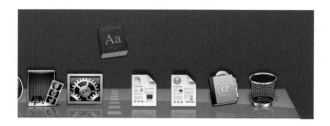

Click the dictionary and drag it away from the Dock. A small cloud appears below the icon. When you let go of the icon with this cloud visible, it will disappear in a puff of smoke. Don't worry, though – you haven't uninstalled the app itself, as you will see by opening the Applications folder again. The Dictionary app is still there.

TWEAKING THE DOCK

You can change the Dock itself in many ways. Move your mouse pointer over the divide between the two halves and you will see that it changes into a horizontal bar with arrows above and below it. Click here and drag your mouse up and down to make the Dock larger or smaller, with the icons themselves resizing to fit.

Left: Drag items out of the Dock to remove them. When you let go of the icon it disappears in a puff of smoke, but remains installed on your system.

Imagine what you can do

You've got big ideas. We've got what you need to take them to the next level. Office for Mac 2011 is packed with great features that help you create professional documents and presentations with the most-used productivity software for the Mac. And since Office for Mac 2011 is compatible with Office for Windows, you can work on documents with virtually anyone, anywhere.

To experience great features and get started with Office Mac 2011 straight away, **buy your copy at www.microsoft.com/uk/mac/buy**
Or, if you'd like to take a test drive before you buy, you can **download a FREE 30-day trial from www.microsoft.com/uk/mac/trial**

Compare previous versions of Office for Mac	Office 2011	Office 2008	Office 2004
Outlook*	✓		
Office Web Apps integration	✓		
Online Coauthoring	✓		
Intel-based Mac support	✓	✓	
Current Office file format support	✓	✓	
Ribbon user interface	✓		
Template Gallery	✓		
Publishing Layout view in Word	✓	✓	
Full Screen view in Word	✓		
VBA Macro support in Excel	✓		✓
Formula Builder in Excel	✓		
Conditional Formatting and Sparklines in Excel	✓		
SmartArt graphics in PowerPoint	✓	✓	

*Outlook is available with Office for Mac 2011 Home and Business Edition.

Microsoft

Right-click the Dock divider to change the way it behaves as you roll your mouse across it.

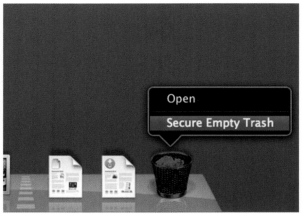

Securely emptying the trash writes over the space that was previously occupied by your files.

Click here while holding Control to call up the Dock menu. Here you can set the Dock to disappear as you move your mouse away from it by selecting 'Turn Hiding On'. After doing this, moving your mouse to the bottom of the screen will make the Dock reappear.

Turning on magnification will cause the icons on the Dock to enlarge as you move your mouse.

You can also change where the Dock appears, moving it to the left or right of the screen if that's more convenient for you, and you can also change the way that icons are minimised onto the Dock, switching between the genie effect, which shrinks the lower portion of the icon and sucks it in, with the upper half reducing in size slightly later, and the scale effect, which shrinks the application window in a uniform manner.

Note that if you move the Dock to the left or right of the screen, it loses its 3D appearance and adopts a smoky background with a white border.

■ EMPTYING THE TRASH

As you work with your Mac, you'll notice that the Trash can icon fills with paper as you delete files. This is a safety measure, allowing you to retrieve them should you decide that you need them at a later date. However, the whole time they are sitting in the Trash can they are using space on your hard drive. To reclaim such space you must empty it.

There are two ways to empty the Trash. The first is to hold down Control while clicking on the icon

itself and selecting Empty Trash. The second is to pick Empty Trash from the Finder menu at the top of the screen.

When you delete files by sending them to the Trash in any operating system they remain on your hard drive. Even emptying the Trash doesn't get rid of them entirely but simply removes the file's entry in the index that your Mac uses to navigate your file system.

Because your Mac will no longer know where they are, it will know that it can reuse the space on the drive that they occupy, thus writing over the top of them. The process of actually removing files from your drive, rather than simply 'deleting' them is therefore a slow, passive one.

Marking the location of unwanted files as blank achieves the goal of making their space available for reuse, but isn't entirely secure as it means that given the appropriate tools someone could conceivably – in some cases easily – recover files that you considered to be deleted.

If you need to make the files more difficult to recover for security reasons, hold down Command and Alt at the same time while clicking on the Trash and choose Secure Empty Trash. Your Mac will warn you that files deleted in this way cannot be recovered. If you're certain that you will never need the files again, confirm the option to empty the trash in this secure manner. It will take a little longer to complete the operation as your Mac will not only remove the files from its index, but also write over the space they occupied on the hard drive immediately.

THE MENUBAR

The Menubar is where Mac OS X puts all of the drop-down controls for each of your applications. Unlike Windows, it doesn't attach a different menu bar to the top of each application window.

The Menubar runs across the top of the screen, even when you don't have any applications running. Every application uses the same Menubar, so as you switch between them the Menubar components change.

Like the Dock, the Menubar is split into two halves, but unlike the Dock it doesn't have a divider drawn on it at any point. The menus that relate to your current application occupy the left-hand side of the Menubar, while various status icons and utilities sit to the right. These include the clock, network status, the tool for setting your screen resolution (if you've chosen for it to be visible), Bluetooth status, Time Machine status and the Spotlight icon. If you're using a portable Mac you'll probably also have an icon here that shows the current charge of your battery.

Clicking any of these icons pulls down a menu that lets you change its status. For example, clicking the battery icon shows you further information about the current charge, how long it will take to complete charging if you're currently plugged in, and what the current power source is. You can also change what the icon shows through the shallow submenu, which lets switch between time, percentage, and just an icon.

Like many other menus, though, the battery icon also has hidden information to offer, which isn't shown by default. Click while holding Alt on the keyboard, and you'll see some further information telling you about your battery's health and whether it needs attention. If it says 'Condition: Normal', you needn't worry.

Much of the information hidden in these menus can be useful when diagnosing problems. Click the Wi-Fi menu while holding Alt, for example, and you will see not only the available networks in your area, but also the channel you're currently using, your transmission rate, what security measures are in place on the network you're using, and other information that may help you diagnose a sluggish connection.

THE APPLE MENU

The most important entry on the Menubar is the Apple menu. This is a menu that drops down when you click the Apple icon on the very left-hand side. It gives you access to important tools that help you manage your Mac.

About This Mac

This is the place to look to find more information about the configuration of your machine. It calls up a small window that shows which version of the operating system you're currently running, what processor you have installed, how much memory is installed and the name of the disc from which your machine boots.

There are two buttons on this panel. The first, Software Update, launches another application that checks for new versions of the various Apple applications installed on your machine. We will cover this in greater detail later.

The second button, More Info…, opens the System Information utility for a more detailed analysis of your machine. This has been greatly improved in Mac OS X 10.7, with a toolbar runni across the top giving you shortcuts to informatic about your display, storage devices, memory ar battery. Two further buttons on the right of the toolbar help you find user manuals and online support, and check whether your machine is eligible for professional support from Apple should anything go wrong.

Click the overview button on the toolbar, and then the System Report… button on the panel fc a full rundown of every aspect of your machine.

The system report panel is split into two halve with the sidebar showing various categories, su

as memory, applications and diagnostics, and the main part of the screen showing information relating to each one as you click between them.

Note that not all categories are relevant to every Mac. For example, your Mac may not have a card reader, but the card reader entry will still appear in the categories sidebar. Clicking it will merely bring up a message that your computer doesn't contain any Apple internal memory card readers.

Software Update…

Launch Software Update and your Mac will scan the various applications installed on its hard drive and any connected drives. It will compare the list of Apple applications, including add-ons such as iLife, iWork and Aperture with an online database of recent upgrades. If it finds that any application, parts of the operating system such as Safari, or the operating system itself have received updates since you installed the current version on your machine, it will allow you to download those updates and install them automatically.

Each available update is briefly described, usually with details of the improvements that you will experience if you upgrade. Those that will require a reboot will have a warning telling you of this so that you can choose not to upgrade them immediately if it would interfere with your work.

Click System Report... for a fuller run-down of the hardware and software installed on your Mac, including an illustration of occupied internal slots.

The App Store is built into Mac OS X 10.6.6 and later. It makes buying, downloading and installing software a simple one-step process. You just need an Apple ID and credit card to start shopping.

APP STORE...

The App Store first appeared in Mac OS X 10.6.6, and is incompatible with earlier versions, so it won't run on any Mac that doesn't have an Intel processor. The App Store builds on the success of a similar store that Apple runs through iTunes for iPad, iPhone and iPod touch users, making it easy for them to download software to run on the devices and simple for developers to sell their own applications.

The Mac OS X App Store does the same thing for apps that run on a laptop or desktop computer. It also features in the Dock, and can be accessed by clicking the icon that looks like the letter 'A' inside a blue circle. On a default installation, it sits beside the Launch Pad icon.

To use the App Store you must have an Apple ID, tied to an active credit card. You can then buy applications directly, and they will be installed on your machine without you having to do any configuration yourself.

There are several benefits to buying apps this way, not least of which is the fact that each one has been tested and approved by Apple, so should not cause any problems on your machine.

The App Store will also keep track of those applications you have bought in the past, allowing you to reinstall them on other machines that you own in the same way, and informing you when there are updates ready for download. Much like Software Update, this utility lets you download and install the new versions of your software with little or no further input from yourself.

SYSTEM PREFERENCES...

The System Preferences application controls the very essence of your Mac. It's the place to turn when you need to change a monitor's resolution, swap out your desktop wallpaper, add new user accounts and so on. On a default installation, it can also be accessed from the Dock by clicking the icon showing cogs inside a grey window.

Dock

Here, you'll find the same preferences as we accessed when right clicking on the dividing bar on the Dock itself, allowing you to move it, hide it or activate magnification to enlarge your icons as you move your mouse across them.

Recent items

It's easy to forget that this entry is here, but Recent Items is a very useful feature on the Apple menu. It keeps track of not only applications that you have recently launched, but also documents that you have worked on (including images, spreadsheets and so on) and servers to which you have been connected.

If you accidentally cut a server connection or closed a document before you had finished working on it, this is the place to look to quickly get back online or reopen the document without having to navigate the file system.

If you have been working with files that you don't want anyone else to know about, you can erase the contents of this part of the Apple menu by clicking the Clear Menu option, which appears at the foot of the list itself.

Force Quit Finder

Sometimes your Mac will become unresponsive, and hang. At times like this you'll need to quit the application that's currently running and cleanly relaunch it.

Occasionally it may be the Finder itself – the very essence of Mac OS X – which is causing the problem, and as you can't quit this in the usual way your only option is to Force Quit it, at which point it will immediately relaunch, having jettisoned the code it was running that caused it to hang.

This Force Quit option in the Apple menu is one way to do just that, but you can also hold Command, Alt and Shift while pressing the power button on your system, or by holding Control and Alt while clicking the Finder icon on the Dock, and then selecting Relaunch.

Don't perform either of these actions without due care, as they may cause you to lose whatever data hasn't been saved in your active applications.

Your Mac will become briefly unusable as the Finder restarts itself, but should free itself within a few seconds and be more responsive to your demands.

Sleep, Restart..., Shut Down..., and Log Out...

The last four options on the Apple menu are the ones you turn to at the end of the working day. They control turning off or restarting your Mac.

Sleep puts your Mac into a low-power mode, where the screen will go blank, the drives are shut down and the memory saved so that the next time you open the lid, move the mouse or tap the keyboard it will wake up and be ready for use within a couple of seconds. You will know that your Mac isn't fully turned off because a small light at the front of the case will pulse as though it's breathing.

Note that although this is an extreme energy saving mode, it still uses some battery power, and so if your Mac isn't plugged in to the mains leaving it for too long in that state may put it into deep hibernation to preserve your data as the battery fully drains. It will take slightly longer to restart from this condition, but will not usually lose any of your data as your applications will be suspended in their last known good state.

Restart, as its name suggests, reboots your Mac. If the Mac has been set to demand passwords to logon, you will be required to enter one, along with a valid username, at the end of the rebooting process, so ensure you have these details to hand before restarting.

The restart process safely closes down all of your active applications, which may ask whether you want to save the data on which you're working in each one before the apps close. You'll usually be given the option to cancel at this point if you change your mind once you see what data is in use.

Shut Down... only goes half as far as restart, quitting all your applications and safely closing down the operating system before switching off your Mac fully so that it doesn't draw any more power.

The final option is to log out the current user, with that user's name displayed in the menu.

Selecting this doesn't shut down or reboot the computer at all, but returns you to the login screen. If you plan on leaving your Mac switched on for any length of time, it's worth using this option to log yourself out of your account and leave your Mac in the state where anyone who comes across it will be required to enter a password (if you have applied passwords to your account) before they can access the machine and your data.

APPLICATION MENUS

Whatever application you're running – even if it's just the Finder – its name will be displayed to the right of the Apple menu. Quite apart from being useful in telling you which application is active even if you have no windows open, this title is a menu all of its own. Click it to pull up specific options for that app. What these options are will vary depending on which application you're using, but the first option will always call up more information about current application, and the last will always quit it. There is usually also a Services menu among the options, which gives you access to central operating system functions.

This application menu is also the place to look if you want to change how the application itself works through its dedicated Preferences tool. Again, the precise options within this tool will vary from application to application, but by standardising on this as the location for that option, the Mac is often easier to navigate than a Windows-based machine. Further, because the menu bar is always at the top of the screen, beyond which your mouse pointer is unable to stray, it may be easier for those with mobility issues to hit the menu accurately than it would be if it was attached to a floating window in the middle of the screen.

The application name in the top left corner of the display has a number of common options, regardless of the app in use, including preferences and options to hide or quit the application in use.

SWITCHING BETWEEN APPLICATIONS

If you already have several applications running at the same time, you may well want to switch between them. You can do this in the usual way by clicking an icon on the Dock.

However, if you just want to quickly copy some text from another application into the app you're currently using, switching back and forth between them in this way is time-consuming and clumsy. It's much more efficient to use a series of keyboard shortcuts.

Hold down the command key and press tab to call up a bezel showing each of your active applications. Keep command held down and continue tapping tab until the application you want is selected. Now let go of both tab and command to switch to that. You can quickly switch back to the last app you're using by tapping command tab just once, so if you are frequently switching between just two applications you know you can perform this operation without even looking at the screen.

If you applications are running in full screen, you can swipe between them using three fingers on a trackpad or Magic Trackpad, and two fingers on Apple's Magic Mouse.

■ QUITTING APPLICATIONS

You can also shut down applications that you no longer need from the bezel. Hold command and tap tap until you reach the application you want to quit, then with command still held down tap the Q key. The application that was selected on the bezel when you pressed Q will be shut down.

■ EXPOSÉ AND MISSION CONTROL

Exposé helps you navigate the clutter of a busy desktop. If you have several applications running at the same time, you may find it difficult to locate the precise window you need without first moving a lot of others, which may be floating on top of it. Using Exposé, you can tell your Mac to rearrange all the windows so that none of them overlap and you can easily locate the one you need.

On recent Macs, Exposé is activated by pressing F3. What happens next depends on which version of the operating system you are running, as Lion – OS X 10.7 – introduces some changes with the addition of a whole new organisation utility.

Holding command while tapping tab lets you cycle through your active applications. Release both buttons when you get to the app you want. Hold shift and command while tapping to cycle in reverse.

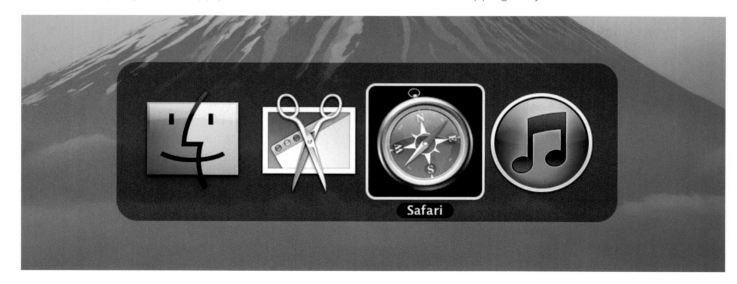

Safari

Mission Control builds in the success of Exposé to group together you active applications and the Desktop spaces on which they are running, allowing you to switch in an instant between them.

If you're running a version of the operating system between Mac OS X 10.3 Panther and Mac OS X 10.6 Snow Leopard, it shrinks all of your open windows and rearranges them so that they can be seen on screen in their entirety. You can then click with the mouse on whichever one you need.

If you are running Mac OS X 10.7 Lion, you will have activated Mission Control, which groups your Windows by application, so if you have several browser windows, two Word documents and three iChat sessions active, the Safari windows will be grouped separately from the Word documents, which in turn will be kept away from the iChat sessions.

At the same time, the Desktop will shrink to make room for each of your active Spaces at the top of the screen, and the Dashboard. We will explore Spaces and the Dashboard later. For the moment, though, you should notice how the windows within the shrunken desktops remain active at all times, so if any of them includes video, for example, it will continue to play even in this thumbnail view.

Whichever version of Mac OS X you are using after 10.3, holding control while pressing alt F3 shows you only the windows of the current active application, so if you have several browsers open within Safari, for example, each of them will be organised so that you can pick the one you want, without also seeing your windows from Word, Keynote or iPhoto.

Holding command while pressing F3 will shuffle all the windows of the screen to reveal the desktop (you can achieve this by unpincing five fingers on the trackpad). You will notice that they remain visible poking from the sides of the screen, and they will stay there until either you click one of them where it is poking in, or you press command F3 again. This lets you manipulate documents and files on the desktop without closing down your applications or minimising them to the Dock.

TOP PERFORM
& DOUBLE SEC

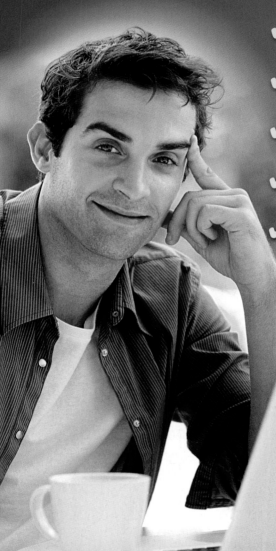

✓ **Maximum security:**
Geo-redundant data centres!

✓ **High performance:**
Latest server technology!

✓ **Super-fast:**
210 GBit/s connectivity!

✓ **Future-proof:**
Over 1,000 in-house developers!

✓ **Environmentally responsible:**
Powered by green energy!

1&1 DOMAINS
.eu
now only £0.99 first year*
.co.uk
now only £2.49 first year*
.com
now only £4.99 first year*

1&1 offers expertise, qual
Experience outstanding w

1&1 STANDARD

- ■ NEW: 50 GB Web Space
- ■ UNLIMITED Traffic
- ■ UNLIMITED 1&1 Click & Build Apps
- ■ 10 MySQL 5 Databases (1 GB each)
- ■ 3,000 IMAP/POP3 E-mail Accounts
- ■ 1&1 SiteAnalytics
- ■ NetObjects Fusion® 1&1 Edition
- ■ 24/7 Phone & E-mail Support

For 3 months
~~£4.99~~
£0.00
per month,
then £4.99/month*

ANCE
URITY!

double website security through 1&1 Dual Hosting.
ting now and get up to 6 MONTHS FREE:

1&1 UNLIMITED

- 1 .uk Domain Included
- UNLIMITED Web Space
- UNLIMITED Traffic
- UNLIMITED 1&1 Click & Build Apps
- 100 MySQL 5 Databases (1 GB each)
- 5,000 IMAP/POP3 E-mail Accounts
- 1&1 Newsletter Tool
- 1&1 SiteAnalytics
- NetObjects Fusion® 1&1 Edition
- 24/7 Phone & E-mail Support

For 3 months
£~~6.99~~
£0.00
per month,
then £6.99/month*

1&1 BUSINESS

- 1 .uk Domain Included
- UNLIMITED Web Space
- UNLIMITED Traffic
- UNLIMITED 1&1 Click & Build Apps
- UNLIMITED MySQL 5 Databases (1 GB each)
- UNLIMITED IMAP/POP3 E-mail Accounts
- UNLIMITED Mailing Lists
- GeoTrust Dedicated SSL Certificate
- Choose between NetObjects Fusion®
  1&1 Edition and Adobe Dreamweaver® CS4
- Free 0800 24/7 Emergency Support
- DOUBLE SECURE WEBSITE:
  GEO-REDUNDANT DATA CENTRES!

THE BEST CHOICE FOR YOUR BUSINESS!

The 1&1 Business package with performance-class features will ensure your website runs smoothly and securely. Enjoy uninterrupted service, lightning-fast connectivity and peace of mind while taking advantage of our geo-redundant data centres.

For 6 months
£~~9.99~~
£0.00
per month,
then £9.99/month*

1&1

Call **0844 335 1211** or visit us now

www.1and1.co.uk

SPACES

Spaces lets you create up to 16 virtual screens on which to run applications, and even switch between them using either the keyboard or an icon on the menubar.

■ ACTIVATING SPACES IN MAC OS X 10.6 AND EARLIER

Spaces is switched off by default, so in its newly installed state your Mac has only one screen to play with. Turn on Spaces by opening system preferences (you can find this through the Apple menu or by clicking its icon in the Dock) and clicking Exposé & Spaces on the top row. Click the Spaces button to switch to the Spaces settings.

Click in the checkbox beside Enable Spaces to activate this feature. By default you will be given four spaces to play with, but you can increase this to a maximum of 16 by adding new rows and columns by clicking on the plus and minus buttons to the side of the Spaces layout.

You can switch spaces on and off using F8. Note that if you are using a keyboard with multimedia functions, such as the one built into Apple's laptops or modern Mac keyboards which use F7, F8 and F9 to control rewinding pausing and fast forwarding music, you will need to hold the function button (which has 'fn' stamped on it) to access F8 without pausing or playing your music.

You can choose whether or not to display the Spaces icon on the menubar. If you do, then clicking on it will let you switch straight to whichever space you want by picking it from the list. You can also switch directly to a Space without using this menu in two ways, so if your menubar is starting to become cluttered then you may want to skip this option and use the keyboard instead.

Your first choice is to use control with one of the keys on a numeric keypad to switch between up to nine of your Spaces, and the second is to hold

down control and use the arrow keys to switch from one space to those adjacent to it. For example, if you have six spaces organised in three rows and two columns, then to move from space 2 to space five you would hold control and tap down, down, left. To then go to space one, you would hold control and tap the up key twice.

If you can't quite remember the layout of your spaces then it doesn't entirely matter, as moving in this way calls up a bezel that shows their layout, helping you to navigate from one to another.

■ MAC OS X 10.7 AND LATER

OS X Lion uses Mission Control rather than Spaces, mixing a selection of numbered Desktops with full screen applications. You don't need to switch it on. You can, however, tweak the way that it works by deciding whether or not full screen applications really should be considered equivalent to a Desktop in their own right, and whether the Dashboard should be shown in the overview mode. We would recommend that you do opt to show it, as it makes it a lot easier to access your Widgets and keep an eye on what they're up to than it ever was in Snow Leopard and earlier versions.

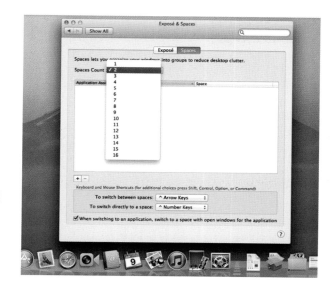

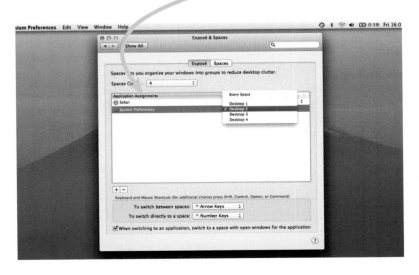

Above: add applications to default Spaces by clicking the '+' and choosing the application from the Finder window. When you return to the Spaces dialogue assign it a Space.

There is no option to display a Spaces icon in the menubar, and the layout of your Desktops is linear, with each of them arranged in a row. To switch between them, then, you can either hold control and press a number key, or hold control and use the left and right cursor keys to scroll along the row. If you scroll to the left of Desktop number 1, you will enter the Dashboard.

ASSIGNING APPLICATIONS TO SPACES

Spaces can be used to make your Mac more predictable. You will already have worked out for yourself that it can stop your screen becoming too cluttered by allowing you to concentrate on one application at a time, but it can also make those applications easier to find.

If you always have Mail, Excel, Safari and iCal running throughout the day, then why not assign them each to their own particular space so that, for example, whenever Mail launches it is on Space one, Excel is on Space two, Safari is on Space three and iCal is on Space four. That way you know that if you ever want to use Safari you only need to press control-3 to switch straight to it.

You do this through the application assignments window within Exposé & Spaces in Mac OS X 10.6 and earlier. Click the plus below the empty panel and it will display a list of your current applications. Choose one and it will be assigned to the current active Space. You can change this by clicking the desktop name and picking a new one from the list. You can, alternatively, specify this application should appear on all Spaces. For example, you may want to keep iChat visible at all times whatever else you are doing. You can also add applications that are not currently running. Again, click the '+' button and choose 'Other...' from the menu. This will open a file browser showing your applications folder from which you can pick the application you need and click add to assign it a space. When you're done, press command-Q to quit System Preferences.

Spaces remembers how these applications have been designated even if they are not currently running, so the next time they launch their will be sent to the appropriate Space.

DASHBOARD

The Dashboard is a hidden layer of Mac OS X. In version 10.6 and earlier it sits behind the operating system Windows. In version 10.7 and later, it sits to the very left of the first Desktop.

In 10.6 and earlier, there is a Dashboard icon on the Dock, unless you've chosen to remove it. By default it sits to the right of the Finder icon, just where Launchpad is found on Mac OS X 10.7. If you want this icon in 10.7, you will have to put it there yourself, by dragging it from the applications folder onto the Dock.

A similar icon also appears on Apple keyboards, usually on the F4 key. Pressing it calls up the dashboard. In Mac OS X 10.7, you can also enter the Dashboard by holding the control key and pressing the left arrow keys to go one step further than the first Desktop. You know you're on the Dashboard because the background changes, some small applications appear on screen and there is a plus in a circle in the lower left-hand corner.

■ OPENING NEW DASHBOARD WIDGETS

These applications are called Widgets. Your Mac ships with a number already installed and you can download others from various sites, including Apple's own website. Click the plus in the lower left-hand corner of the Dashboard to access the other Widgets installed on your system.

Open the Dictionary Widget either by clicking its icon or dragging it onto the Dashboard. Do the same with the Stickies Widget, which replicates a

Click a Widget's 'i' button to flip it over and change the settings and options.

popular utility from Mac OS X itself. You can rearrange the Widgets by dragging them around the Dashboard, and close the springboard by pressing the 'x' just above it.

■ MAKING WIDGETS WORK FOR YOU

Many Widgets can be customised by flipping them over and using controls on the back. Hover your mouse over the stickies Widget on the Dashboard and you'll see a small 'i' appear in the bottom right corner. Click this to spin the Widget around and you can change the paper colour, the font or the text size used for writing notes. Click done to return to the front and continue using the Widget.

Try typing something into the Dictionary Widget and you'll see that the Widget enlarges to provide a definition, and that when you move your mouse over it the lower case 'i' now appears in the bottom left hand corner. Clicking it again turns over the Widget, but this time your options are

Widgets live in a springboard at the foot of the Dashboard display. Scroll by clicking the arrows, and then click the icon for the Widget you want to use to drop it onto the Dashboard itself.

Close a Widget by holding alt as you hover over its face, and then click the 'x' in the top corner.

Manage your Widgets by checking and clearing the boxes beside their names.

more limited, stretching only to changing the font size.

CLOSING DASHBOARD WIDGETS

These applications remain active even when you're not looking at the Dashboard, so it pays to close them down when not using them to free up the memory that's allocated to them. You can close an application on the Dashboard by holding the alt key and moving your mouse over the app. You will notice a cross appear on the top left corner of the application. Clicking this removes it from the Dashboard.

MANAGING YOUR WIDGETS

Widgets don't consume any resources other than a very small amount of disk space when they aren't running, but still you might want to uninstall some that you have previously added to your system. Only third-party Widgets that you have installed yourself can be removed entirely. The

Widgets that came as part of Mac OS X can only be hidden from view.

To manage Widgets, press the plus in the lower left corner of the Dashboard and then either click 'Manage Widgets...' or click the Widgets icon on the springboard.

To disable Apple Widgets, clear the checkbox beside their names. To remove third-party Widgets entirely, click the delete icon beside them. Your Widgets will not disappear immediately from the springboard, so close the management bezel and then close the springboard by pressing the 'x' just above it. The next time you reopen the springboard the Widgets should not be present.

LEAVING DASHBOARD

You can exit the Dashboard on all versions of Mac OS X by pressing the Dashboard button on your keyboard. On Mac OS X 10.7, holding control while pressing the right cursor key also brings you out of the Dashboard and takes you to the Desktop number 1.

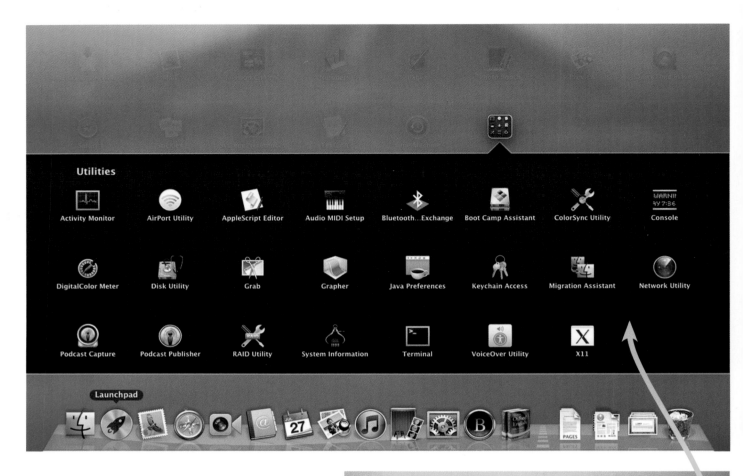

LAUNCHPAD

Launchpad has a permanent spot on the dock, appearing just to the right of the Finder icon. It looks like a silver button with a rocket on it.

Click on the Launchpad icon and your Desktop and running applications will be blurred into the background. In their place will be icons for each of the applications installed on your Mac. You can then click them to launch the associated apps. This makes it easy to launch new applications without going through a Finder window.

Any folders within your application folder, such as the utilities subfolder, are shown as a grey square among the application icons. Click them to open them up. Their contents drop-down in a grey panel that seems to split the screen, with the folder itself shifting up the screen if necessary to make space.

As soon as you click on an icon in launchpad, the associated application launches and Launch Pad itself disappears.

Step 2

Step 1

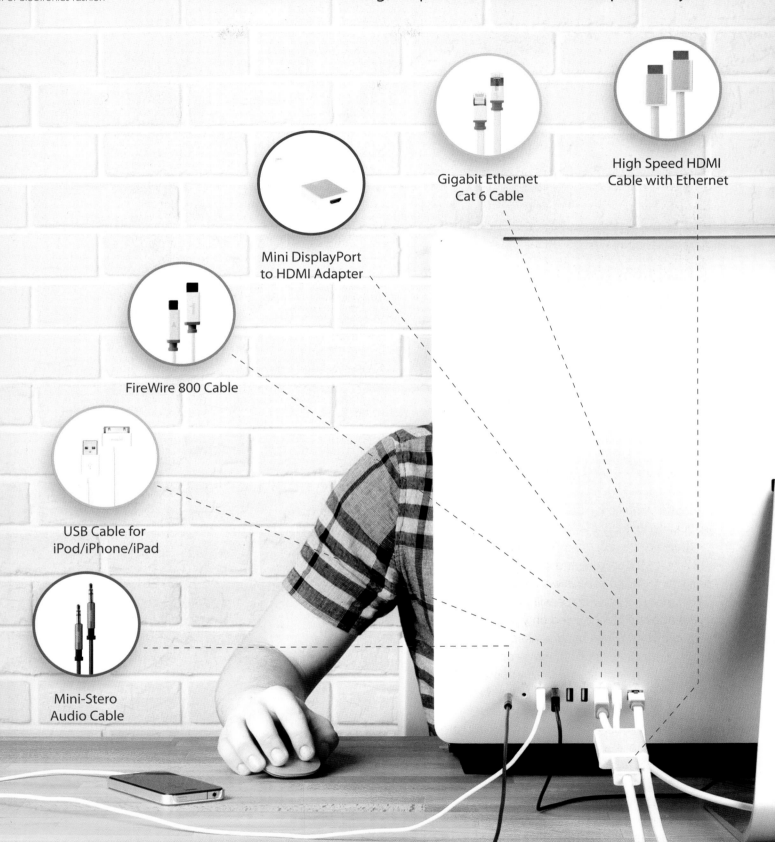

Connect with Moshi

Moshi offers a full range of premium cables and adapters for your Mac.

moshi
or of electronics fashion

Gigabit Ethernet
Cat 6 Cable

High Speed HDMI
Cable with Ethernet

Mini DisplayPort
to HDMI Adapter

FireWire 800 Cable

USB Cable for
iPod/iPhone/iPad

Mini-Stero
Audio Cable

 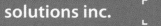

SEARCHING YOUR MAC

Mac OS X boasts some very impressive search tools that help you to pinpoint resources throughout your system.

■ SPOTLIGHT

Spotlight is Apple's system-wide search tool, which can be used not only to hunt out files on your system, but also to find and launch applications.

■ SEARCHING WITH SPOTLIGHT

Spotlight lives behind the magnifying glass icon on the right-hand side of your menu bar. Click it, or press command-space, to open its search box.

As soon as you start typing into the box, Spotlight starts searching, continually refining its results as you continue to type, so the more you enter the more accurate the results will become. The results are drawn from all parts of your Mac's file system, including folder names, documents, spreadsheets, images and even web pages you have recently visited, and a record remains of which in your browser history.

Once the file you're after if displayed in the list, click it with the mouse or use the cursor keys to highlight it and then hit return.

If your search turns up several very similar results – perhaps several files with the same name – and you're not sure which one you need, then in OS X Lion you can hover your mouse over each one in the list of results and a preview will pop out from the left-hand side of the Spotlight drop-down.

■ EXPANDED SEARCH RESULTS

If Spotlight doesn't immediately find what you're after, or it appears so far down the list of results that it is not displayed within the drop-down menu, click the Show All in Finder entry immediately below the search box. This opens a regular Finder menu showing only those files that match your

requirements. From here you can refine the search criteria and save the results for future reference. See 'Searching from the Finder' and 'Saved searches', later in this section, for more information.

■ REFINING THE SPOTLIGHT INDEX

Spotlight searches everything from applications and documents to email messages and addresses. This can make it the first place you turn to find anything on your Mac, but it can also make the results unwieldy, and the underlying index itself bulky and resource-hungry.

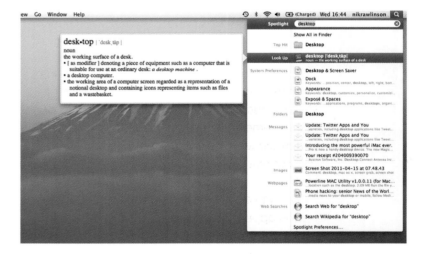

Deselect those items you don't want to see in your Spotlight results to refine the search.

Spotlight searches not only the files on your computer, but also emails, folders and apps.

You can trim the range of assets that Spotlight indexes through its Preferences pane (System Preferences > Spotlight). This presents a list of all of the elements it will search in a list, with each accompanied by a check box. Clear that box for the elements you don't want to see in the results list.

You can also change the order in which the results appear in the Spotlight menu by clicking and holding on the entries and dragging them into a new order. If most of your Spotlight searches will be focused on finding documents, it therefore makes sense to drag this to the top of the list so that they appear in the most accessible location within the results list. You then don't need to step through many entries before opening them using the keyboard.

IMPROVING SPOTLIGHT'S SEARCH PERFORMANCE

Spotlight searches not only on file and folder names, but also the contents of your files, so if you know that you wrote about fly fishing in a Pages document, you should be able to search for words related to that subject and turn up your documents. Likewise, any emails exchanged on that subject, spreadsheets recording your catches and electronic receipts for fly fishing supplies will all be found if they include the keywords you supply.

It's by no means guaranteed that all of the files relevant to your search will include the search terms you enter within either their file name or their actual contents. You may be looking for photos of your friend holding a particularly large fish they caught, but unless you have catalogued the image in iPhoto or Aperture, or have renamed the file manually they will probably still be identified only by the serial numbers they were given by the camera when shot. Your chances of finding them through Spotlight would therefore be very slim indeed.

In instances such as this you should use Spotlight metadata to catalogue your files and thus increase the relevance of your search results.

Adding metadata is the equivalent to tagging your assets with hints about their subject, or their relationship to other assets on your Mac. When adding metadata, try to think of the keywords you might use when trying to find it through Spotlight.

■ HOW TO ADD SPOTLIGHT METADATA

1. Select the file to which you want to add the metadata and either press command-i, or right-click and pick Get Info from the menu.
2. Find the 'Spotlight Comments' section at the top of the information panel. If it is a single line, click the disclosure triangle on its left-hand side to expand it.
3. Enter keywords that describe the file. These need not be as literal as 'photo', 'fish', but could instead be related to a project for which the file is an asset.
4. Close the Info panel by clicking the red lozenge at the top of the dialogue.

■ EXCLUDING DRIVES AND FOLDERS

By default, Spotlight indexes everything it can find on your system. However, there are many reasons why you may not want to do this. You may, for example, have a folder of older documents that you are keeping as a backup while you work on more up to date versions. You'd be wise to remove the older documents from the Spotlight index so that only the current edition of each one appears in the results and your chances of opening and working on the wrong one is reduced. You might also want to exclude whole drives that are used for backup purposes if you'll never need to manually open the backup archives.

To exclude folders or drives in this way, switch to the Privacy tab in Spotlight's Preferences pane and click the '+' at the foot of the dialogue. Navigate to the folder or drive you want to exclude and click Choose. You will be returned to the Privacy dialogue, with the selection added.

To later return that folder or drive to the Spotlight index, select it within the dialogue and click the '-' button to remove it from the list of excluded locations. Note that its contents won't immediately be visible within Spotlight searched as they must be rewritten to the index.

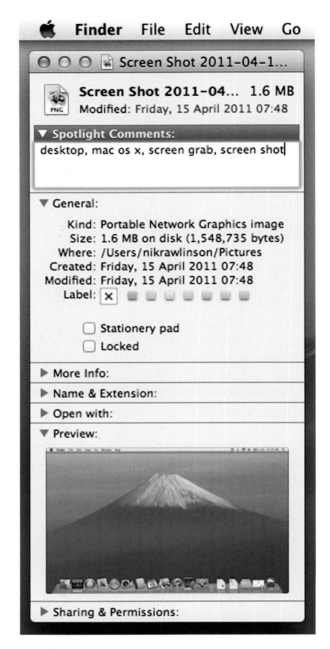

By making entries in the Spotlight comments box that accurately describe your file you can improve the effectiveness of the OS X search engine. Here, we have captioned a screen grab.

■ REBUILDING THE SPOTLIGHT INDEX

This method of excluding locations from Spotlight has a secondary use, forcing Mac OS X to reindex that location when you return it to the list.

If Spotlight is not finding applications, files or folders that you know to exist, you can force it to re-index a particular part of your drive this way:

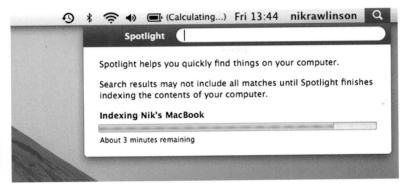

Return an excluded drive to Spotlight and OS X will re-index its contents for full searching.

1. Add the folder containing those files that Spotlight can't find to the list of excluded locations within the Spotlight Preferences Privacy tab.
2. Quit System Preferences, and then re-open it and return to the Privacy tab.
3. Remove the excluded item, and again quit System Preferences. Spotlight will rebuild its index of that folder.

You can reindex anything from a single folder to a whole drive in this way by excluding and then including whatever is relevant.

USING SPOTLIGHT TO LAUNCH APPLICATIONS

You will have noticed when looking at Spotlight Preferences pane that Applications appear by default at the top of the search list. This makes Spotlight a great app launcher.

Rather than clicking to the Finder and then navigating through your folders to find the application you need to use, press command-space to call up Spotlight, enter the first two or three characters of the application's name and it will most likely appear at the top of the results list, already highlighted. You now need only press return to launch it.

Because Spotlight's search results are refined over time to reflect your search patterns, the applications you use most often will quickly work their way up to the very top of the list and you may soon find that you can launch an application by entering only the initial letter of its name.

SPOTLIGHT'S HIDDEN FEATURES

Spotlight does more than just search your Mac; it can also search the web, OS X's built in dictionary and your address book, and can also perform impressive, complex maths.

SPOTLIGHT MATHS

Spotlight's maths functions range from the simple to the complex. Type 2+2 and the search result will be 4. Perform 2*3 and it will be 6. However, Spotlight also understands parentheses and many spreadsheet-like functions.

2*(4*4), for example, would give you 32, whereas sqrt(4*9) would give you the square root of four times nine, which is six. 'cbrt', as you may be able to guess, gives you the cube root.

You can apply powers to numbers by using the caret symbol (^). So, six to the power of two would be entered as 6^2, and give you the result 36. Seven to the power of three would be 7^3.

Spotlight understands percentages, giving you an easy way to find a particular percentage of a number. For example, 50*20% gives the result 10, since 10 is 20% of 50. You can of course use this in conjunction with other sums in parentheses so if, for example, five people contributed 10, 20, 25, 15 and 35 items respectively and you wanted to find 35% of the total, the sum would be (10+20+25+15+35) *30%.

USEFUL MATHS FUNCTIONS FOR USE IN SPOTLIGHT

*	To multiply two or more numbers. eg, 2*3
/	To divide two or more numbers. eg, 2/3
-	To subtract one number from another. eg, 3-2
+	To add one number to another. eg, 3+2
^	To apply a power to a number. eg, 4^16
%	To work out the percentage of a number. eg, 50*20%
sqrt	To find the square root of a number. eg, sqrt(16)
cbrt	To find the cube root of a number. eg, cbrt(9)
cos	To calculate cosine of a number. eg, cos(15)
tan	To find the tangent of a number. eg, tan(20)
sin	To find the sine of a number. eg, sin(25)

If you need to use the result of your sum in a document, highlight it in the Spotlight result list and press command-c to copy it to the clipboard. Return to the document where you need to use it and press command-v to paste it in place.

Spotlight uses the Math library that underpins the operating system to perform these functions. You can pull up a full list of its functions by opening Terminal and typing *man math* at the command prompt.

■ SPOTLIGHT WEB SEARCHING

Spotlight searches can be directed to the web where they will be fulfilled by Google or Wikipedia, depending on where you choose to send them. You'll see links to each of these services at the bottom of the Spotlight results list – simply click the one you want to forward your keywords to the relevant service.

■ SEARCHING FROM THE FINDER

Spotlight's search tools are also accessible within regular Finder windows. Open a new window and you will see a large search box in the toolbar at the top of the dialogue. Enter some keywords and your Mac will immediately start searching for matching results.

At the same time, a new bar will appear below the toolbar allowing you to refine your search criteria. By default, the name of the current folder, and 'Contents' will already be selected on this bar, indicating that it is searching only the folder displayed within that Finder window and focusing on the contents of those files rather than simply names.

To search the whole of your Mac, click 'This Mac', and to search only on file name, ignoring the actual contents of your files or the Spotlight meta data you have added to them, click 'Filename' on the right of the divider.

You can change the way your Mac displays the results in just the same way that you can change how it displays files in a regular Finder window. Click the item arrangement button on the right of the central group of controls on the toolbar and pick the method you would like the Finder to use to organise your search results, choosing from kind, application, size, label or the dates of modification, creation, addition, or last opening.

However you organise the display of your files,

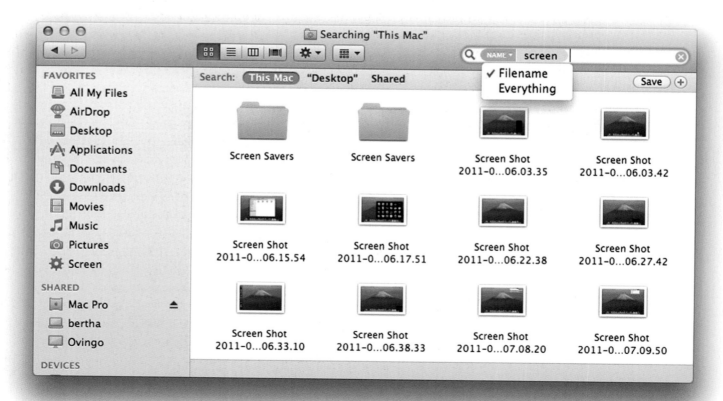

| DESKTOP LUXURY |

Introducing the world's first full-digital USB multimedia speaker system. As a true hi-fi speaker with captivating design, cubik makes an ideal partner for your Mac. It's high-resolution digital amplifier and lossless digital USB streaming interface deliver jaw-dropping sound.

"Cubik is backed by speaker power unmatched by other speakers in its class. It delivers on every level."
- Myteklife Magazine -

"They are compact, connect easily, and the sound is great."
-JK from Newport News -

"I bought these speakers last week and all I can say is WOW! "
- AT from San Fransisco-

cubik

High-end Computer Audio

clicking any one of them will display its location in the bar at the bottom of the Finder window. It may be buried fairly deep within the file system, in which case you are likely to see a line of folders whose names have been shortened to fit them all in, with your chosen file on the far right hand side. As you roll your mouse pointer across these folders, they will shuffle about so that you can read the full name of each one as you pass over it. Double-clicking a folder will open it up within the Finder window, allowing you to navigate the folders manually to find other files that may be related and stored in the same location.

■ SAVING YOUR SEARCH RESULTS

If you find yourself frequently making the same searches, you can save time when conducting the same search in the future by saving them to the sidebar. Perform the search you need and then click the 'Save' button on the toolbar (Step 1).

Mac OS X will ask you to give the search a name, and although it will suggest one this may not be the most appropriate description for your search results (Step 2). Enter whatever makes sense and will allow you to easily find the search again in the future and make sure the option to save the search to the sidebar is checked. When you click the save button you will see your search appear in the coloured panel on the left of the Finder window, with a cog icon beside its name.

This icon indicates a smart folder, and if you are to open its parent folder in the Finder, you would see that whereas regular folders are coloured blue and have no icon stamped onto them, a smart folder is purple and also bears this cog icon.

Smart folders update themselves every time you open them, so while it will always contain an up-to-date list of those files which satisfy your search criteria, they are never physically stored within that folder. Instead, they are merely referenced from that point, and so clicking on any file within the smart folder will again pull up its location information at the bottom of the window.

The best way to think of a smart folder is in the same way you consider a playlist in iTunes: it's merely a representation of resources stored elsewhere.

■ DELETING SAVED SEARCHES

To remove a saved search from the sidebar, right click its name and select 'Remove from Sidebar'. That this doesn't remove the smart folder from your Mac entirely. To do this, instead select 'Open Enclosing Folder'. This will open the Saved Searches folder inside your Library folder, with the saved search already selected. Delete it by dragging it to the Trash, or holding command and pressing backspace.

Note that although you've removed the search folder, because it only ever referred to the locations of your original files, they are still safe. The search folder itself never actually held any contents, and so by deleting it all you have done is remove the search term, not the files that satisfied the search itself.

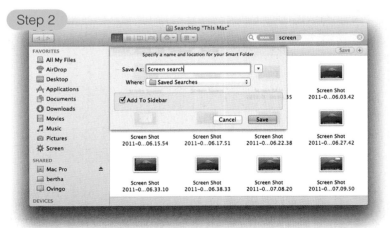

Save searches straight from the Finder and you'll be able to find your most commonly-used files and folders more easily in the future.

BACKING UP YOUR MAC

Your data is your most valuable possession. It may not exist as anything more than ones and zeroes on a disk platter, but if you were to lose it, it would be almost impossible to replace.

All disks fail after a certain amount of time, and when they do they'll take a greater or lesser amount of your data with them. If you're really unfortunate, they'll fail catestrophically and rob you of everything. Even if you were able to recover some of your data with the assistance of a data recovery professional, their services don't come cheap, and it could cost you more than the full value of your Mac.

It's far better, then, to seriously consider backing up your data in advance of any catastrophe. Fortunately Apple provides two industry-grade backup solutions in the shape of Time Machine and Backup.

■ TIME MACHINE

Time Machine first appeared in Mac OS X 10.5 Leopard and has been carried through to each edition since then. The first time you enable it, it creates a full back-up of your Mac, and then every hour after that when your Mac is switched on, so long as the drive remains attached, it will copy any subsequent changes to the archive.

Time Machine is designed to remain running at all times, rather than performing periodic backups to a drive you might unplug from your system between operations. You should therefore leave your Time Machine backup drive attached to your system whenever your Mac is turned on.

As the months pass by, Time Machine will start to fill up your backup drive and so will start to reorganise your older backups, maintaining hourly

With Time Machine on your Mac you need never worry about losing a file as OS X will automatically create backups each hour of your working files, applications and current system state.

snapshots of your system covering the last 24 hours, daily backups for the past month and weekly backups for everything else.

TIME MACHINE STORAGE OPTIONS

Time Machine can back up your files to either a drive attached directly to your Mac, or to Apple's dedicated Time Capsule, which is a combined network router and network attached storage (NAS) device.

Locally-attached drives must conform to the following standards:

- be formatted as journaled HFS+
- be connected by USB or Firewire, depending on the ports available on your Mac
- or be a folder on another Mac on the same network running Mac OS X 10.5 or later

Time Capsule connects to your broadband router using a regular Ethernet cable and allows other devices to be attached using one of the three Ethernet ports, the built-in USB port or wirelessly using 802.11n Wi-Fi. The USB port is not used for connecting a Mac or PC, but for sharing a printer between several computers on your network.

Your first Time Machine backup, whether to a locally-connected drive or a Time Capsule, will be time consuming, but subsequent incremental backups should be barely noticeable. Notebook users using Time Capsule will need to connect their MacBooks to a mains power supply to perform the larger initial backup.

ENABLING TIME MACHINE

1. Connect the drive you intend to use for backup or, if you will be using Time Capsule, ensure your device is switched on.
2. Open System Preferences > Time Machine.
3. Enable Time Machine by clicking the OFF / ON slider on the interface to call up the disk selection window.
4. Choose the disk you want to use and click Use Backup Disk. Although you can create local snapshots of your files using first option in the dialogue this isn't to be recommended if

you need a rock-solid backup routine as any failure of your primary drive will affect your snapshots as well as your original files.
5. Click the 'Use Backup Disk' button to perform the first backup.

EXCLUDING FILES FROM YOUR TIME MACHINE ARCHIVE

Large files that change frequently will quickly eat up your backup drive as they must be backed up in their entirety. If you use a virtualisation product such as Parallels Desktop or VMWare Fusion to run a guest operating system on your Mac it will save the whole operating system image, including all of the applications installed within it and all files, photos, documents, music tracks, movies and so on, in one single file.

Change just one small part of this file, such as the name of a photo within the guest operating system, or its desktop wallpaper, and Time Machine will see the whole file as having changed and write a fresh backup to its archive. This will be time-consuming, and if you're using a Time Capsule rather than a locally-attached storage device, will also increase your network traffic.

You should therefore exclude such files from your backup, and can optionally exclude whole folders or drives.

1. Open System Preferences > Time Machine and click the 'Options...' button. (*right*)

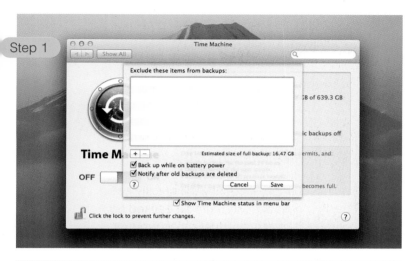

Step 1

Step 2

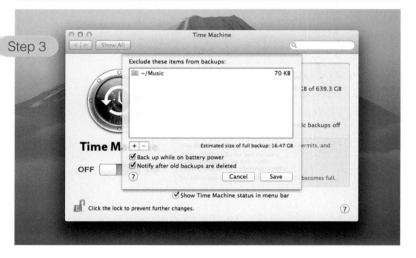

Step 3

2. Click the '+' button on the pane that pops up and navigate to the file, folder or drive you want to exclude from the backup. (*above*)

3. Select the item to be excluded and click 'Exclude'. The item will be added to the exclusion list on the original dialogue. (*above*)

4. Repeat steps 2 and 3 for each additional item

you want to exclude from the backups, and then click Save to return to Time Machine's overall settings pane.

5. To resume backing up these items, return to the options pane, select the item you want to back up from the exemption list and click the '-' to remove it, then once again click 'Save'.

■ RUNNING MANUAL BACKUPS

Time Machine is a true 'set and forget' system. It works best if you set it up once and then leave it to run in the background while you get on with using your Mac as usual. However, if you detect an impact on your system performance, or prefer to manually manage when backups occur, you can control them from the Time Machine icon on the toolbar.

1. This icon looks like a small clock, surrounded by a curved arrow. If it doesn't appear on your menu bar, enable it by opening System Preferences > Time Machine and checking the box beside 'Show Time Machine status in menu bar'.

2. Click the Time Machine icon and select 'Back Up Now'. The icon will animate to show that it is working. When the animation stops, the backup process has completed.

■ RESTORING FROM TIME MACHINE

Restoring a file is a simple matter of stepping back through your file system using Time Machine's graphical interface. This is accessed by clicking the Time Machine logo on the Menu bar and selecting 'Enter Time Machine'.

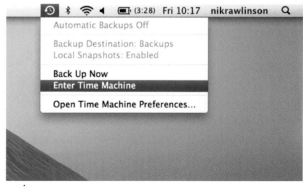

Perhaps the simplest backup system on any platform, Time Machine presents you with familiar system interfaces through which you choose the files you want to restore to a previous state.

1. Your applications and background will slide off the bottom of your screen to leave only your current Finder window in place, or a new Finder window if you don't already have one open.
2. If you are restoring a file that has gone missing, navigate to the location where you know your missing file once existed and then use the timeline on the right-hand side of the screen, or the forwards and backwards arrows beside it, to step back through time until it reappears in the Finder window. You can press the space bar here to invoke Quick Look and preview the file.
3. Click the restore button. You'll come back out of Time Machine and the file will be restored to its original location.

You can do the same thing to roll back an existing file to an earlier state – to undo some erroneous editing, for example. Select the file in its current state in a regular Finder window and the enter Time Machine through the Menu bar. Leave the

file selected in the Time Machine interface, but step back through time to its last known good state and again click Restore to return the old state of the file to your current file system, overwriting the one that currently exists.

Using Time Machine to restore other data

Time Machine isn't only used to restore files in the Finder: it also works with several of Apple's core products, including Address Book and iPhoto.

Restoring to Address Book

1. Open Address Book and then enter Time Machine by selecting it from the Menu bar icon. Everything but Address Book and the galaxy background will disappear from your screen.
2. Use the regular controls to step back through the Time Machine archive until the contact you need reappears in the version of Address

Time Machine works with several compatible applications, and will restore lost or edited images from an iPhoto library, and contact details to the OS X Address Book, all through the application interfaces.

2. Use the timeline controls to step back through the Time Machine archive until the image or images you need to recover appear in the iPhoto interface.
3. Select the assets in question and then click Restore. Alternatively, if you have lost your whole library click 'Restore All'.
4. iPhoto will re-import your images as though they were new assets on a memory card.

RESTORING EMAILS

1. Open Mail and enter Time Machine. Mail will be isolated on the screen against the galaxy background.
2. Navigate your mailboxes in the regular way within the Time Machine interface to find the message you want to recover. Note that any smart mailboxes you have set up will be greyed out. Click Restore.
3. The message will be retrieved and saved in a folder called Recovered Messages inside On My Mac > Time Machine in the Mail sidebar.

Book displayed within the Time Machine environment.
3. Select the identified contact and click the Restore button.
4. The regular Mac OS X environment will reappear and Address Book will ask you to confirm that you want to add the contact.

RESTORING A PHOTO TO IPHOTO

1. Open iPhoto and then enter Time Machine. iPhoto will be isolated on the screen.

VERSIONS

Versions builds on the success of Apple's existing backup technologies, giving every document on your system its own personal Time Machine.

All the time you are working, OS X is watching what you're doing, and when it notices that you're paused it'll use that downtime to save a copy of the file's current state.

The upshot is that it will build up a trail of changes that illustrate how your file has changed over time, from the very first moment you started work on it, right up to the present state.

If you forget to save your work and have a catastrophic crash – or perhaps a power outage that shuts down your system without warning – you'll not lose anything. As soon as you get your Mac back up and running all of those versions will be waiting for you in the archive, ready to be recovered so that you can carry on working as though nothing had happened.

However, Versions is more than a simple backup tool – it's also an aid to creativity, allowing you to experiment with whatever you're working on, safe in the knowledge that you'll be able to unwind any unwise changes.

As soon as OS X has saved its first copy of any one of your files you'll notice that a discreet new button appears on the toolbar. Click this and you'll be presented with the Versions menu. From here, clicking Browse All Versions... takes you into the full Versions interface, which bears more than a passing resemblance to Time Machine. The document's current state is shown on the left side of the screen, with the various versions stacked up on the right. Either roll back through each one

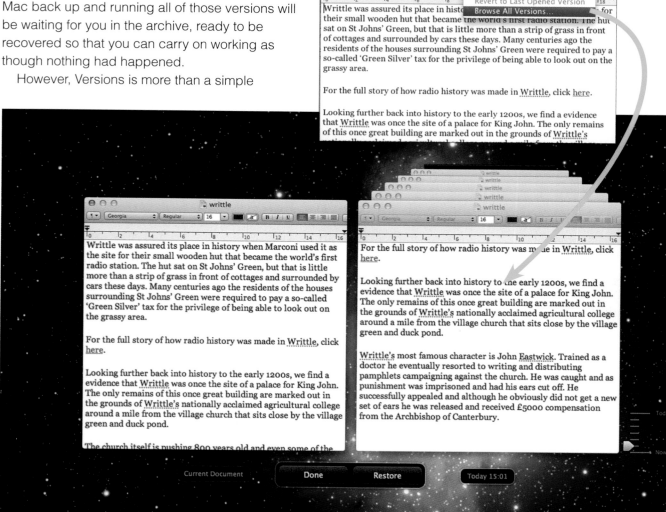

by clicking on their window headers or scroll the timeline, which is notched to mark every iteration of the document.

When you have found the version you want, click the Restore button and the Versions interface will gracefully slide away. Your document window will return to its original position and you can continue working on your earlier edition.

ROLLING BACK QUICKLY

If you know right away that the last state at which you pressed save was the best version of your file so far, you may be tempted to close it and open it again, without saving another time in between, but with Versions there's no need, as there's a dedicated Revert to Last Saved Version command on the Versions menu, which will skip the whole process of stepping back manually and instead repair to the last known good state.

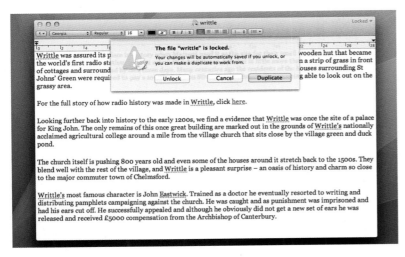

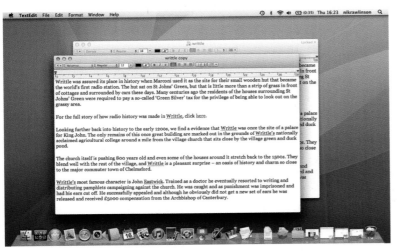

ANOTHER USE FOR VERSIONS

When you have created a document with which you're happy, you can lock it by selecting the Lock option from the Versions menu. This will stop you – or anyone else – from making accidental or unintended changes to the file in the future. Locked files are marked as such in the title bar, just beside the file name (below).

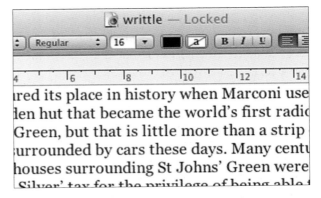

If you try to edit a locked file, Versions warns you, and give you three options: unlock the file, cancel the edit or create a duplicate (*left*).

Unlocking the file makes it available for editing and incorporates your changes, making further Version backups as it goes on. Cancelling obviously cancels your edit, and duplicate creates a second copy of your file, which literally bounces out of the locked version, is blessed with the extension 'copy' and sits in front of the original, ready for editing (*below left*). By locking your original document you have effectively created a template that can be used to spawn further versions, each with standard base components.

Note that new versions don't carry across your previous changes, so it's safe to pass them on to other users without them being able to see earlier revisions of your work, and any placeholder notes you may have included.

If you share your work by email, iChat, or by sending it to another user through Lion's new AirDrop feature, OS X automatically strips out all previous versions, so you don't need to perform this manual copy. This is an excellent safety feature, but shouldn't be taken for granted, as you may still transfer old data should you share using FTP.

FULL SCREEN APPLICATIONS

Many applications, including Apple's own Pages, Aperture and iPhoto, have had full screen modes that give over all of your desktop pixels to displaying just their own interfaces.

Working in this way lets you block out the distractions that may be provided by your other apps – particularly if those other apps are Twitter, Mail, or other forms of communication that encourage you to interact with them as soon as an incoming message appears.

Useful though this feature is, it relies on developers coding it themselves, which in turn increases their workload and risks pushing back the release date of their products. No wonder so few have seen fit to employ it to date.

Mac OS X 10.7 and later makes implementing full screen modes far simpler as it is supported within the very core of the operating system. This is good news as it means we'll likely see it employed by ever more developers in the future.

It's by no means compulsory for developers to use it, and in many cases it's not appropriate either – why would you want to use full screen to display System Preferences, for example – but for those that do, it adds a subtle double-ended arrow button to the upper right corner of their application toolbar [1]. Clicking this expands the window to fill the screen, in turn hiding the Menu Bar and Dock [2] and giving the application a screen of its own in Mission Control [3].

Moving your mouse to the top of the screen makes the menu bar slide back into view so that you can access your app commands; sliding it down to the very bottom calls up the Dock.

When you've finished working in full screen mode, switching back to the regular application windows is as simple as invoking the mode in the first place: move up to the menu bar and click the blue squeeze button on the far right of the bar to slide everything back into place [4].

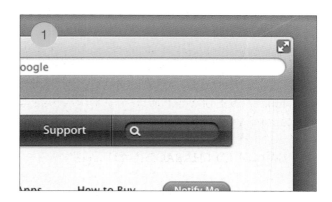

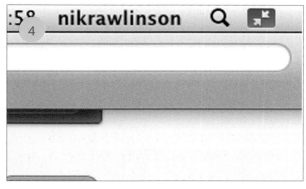

BEST OF THE REST

In all, Apple lists 250 new and improved features that have been rolled out as part of OS X Lion. Many of these sit below the surface and have no visual impact on the way you use your Mac, but for our money the must-have improvements that make it a hugely worthwhile upgrade include:

■ RESTORE

Applications restart in their previous condition. So, if you were using Pages and had three documents open when you quit the last time around those same three documents will open up automatically the next time you start working.

For anyone who uses a standard set of files every time they open a particular app – say three planning and finance spreadsheets – they'll always be waiting for you whenever you start Numbers without you having to hunt them down.

Likewise, after applying updates and patches, when you restart your Mac, OS X will reboot with whatever it was you were last running when you shut it down. That's impressive.

■ SPOTLIGHT

Spotlight now searches both Wikipedia and the wider web for answers to your queries, so it's no longer just a file finder and app launcher. It also previews your results as you hover over them.

■ READING LIST

Apple takes a leaf out of Instapaper's book and introduces Reading List.

Already Safari had the reader pane, which extracted the main body of a web page into a separate layer, dimming the rest of the page and often filtering out the ads so that the results were easier to read. Now it recognises that we don't always have time to read everything we turn up on the spot. Reading List therefore saves a copy of the page you are on to come back to later.

■ AIRDROP

There's no need to set up a bespoke local network to share files with other Mac users. AirDrop recognises other Macs running OS X Lion or later that are within Wi-Fi range and lets you drop files straight onto their hard drives without any configuration. Bonjour went some way to making this painless, but AirDrop finishes the job.

■ A WELCOMING HAND FOR WINDOWS USERS

Lion has a Windows migration tool, making it easier than ever for the growing band of PC switchers to bring all of their existing data with them when they come to the Mac.

■ EASIER EMAIL SETUP

Not only has Mail itself been given an overhaul, but it's now easier than ever to set up accounts with the most popular online services, including Microsoft Exchange, Gmail and AOL. Here, Apple is again drawing inspiration from the work it has done in developing iOS for the iPad, iPhone and iPod touch, each of which include a simple means of integrating your existing online services.

■ IMPROVED CHARACTER CHOOSER

Using international, accented characters in your documents previously required the use of three keys: the letter you wanted, a modifier, and the key that produced the accent. If you didn't know where the accent character was found this was a tricky work-around. OS X Lion takes its lead from iOS again here. Now you only need hold down the character you want to modify and all of its possible configurations will pop up, ready for you to click the one you want. Finally the character viewer can disappear from our menu bars forever, and hunt and peck will be a thing of the past.

GESTURE GALLERY

Two-finger scrolling. Drag up or down with two fingers within an app window to scroll its contents.

Three-finger switching. Drag left and right with three fingers to switch between full screen apps

Drag down with three fingers to enter Mission Control and view your desktops.

Just like Safari on the iPad or iPhone, double-tap with two fingers to zoom on a website.

Unpinch to stretch. Enlarge an image or website by unpinching two fingers on top of it.

Back off by pinching. Pinch back in again to zoom out of a web page or application window.

Swipe to turn pages. Slide two fingers sideways across the trackpad to leaf through documents.

Grip to launch. Put all five fingers on the trackpad and close them up to open Launchpad.

iCloud

Having invested hundreds of millions of dollars in multiple online data centres, Apple wants us to move as much of our data as we can into the cloud. Its aptly-named free service, iCloud, is what it wants us to use.

. . . .

◼ WHAT IS ICLOUD

iCloud is free. iCloud is online. iCloud is a backup service, a music streaming service, webmail and so much more. In short, iCloud is your life online, or at least that's what Apple would like it to be.

Steve Jobs announced iCloud at the WWDC – Worldwide Developers Conference – in San Francisco in June 2011, and he didn't mince his words. It followed on from MobileMe, a service that even he admitted had not lived up to many peoples' expectations. That's a shame, as MobileMe itself was a replacement for (and improvement upon) the company's former long-standing online service, .Mac, pronounced dot-Mac.

The name change came about when Apple realised that a lot of PC users running Windows might be put off using a service that appeared to be very obviously Mac-focused, but which in fact was entirely platform agnostic. It did hook in to the Mac's backup application and worked very well with the integrated email and calendaring applications in OS X, but its real value came in using it as an online synchronisation and storage service for your iPhone or iPad, hence the change of name and slight change of focus.

Still, though, MobileMe failed to impress one and all, and Apple turned its energies towards developing something entirely new. The result is the shiny new iCloud.

With several months still to go before its full launch, some details of iCloud remainedsketchy as we went to press, but several of its component parts were already up and running and available for use – in Beta form, at least.

◼ UNIVERSAL SYNCHRONISATION

One of iCloud's headline benefits is the painless synchronisation of all of your devices, whether they be iPhones, iPads, Mac or PCs – or indeed a mix of all four. When all logged in to the same iCloud account, the changes you make on any one device will be reflected on all the others. So, download an app to your iPhone and it will appear on your iPad. Download one through iTunes on your PC, and the next time you turn on your iPhone it'll be sitting there waiting for you to tap and go.

Although one of the core features of iCloud, this isn't enabled by default. If you are an iPhone or iPad user, therefore, you'll need to turn it on by tapping Settings > Store, and then tapping the sliders as appropriate to activate the various services (see image, far right).

Note that as well as synchronising your app downloads, it will also keep track of which electronic books you have downloaded, and even which page you are on when you're reading them, allowing you to pick up on the iPad where you left off on the iPhone.

Right: applications like Numbers, right, will use iCloud services to synchronise your data between your Mac and an iPhone or iPad.

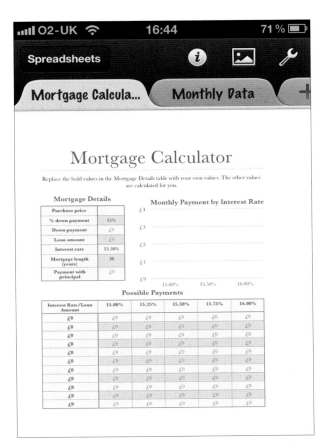

DOCUMENT SYNCHRONISATION

As well as synchronising this third-party content, though, iCloud can synchronise your own work. Its photo stream service will automatically copy your 1000 most recent images between each of your devices, so there's no longer any need to connect your iPhone to your Mac or PC to download your snaps. Set up iCloud and they'll appear automatically on every device, no matter what you used to create them in the first place.

If you use a compatible office suite, such as Apple's own iWork, even your documents, spreadsheets and presentations will be synced, so you can break off from working on a document on your Macwhen the clock strikes five and finish it on the train home, without even consciously copying it to your iPad.

At the time it was announced, the service naturally only worked with Apple's own software, but the company has issued a Software Development Kit (SDK) that will allow third-party coding houses to adapt their own applications so that they, too, can make use of online synchronisation between multiple devices.

APP SYNCING

As well as simultaneously installing downloaded apps on multiple iOS devices, iCloud lets you retrospectively install those applications you have downloaded to one device on a second iOS product. You can now use the iOS App Store on your iPhone and iPad to check which apps aren't present on the device you're using, and install them from the cloud without paying again.

ITUNES SYNCING

Perhaps the most exciting possibility, though, is the ability to synchronise your music.

The inclusion of this feature wasn't a great surprise, as in the lead up to iCloud's

Enable synchronisation through the Store tab in iTunes' Preferences and you'll keep all of your devices in line with one another.

announcement Apple had bought a company called Lala, a cloud-based music streaming service. It is likely that the Lala technology underpins its online music service.

As with applications and books, as soon as you buy a track from the iTunes Store it will be downloaded to all of your devices so that you can listen to them wherever you happen to be. On top of that, if you pay to use iTunes Match – the only charged-for part of the iCloud service – your music will also be available online.

But what of those tracks in your library that you ripped from your existing CDs, or you bought from an alternative online store? Not a problem.

iTunes Match will examine your music library and copy any tracks it finds that you own from the iTunes Store to your iCloud space so that you can listen to them on any device, wherever you happen to be. All of the tracks in your iCloud space will be high quality 256Kbps tracks, even if the versions in your library are of a much lower quality.

With the iTunes Store boasting a catalogue of 18 million tracks to date there's a very good chance that it will have copies of everything you've ever downloaded or copied from CD, but if there are any that it doesn't have already, it will copy them from your local library up to the cloud where they'll join the tracks grabbed from the store. The result will be a comprehensive online copy of your local library to be enjoyed whenever, wherever you want.

As Apple points out, this way of working has several benefits over the method employed by rivals Amazon and Google. They both rely on you uploading the whole of your library to their cloud drives, which can be a lengthy process and will tie up your broadband connection for hours, days or even weeks, depending on the speed of your connection.

How much does iCloud cost?

This depends to a large degree on which services you want to use. On the whole, iCloud is a free service, offering you 5GB of online storage for your documents and backups, and to synchronise your data at no charge.

Only if you want to use iTunes Match will you be charged a fee, which Apple has set at a very reasonable $24.99 for up to 20,000 tracks. How does this compare to the competition? One Apple's own comparison table, Amazon is shown to charge $50 for 5000 tracks and $200 for 20,000 tracks (1 cent per track, in effect. Google's offering, meanwhile, was shown to have not yet set its pricing, so an unknown quantity.

How do I enable iCloud?

At present it is necessary to manually opt in to some of the synchronisation services yourself. As we have already shown, you can enable iCloud syncing of books and Apps in the iPad and iPhone Settings application, but the same setting also appears in iTunes. To enable it check the Store tab inside iTunes > Preferences (see image, above left).

HENGE·DOCKS

SRP from
£59

Clean Up Your Desktop

Henge Docks has created the first truly comprehensive docking station solution for Apple's line of notebook computers.

Henge Docks quickly, easily and cleanly, puts all of your connections in one place, freeing up desk space. This system does not require any hardware, software or settings changes to your computer. In fact, every current MacBook is compatible with our system, right from the factory.

Dock Size: 13" SRP - £59 • 15" SRP - £69 • 17" SRP - £79

PROTRONICA
LIMITED

www.protronica.co.uk

Mac OS X
Applications

Mail

Mac OS X has included a first-class email application from its very inception and while it has been slowly evolving in the decade since then, OS X Lion sees perhaps the most radical rethinking yet of how it works.

. . . .

> *Few of us could manage without an email client today. Almost every computer user – and the vast majority of the online population – has access to an email address through which they can communicate with friends, family and work colleages. Many of these will be online accounts accessed only through webmail interfaces, but for those of us who prefer to use a locally-executed application a powerful email package is an absolute must, whatever operating system we might choose.*
>
> *Mac OS X 10.7 Lion includes the fifth incarnation of Mail, Apple's own email client, which justifies its hiked version number with an impressive selection of new and advanced features.*

■ A BETTER MAIL FOR OS X

Email has quickly established itself as perhaps the most important business and personal communications medium of the modern age. It's not surprising, then, that there are myriad email clients to choose from for every computing platform. Neither is it surprising to see that to encourage us not to switch Apple has given Mail a serious overhaul in 10.7.

Apple seems to have been thinking along similar lines to the developer of Sparrow, making the interface more flexible, more functional in smaller spaces, and better able to take advantage of wide screens when maximised, thanks to a full-height preview pane.

All together, these subtle changes add up to a far more accommodating communications tool for day to day use.

. . . .

■ NAVIGATE THE MAIL TOOLBAR

Check mail

New email / New note

Delete / Junk

Reply / Reply All / Forward

Related messages

Flag message

Search

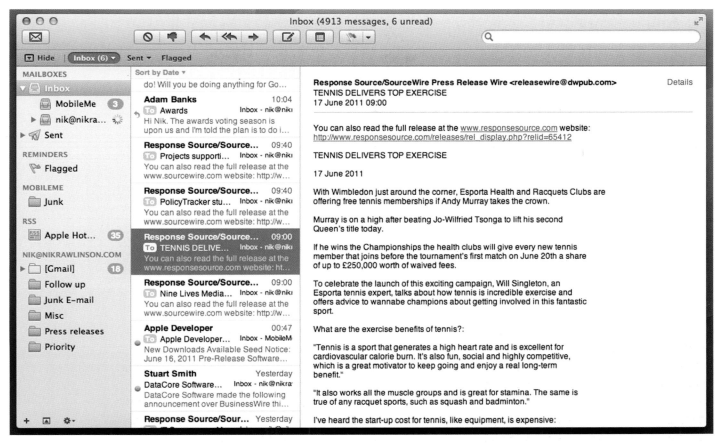

Mail sports a refreshed interface in Mac OS X 10.7, with less obvious visual dividers between the different panes and a full-height preview area that should result in less scrolling.

■ THE NEW INTERFACE

Mail's new interface is far lighter than its previous incarnation, with no firm borders between the parts. As ever, it has a unified inbox in the left-hand mailbox channel which, when clicked, displays all of the messages in all of your inboxes.

Clicking 'Hide' removes it entirely and devotes the whole of the application window to your message list and the preview window.

Previously the preview window used to sit below the message list, which was largely wasteful. The message list didn't need to occupy almost the full width of the application interface, yet in doing so it reduced the amount of space you could devote to actually displaying your messages, forcing you to do more scrolling to preview each one.

You can close the preview pane entirely by reducing the size of the application window and dragging the message list channel to the right so

that it occupies the whole of the available space, leaving you with just the list and your mailboxes in view (below). Double-clicking a message opens it in a separate window, which can be resized however is most is appropriate.

◼ HOW TO SET UP MAIL ACCOUNTS

When Apple announced Mac OS X 10.7 it claimed that it took the best of iOS and rolled it in to the regular desktop operating system. One of those features was an improved setup routine.

You can still define your mail accounts using Mail's Preferences pane, but if you have an online account from MobileMe, Gmail, Yahoo or AOL, or your company employs a Microsoft Exchange server, you'll find it far simpler to head for the Internet Accounts section of System Preferences.

Because OS X already knows how to work with these services the setup is greatly simplified. Opt to set up a new account by keeping your account details to hand and clicking the service name on the right of the interface [1].

The exact details required will differ depending on the kind of account you are setting up. If you are setting up an Exchange server account, for example, which will could theoretically be hosted anywhere, you may need your server address if OS X can't find it automatically.

At the bare minimum, however, you need to enter your full name, email address and password, and give the account you're setting up a description, which will appear in the Mail sidebar. [2] Mail will then head off using the details you have entered and try to find a matching server that will let you use those credentials to set up your account. If it can't, it will ask for clarification on whichever points seem to be incorrect.

Assuming all went well, OS X knows which services each server can provide, and it will give you the chance to opt in and out of each one. Here we're setting up a Gmail account that uses hosted services to manage our own domain. We also use this account to keep track of our appointments and addresses, and occasionally use Google's jabber-based messaging services, so we have chosen to leave the Mail, iCal and iChat options checked to integrate our Google account with each application on our Mac. [3]

Conventional Pop3 and Imap services can be set up by clicking the 'Other' entry at the bottom of the interface and entering the required details manually.

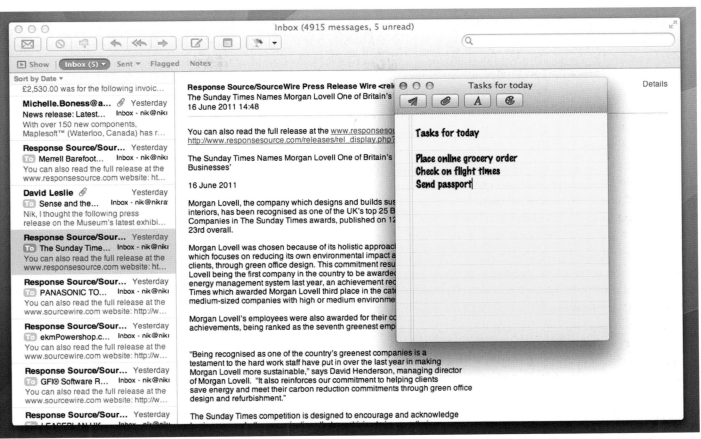

Beyond messages, Mail can also handle notes synchronised from an iPhone, iPad or iPod touch or created on the spot. It is also now the app through which you should subscribe to feeds on the Mac.

MANAGING NOTES IN MAIL

As well as conventional email messages, Mail is the app that OS X uses to organise notes on your system. It's also where iTunes files any notes that you have created on an iPhone, iPad or iPod touch which you have synchronised.

Notes have their own entry on the toolbar – a square lined notepad – and a category in the mailbox channel. Use the toolbar to create notes and the mailbox to view notes already in place.

As well as being a useful jotter for ideas you need to keep track of, Notes is a jumping off point for reminders you might want to send to friends. Click the Send button and it will be dropped into a new mail message in all its graphical glory, to be sent to your intended recipient (*right*). You can also add attachments, which will be sent along with it, by clicking the paperclip icon and selecting the file to be attached from your Mac or a connected drive.

Notes have a particular style, based on yellow legal pads that are a common sight in the US. You can't change the background colour, but you can change the colour of your writing by clicking on the palette icon on the Notes toolbar and selecting an alternative using the regular OS X colour picking dialogue. You can also change the font face by opening the typography panel, either by clicking the slanted A or using the keyboard shortcut command-T.

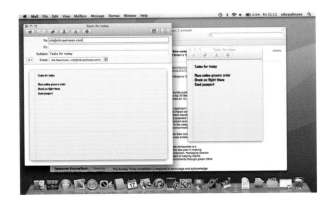

◼ USING MAIL TO READ THE NEWS

Mail is now the default built-in tool for subscribing to RSS feeds, which appear in the sidebar among your mailboxes in a dedicated RSS section.

You can subscribe to feeds either directly within Mail or from Safari, which displays their contents but can't handle the subscription directly except as a bookmark.

To subscribe in Mail to feeds whose address you alread know, click the '+' button at the foot of the dialogue and select Add RSS Feeds...

Enter the address of the feed and Mail will check that it exists and, if it does, add it to the section. Note that the feed address is different to the website URL, and Mail doesn't go to any effort to find the feed location on the basis of the site address like some other feed readers do.

To subscribe to a feed from Safari, visit the site in question and click the RSS button in the address bar. When the address is displayed in place of the site content, use the Subscribe in Mail link on the right side to add it to Mail.

Each of your feeds is shown as a summary in the main pane of the application; double-clicking then opens them in a window of their own so that you can read them in full.

Mail checks in with each of your subscribed feeds periodically to see whether they have been updated and displays a badge showing how many new entries appear in each one. Optionally, however, you can integrate the feeds directly into your mailbox so that updates show up among your messages. While this will ensure you don't miss any important postings, some users may find it confusing to mix direct, personal messages with online postings made to the world at large.

Fortunately, feeds added to the inbox are only mixed in with your messages if you select the overall Inbox entry in the mailboxes sidebar. To view the inbox without your updates included among your incoming mail, yet without removing them from Mail's Inbox section, select your individual accounts either one by one, by holding command while clicking on each one, or using shift as a modifier to select a range.

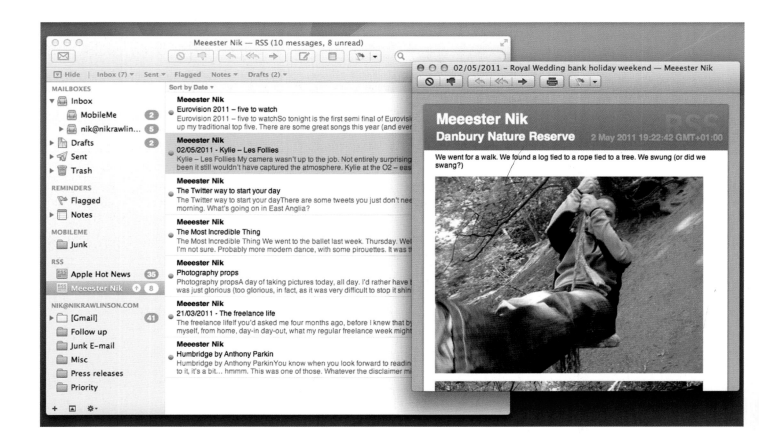

■ HOW TO USE MAILING GROUPS

If you regularly need to send messages to the same group of people, it makes sense to set up a mailing group so that you can email them all at once without entering each address individually.

Your starting point is not Mail but the OS X Address Book. This opens showing the contacts in your database; click the red marker tag at the top of the page *[1]* to switch to the groups view, and then click the '+' at the foot of the facing page to create a new group *[2]*. Give your group a name *[3]*. Choose something logical here as you'll use it to select the group when writing your email.

Now that you've created your group you need to populate it with the contacts who will be receiving your messages. Click All Contacts at the top of the list to show a list of your full address book in the right hand pane. Drag the ones you want to include in the list onto the new group *[4]*.

When you have built up your list, you can click the group name to see only those names that it includes on the address book's facing page to check that it includes everyone you want.

To use your group, switch to Mail and start a new message. Start typing your group name and Mail will offer up suggested completions drawn both from individual entries in the Address Book and your group names. Here it has correctly suggested that we want to send a message to our Games Night group *[5]*. Hit Return to accept the suggestion and it will populate the To field with the addresses from the group *[6]*.

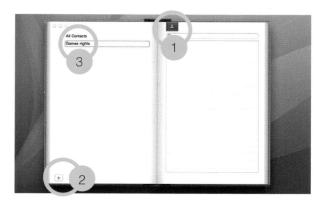

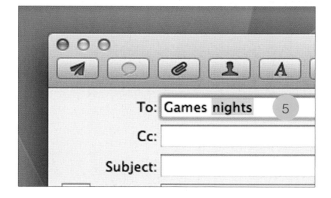

Safari

Few computers – at home or at work – now exist as an island all on their own. The massive growth and uptake of the Internet means that a browser such as Safari is an essential piece of kit, not merely a nicety.

. . . .

"

The number one requirement for any web browser isn't a pretty interface, but broad compatability. As we venture out onto the web we need to be confident that any site we visit will be rendered accurately, and look broadly similar in our chosen browser to the way it looks in any other.

Safari is one of the most accomplished browser choices in this respect, scoring well in online compliance tests, and frequently integrating the latest web technologies well in advance of its rivals, making the Mac one of the most stable, compliant – and often fastest – web platforms money can buy.

"

Safari is Apple's own web browser. It was first introduced in January 2003, and became a part of the operating system with the release of Mac OS X 10.3 Panther. Before then the platform's default browser had been Internet Explorer. With the introduction of Safari, Microsoft no longer actively develops IE on the Mac.

Safari is built on the Webkit rendering engine, which also underpins a lot of other key OS X technologies, such as the iTunes Store, and is found on Apple's iOS devices – the iPad, iPhone and iPod touch. In the last couple of years, since these devices have proved themselves to be equally popular with PC users, Apple has also been shipping a version of Safari for Windows.

Support from web site developers was initially patchy, with online banks particularly slow to allow their users to access their services through it. However, as its popularity has grown and it has

. . . .

■ Navigate the Safari toolbar

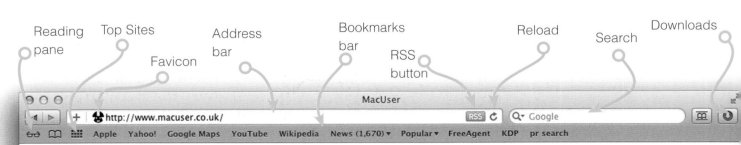

Reading pane
Top Sites
Favicon
Address bar
Bookmarks bar
RSS button
Reload
Search
Downloads

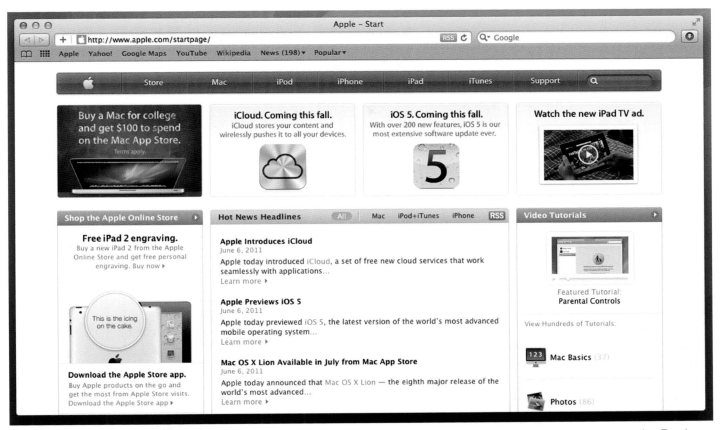

Safari is Apple's default web browser. It's installed as part of OS X and has its own spot on the Dock, unless you choose to remove it. You can replace it with alternative browsers should you choose.

appeared on an ever growing number of increasingly important mobile platforms support has improved to the point where, now, it is as widely accepted as its major rivals, Firefox, Chrome and, on Windows machines, the most up to date editions of Internet Explorer.

Safari is installed by default as a component of Mac OS X, and as such appears on the Dock of a Mac in its standard configuration, represented by a blue compass icon.

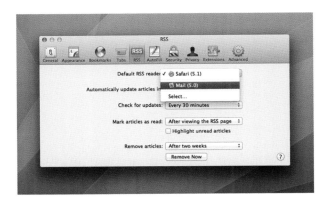

CHOOSING AN ALTERNATIVE BROWSER

If you already have a favourite browser other than Safari, perhaps because you use it on Windows or an alternative platform, it's easy to change OS X to direct links to that instead.

Download and install your chose browser and open Safari > Preferences. The first option on the General tab is Default Web Browser, which will currently be set to Safari. Click this to drop down the menu of alternatives and your newly-installed browser should appear in the list. If it doesn't, pick Choose... and navigate to the browser in your Applications folder.

Safari is also used to view RSS feeds when you click the RSS link that appears in the toolbar for those sites that include a feed. However, you can change this in the same way. Click RSS and then choose your alternative from the Default RSS reader drop-down menu (left). Close the Preferences dialogue to save your changes.

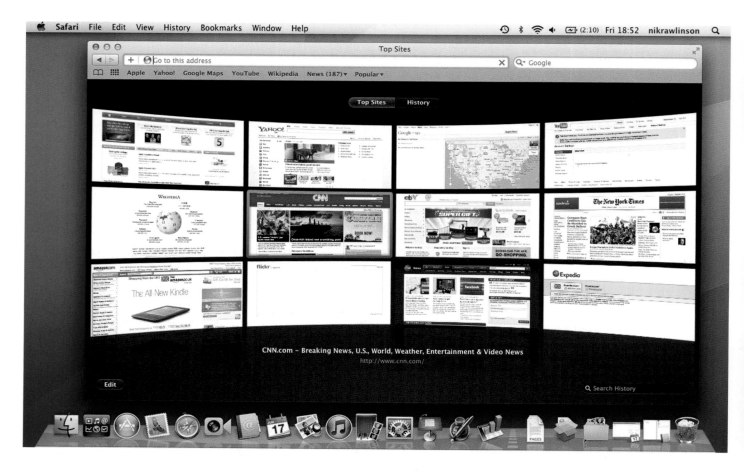

TOP SITES

One of the most beautiful ways to keep track of your most-visited sites is Top Sites (*above*).

This is a self-popularing area within the browser that displays thumbnail images of the sites you visit the most. Over time the make-up of the page will slowly change as your browsing habits evolve, but if you want to keep one or more of your sites permanently within Hot Sites so that you can always find it and skip to it quickly, you can pin it.

To do this, click the Edit button at the bottom of the display and Safari will overlay each one with two buttons: a 'x' for removing the thumbnail entirely from Hot Sites, and an image of a thumb tack which, when clicked, will pin the site to the display. The pin turns blue and the site won't disappear as your browsing habits evolve.

It makes sense to put the sites you want to find most quickly in the top row of Top Sites – an operation that's as simple as dragging the thumbnails into the order in which you want them displayed. Dragging a site automatically activates

its pin so that it will be anchored to its new spot.

The precise number of thumbnails displayed on your Top Sites page will be determined by your screen resolution, but if you want more or fewer than the default, pick Small, Medium or Large icons from the corner of the Edit pane.

By default, new tabs open with a display of Top Sites. This is helpful but can slow down your browsing. To change this setting so that new tabs open with an empty page, select the appropriate option from the Safari > Preferences > General tab.

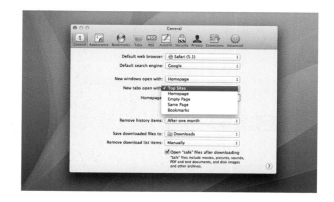

RE-VISITING SITES IN YOUR HISTORY

The forward and backward buttons on the toolbar let you navigate the series of links you followed to get to your current page, but as soon as you close the tab or window through which you're currently browsing, that series is lost.

Fortunately all browsers maintain a more permanent list of the addresses you have visited over time in your Browser History so that you can re-visit them later. You can access your Safari history in two ways. Either click the open book icon below the address bar to display thumbnails of the sites in a CoverFlow stream through which you can leaf, or use the History menu.

If you have upgraded to OS X Lion you can also use a gesture to navigate through your history list. Put two fingers on the trackpad, or one on a Magic Mouse, and swipe right to step back through your history, and then left to move forward once again as far as your current page.

BROWSER SECURITY

Whatever your browser, you'll leave behind a trail of information as you move about the web. The data left behind can be both helpful – saving you from logging in to some sites every time you pay them a visit – and a security risk, helping sites to identify you and serve advertising on the basis of your previous visits. Use the Safari > Preferences > Privacy tab to periodically clear out cookies for sites that you won't be visiting in the near future, and advertising networks you would rather not have following your movements.

Also consider refining the settings in the Security tab, from which you can disable plug-ins that play third-party media on some sites, as well as enabling or disabling Java, JavaScript and pop-up windows. The latter is a particularly important consideration as some less scrupulous sites use pop-up windows to serve adverts that, once closed, merely pop up another window containing yet another advert. By halting them in their tracks you can save yourself the frustration of tackling them one by one later on.

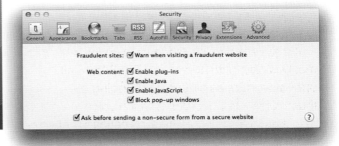

■ MANAGING DOWNLOADS

The way Safari handles downloads has changed very slighly in OS X Lion. The result is far more discrete than it was in previous incarnations. It still has the traditional Downloads pane (*below left*), but this doesn't automatically pop up when you start downloading a file. Instead, the downloads icon to the right of the address bar adopts a progress gauge showing you how far through it has progressed through the overall download.

Clicking the icon drops down a panel showing you further details.

Downloaded files are still saved to the Downloads folder within your User folder by default. This is traditionally positioned on the Dock, to the right of the divider, and will sport a progress indicator that matches that found in the Downloads drop-down, if you would rather keep an eye on the progress of your files without opening the overlay window itself.

■ TAKING SAFARI FURTHER

Safari is already an advanced and accomplished browser as soon as it's installed, but Apple has provided the necessary hooks for third-party developers to code add-one called Extensions.

You can find various Extensions by searching for them online, but the easiest way to install approved ones is by Apple's own Gallery.

Open Safari > Preferences > Extensions and ensure Extensions are turned on, or else you won't see the rest of the interface. If it is, click the Get Extensions button at the foot of the display. *[1]*

This takes you directly to the Gallery at https://extensions.apple.com *[2]* where Apple highlights notable Extensions at the top of the page and splits others into categories.

Here, we're going to install an Extension that will let us post to Twitter without ever leaving our browser. This appears within the featured section at the top of the page so, after selecting it, we only need click the Install button below its description to start the process. *[3]*

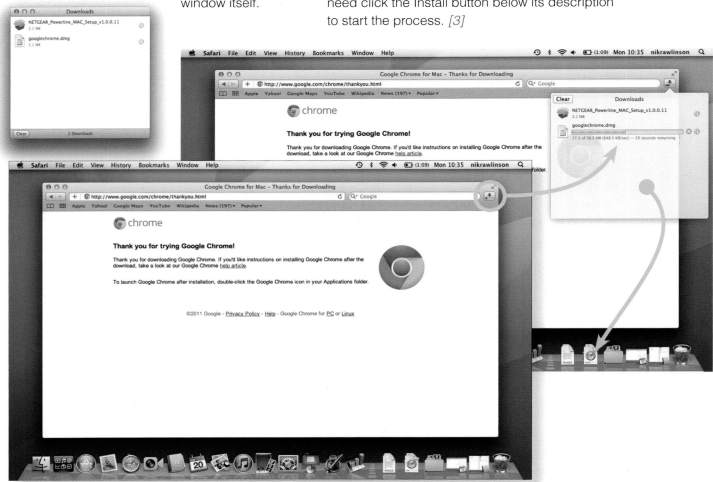

Safari downloads the Extension and automatically installs it in the browser, adding a toolbar above the main page window.

At the same time it also installs a configuration pane in Safari > Preferences > Extensions. *[4]* The exact make-up of the preferences will differ from Extension to Extension, but here we can enable or disable the extension and choose how we post tweets to Twitter.

If you later want to remove the Extension because we find we're not using it, we need only click the Uninstall button *[5]* and confirm that we do indeed want to remove it from our system *[6]*.

If an installed Extension is causing problems for your Mac but you can't identify which one, consider switching off all of them at once by disabling Extensions entirely using the OFF/ON switch at the top of the Preference pane.

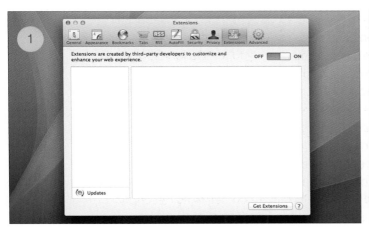

iTunes

More than a simple music player, iTunes sits at the heart of Apple's portable, digital strategy, handling device synchronisation, App purchases and video downloads.

. . . .

iTunes is one of the most important pieces of software Apple has ever shipped. At heart it is a music organisation and playback tool, but despite its rather focused name, it has grown over the years to encompass a downloads store, video playback, podcast subscriptions and, crucially, a hub through which you can manage the Apps, music and data stored on your iPod, iPhone or iPad, whatever its model or capacity.

iTunes, which was once part of iLife, appears on the Dock by default for very good reason. It'll be such a central part of your Mac-using life, we're pretty sure that's just where it'll stay.

iTunes is far and away Apple's best known application on any platform – not just the Mac. Apple released a Windows version for iPod users on the PC, which in the process gave PC users a small taste of the Mac experience.

Working together, iTunes and the iPod have drawn some people to switch from Windows. Anyone doing so would be relieved to know that iTunes has the same look and feel on the Mac as it does on Windows. The majority of features on iTunes such as ripping CDs, buying music from the iTunes Store and transferring music to an iPod, iPhone or iPad, all work in the same way.

iTunes allows you not only to buy music, apps, movies and TV shows from the iTunes Store, but also to catalogue your media using metadata that describes each item in your library.

Tracks can be rated to make it easier to pick out the ones you want to find and play at a later

. . . .

■ NAVIGATE THE ITUNES TOOLBAR

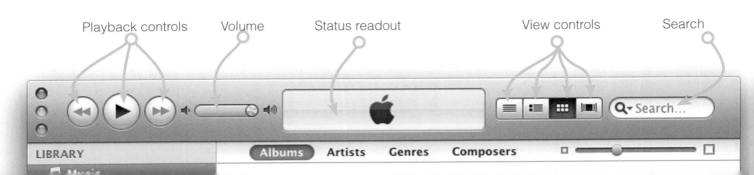

Playback controls   Volume   Status readout   View controls   Search

LIBRARY   Albums   Artists   Genres   Composers

There are many faces to iTunes, but one of the most attractive is the cover art view, which represents each album or single with an image of its cover. This artwork is the same as is transferred to an iPhone, iPod or iPad when you synchronise your music to your portable device.

date, and to build smart playlists that allow you to pick out specific tracks based on your own defined set of criteria. Adding genres, ratings and other details to tracks in the library lets you harness the full power of iTunes to create the perfect mix for any party, or to burn to CD.

With every new version, Apple adds new features, and latterly it has introduced Ping, its own media-focused social network that lets you share your music tastes and see what your friends are buying and listening to. This works alongside Genius, its technology for building playlists of tracks that work particularly well together based on not only their physical characteristics such as tempo, but how other iTunes users have used those tracks alongside others in their libraries.

With the arrival of iCloud, Apple's online synchronisation service, comes iTunes newest feature: iTunes Match. This clever tool examines the contents of your iTunes library and, if it can

match those tracks to songs that are available for download from the iTunes Store, makes them available online without any further user action. Any tracks that aren't sold through the Store can be uploaded to the cloud service to make them available alongside the rest of the library. This lets you listen to your music wherever you happen to be by streaming it from the Internet, even when you don't have access to your local iTunes library. Although iTunes itself is free, the iTunes Match service is charged-for.

iTunes was very aptly named when was first developed, but as it has grown and matured, and its range of features has been extended and expanded, it now sounds like a fairly limited description. Don't underestimate the power of this app purely on the basis of its name, though. From the very first time you import a piece of media to your Mac it's likely to be the home of that movie or track for as long as you own it.

■ How to share your tunes

iTunes has sharing built in. Note that we're not talking about copying your music and giving it to friends – in almost every instance that's illegal – but rather allowing other people on your local network who are also running iTunes to share the music on your Mac.

To enable sharing, open iTunes > Preferences and click the Sharing tab, then check the box beside 'Share my library on my local network' and click OK.

Your iibrary, complete with its playlists, will then appear in the sidebar of any other installation of iTunes running on your network. By default, each user will see the whole of your library.

Despite sharing your library in this way, you retain a great degree of control over what can be seen within your library.

If you don't want to share the more embarassing selections of your iTunes library, you need only gather them in to a dedicated playlist and click on the radio button beside 'Share selected playlists', then check only the playlists you want to share – remembering to omit that embarassing collection of hidden tracks.

You can also restrict the people who are able to access any of your library by setting a password. This is particularly useful if you are running an older Mac that might become bogged down if too many other users start playing music – or TV shows and movies, which are also shared – from your computer.

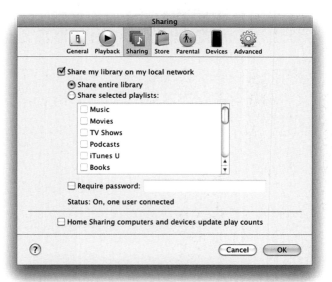

■ How to subscribe to a podcast

iTunes is more than a simple music download tool – it also lets you keep up with your favourite radio programmes.

01 Enter the Store Click iTunes Store in the sidebar to enter the store and type a search term in the box at the top of the window. This could be a keyword related to the subject you're after – such as 'football', for example – or, as in our case, part of the name of the podcast we're looking for. We want to subscribe to the BBC soap, The Archers, so have typed Archers.

02 Read the synopsis Every podcast has a description and each episode has a synopsis. Click the 'i' button beside an episode description to pull up an outline and check that this really is the podcast stream you want.

03 Download an episode You can download individual episodes of any podcast without making an ongoing commitment by subscribing. To do this, simply click the button marked 'free' in the price column. The episode will immediately start to download.

04 Subscribe to the podcast If you know you're going to want to listen to the podcast on an ongoing basis, then instead click the Subscribe Free button below its cover art. You'll be asked to confirm that you really do want to download this and future episodes. Click the Subscribe button to confirm this and iTunes will automatically download all future editions of the podcast as soon as they become available without any further intervention from yourself.

05 The download begins The first episode of your subscription will start to download. If you want to catch up on past episodes that you have already missed, click the Get button beside each one, or Get All, at the top of the column. You can monitor the progress of the downlaods in the status window or if you have several downloads running concurrently, by clicking Downloads in the sidebar.

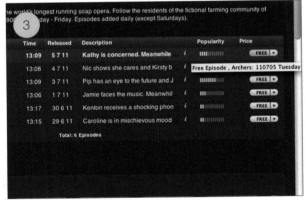

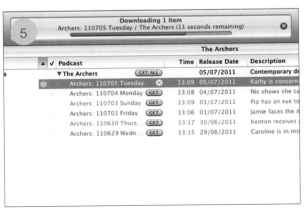

WORKING WITH iTUNES PLAYLISTS

iTunes lets you sort your music into playlists, which can encompass tracks from any number of albums. This lets you gather related music for specific occasions, such as relaxing after work, while driving or for working out in the gym. For this we want to create a playlist of energetic, up-tempo tracks that will keep us feeling motivated. The first step is to create the container for the playlist itself by clicking the '+' button at the bottom of the iTunes sidebar. We can then give our playlist a name that makes it easy to identify in the future. Choose something memorable as this will also be transfered to your iPod.

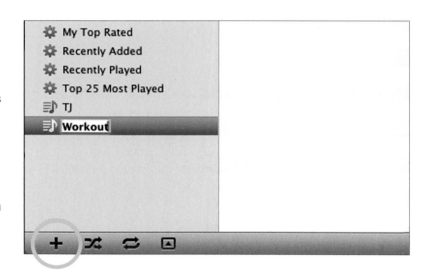

Select the tracks you want to include in your playlist by clicking them in the main track listing window. Use the standard Mac convention of holding command (the 'Apple' key) while clicking tracks to select non-consecutive entries, and hold shift to select a range of tracks that follow on from one another. If you want to create a playlist of a specific duration, keep an eye on the status bar at the bottom of the iTunes application window, which tells you the cumulative length of your selection at the current point. Unless you have your full track listing displayed you'll only be able to select from one album, artist or genre at a time.

With your tracks selected, drag them onto the playlist container you created in the sidebar. A badge on the music icon indicates how many tracks you are adding to the playlist. You can now continue to select other tracks from elsewhere in your library to add them to the ones already in the playlist. To transfer the playlist to your iPhone, iPad or iPod, connect your device and either drag the playlist on to its icon in the sidebar (if you are manually managing your music) or make sure its checkbox is ticked within the music section of iTunes' device configuration pages and then perform a full synchronisation.

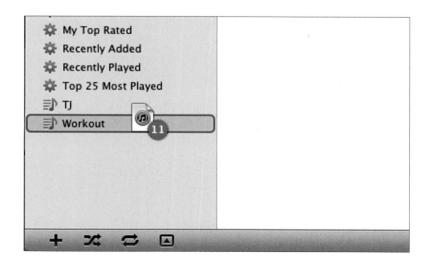

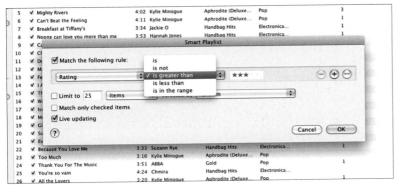

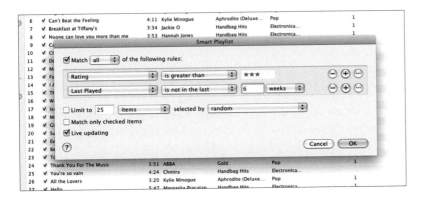

CREATING A SMART PLAYLIST

Smart Playlists use the metadata contained within your tracks to build specific listings based on criteria you select yourself using a series of menus and drop-downs.

To create your first smart playlist, hold alt while clicking the '+' icon at the bottom of the iTunes sidebar. Notice that when you held alt the icon changed to a cog, which Apple frequently uses as an indicator for any tool that helps you make changes or create smart lists.

Unlike when we are creating regular playlists, we don't need to start by giving the playlist a name. Simply jump straight in and start defining the contents of the playlist by using the dialogue that pops up. We are going to create a list of the highest-rated but least-played tracks in our library, so start by specifying that they should be rated higher than three out of five by picking Rating from the first menu, 'is greater than' from the second, and clicking the third dot in the rating box. This will restrict our results to just those tracks with four or five stars.

Click the '+' button at the end of the line to add another condition to the search. This time we are specifying that the tracks should not have been played in at least six weeks, so pick 'Last Played' from the first menu, 'is not in the last' from the second, and 'weeks' from the third. Now type '6' into the box that sits between them.

We don't want to limit the length of the playlist. The only reason we might want to do this is because it should fit within a certain timeframe, perhaps because it needs to be burned to a CD, which has a maximum capacity of 74 minutes, or because we want to create another playlist for, say, a workout, where the end of the tracks would mean that we could finally come to a stop.

You can carry on adding elements to the search criteria that must be fulfilled until you've built a smart playlist that exactly matches your needs. When you're happy with the results, click OK to save them, and give the playlist a name. We have called ours 'Lost Favourites.'

Whenever you add new tracks to your library from a CD or the iTunes Store, they'll be added to the playlist if they match your criteria.

iCal

You don't need a personal organiser – or even a calendar on your wall – when you have a Mac on your desk. iCal, its bundled calendaring application, will synchronise with online services and mobile devices.

. . . .

iCal is one of the smartest time tracking applications you could ever hope to use. More than a simple date book, it also keeps an eye on reminders and due dates, and lets you invite friends and colleagues to meetings.

The version bundled as part of OS X Lion has a striking new look that differs considerably from the interface of previous versions, but under the surface it works in a very similar manner. Anyone upgrading should feel comfortable with the new layout in a matter of minutes.

When you want to track your appointments and jobs in OS X, the first place to turn is iCal. It's a sophisticated calendaring application that ties in with Mail to automatically add appointments and invite attendees to meetings.

When you first launch it, you'll have work and home calendars. You'll find them by clicking the Calendars button on the toolbar; adding any new ones will also position them on this list.

You can turn your calendars on and off by checking and unchecking the tick boxes beside each one, so you can have all of your entries, a few of them, or just the ones that appear on one particular calendar in view at any time.

You'll notice that each calendar is colour coded, and these colours are replicated on any entries you create so that you can see at a glance whether they relate to your personal or professional life. The colours are tweakable, so if

. . . .

■ NAVIGATE THE iCAL TOOLBAR

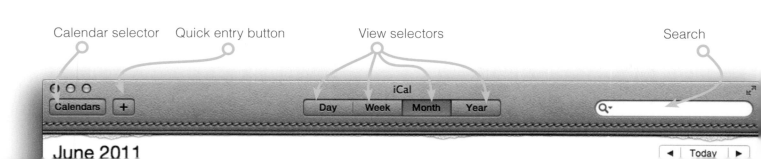

Calendar selector   Quick entry button   View selectors   Search

iCal

Calendars +   Day | Week | Month | Year   Qᐨ

June 2011   ◄ | Today | ►

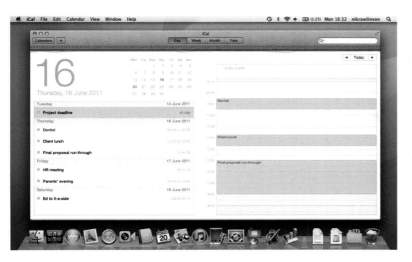

iCal has four views to choose from. The most informative is the day view (above), which shows a mix of listed appointments for the current and subsequent days, and a grid of the current day's timed events. The remaining three views are week view (top right), month view (right) and year (bottom right), each showing progressively less information.

you really don't like the ones Apple has chosen for you, you can change them to meet your need.

In versions of Mac OS X later than 10.5 Leopard, there is a third default calendar – birthdays – that draws data from the birthday field on contacts' entries in your Address Book. It isn't enabled automatically; you'll need to opt into it through iCal > Preferences.

Of course, there are times when two (or three) calendars simply isn't enough. You might want a separate calendar to track fixtures in your local football league, remind you when your recycling is due for collection and when to put the bins out. In that case you can create a new calendar by clicking File > New calendar and choosing where it should be maintained. A bubble dialogue will drop down below the Calendars button asking you to give the calendar a name (below).

iCal reminders

iCal is the place to turn to maintain a list of jobs. They sit in a sidebar called Reminders, which can be ordered by priority, title, calendar, due date or a manual order of your choosing.

To set a new reminder, use the keyboard shortcut command-K and enter a heading. If you want to further customise the reminder, double-click its name in the sidebar and you can give it a due date, add notes and associate it with a URL that links to further online resources. A check box beside each one lets you mark them as completed.

■ ADDING APPOINTMENTS TO YOUR CALENDAR

There are three ways to add appointments to your calendar in iCal. The simplest is to use the shortcut command-N, which does exactly the same as the second method – clicking the '+' button on the toolbar. This opens the Quick Event dialogue through which you can use plain English descriptions to enter new appointments. *[1]*

In our example, we have entered Theatre at 8pm on Wednesday, and iCal has correctly interpreted where and when it should add it to the calendar. If we were to leave off the time – simply Theatre on Wednesday – it would assume that it was an all-day event and mark it as such.

iCal drops our appointment onto the calendar on the next available Wednesday and opens the full entry editing dialogue box. This lets us assign the appointment to different calendars, mark how it should be shown (if you share a calendar this is useful as it lets people know you are busy), set an alarm to remind you of the event a specified

length of time before it's due to take place, and invite other people to attend the meeting or event alongside you. They'll be sent invitations. *[2]*

The third method is simply to move the calendar to the date on which the appointment is to take place and double-click in the appropriate time slot. It can be difficult clicking exactly the right spot, so you can drag your appointments around the calendar once they've been created if you need to re-time them, or double-click them to open the edit dialogue once more and change the time by entering it on the keyboard.

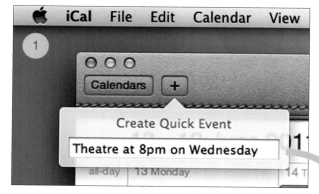

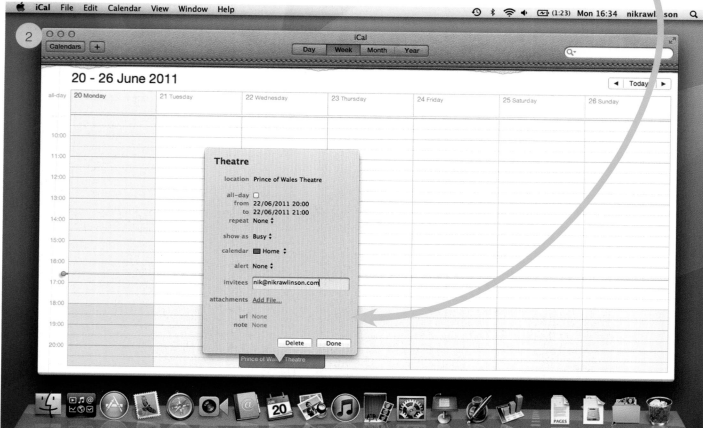

■ SYNC iCAL ONLINE

iCal will work as happily with online calendars as it does as a purely locally-held store of your dates and appointments. Here, we'll synchronise it with Google's free online calendar.

Open iCal > Preferences and click the Accounts tab. Click the '+' button at the foot of the interface to start adding your account [1]. Select Google as the account type and enter the login details for your Google Account (your email address and password) [2]. iCal will check your details with the server, log in and start to retrieve your existing appointments [3]. You need to decide how often you want iCal to refresh its local

copy of the calendars that it pulls down from the server, so select an appropriate interval from the Refresh calendar drop-down menu [4]. The default is to refresh them every 15 minutes, which for most users will be fine, but if you're accessing a shared calendar you may want to shorten the interval so that it immediately reflects' updates.

At present iCal will only be reading changes from the server, not writing to it. To change that, click the Delegation tab and check the box that allows account access for writing to the calendar. It will now synchronise any local changes to your online calendar [5]. Finally, decide which of your online calendars you want to display in iCal from the Calendars button on the iCal toolbar [6].

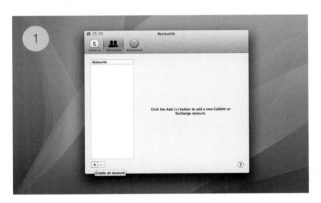
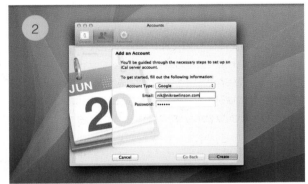

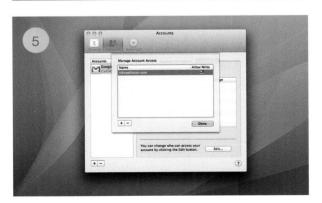
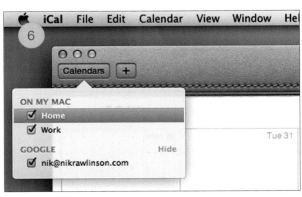

iChat

When speed is of the essence, there's only one place to turn: instant messaging. There are many clients to choose from, but it makes sense to try OS X's built-in messaging tool, iChat, before looking elsewhere.

• •

iChat is Mac OS X's integrated messaging application. The closest equivalent on the PC is AOL messenger with which it is totally compatible. The most popular PC equivalent, however, is MSN Messenger or Windows Live Messenger, thanks to bundling it with Windows.

Microsoft's messaging applications also work on the Mac, so if all your contacts use them they may suit you better, as you won't be able to talk to them using iChat. However, iChat is very closely integrated with the operating system as well as being very attractive.

The first time you run iChat you'll be taken through the setup process, during which will need to enter an existing AOL or me.com/mac.com username. If you don't really have one you get a free AOL address from aol.co.uk or aol.com. You'll also be taken through setting up any built-in or attached webcam, microphone and speakers, which will allow you to use iChat as a simple videoconferencing system with other users on the same system.

iChat videoconferencing features require at least Mac OS X 10.4 if you want to talk to multiple people at once, or Mac OS X 10.3 if you are happy to speak to just one person at a time.

■ BONJOUR

You'll be asked if you want to use Bonjour to connect to other users on the local network. If you're using your Mac home or you're the only Mac user in your office then it is safe to decline, but if you work with other Mac users it allows you to send messages locally without using the Internet.

Contacts with messenger details in Mac OS X's address book will automatically be added to iChat contacts list – assuming these are AOL or MobileMe buddy details. To add your own, click on the plus button of the bottom of the window and enter the necessary details, remembering to select AIM or MobileMe as appropriate from the account type drop-down.

To chat with any of your contacts, simply double-click the name and start typing. The two sides of the conversation will appear as speech bubbles within the chat window. To video conference, click on the green video icon to the right of their name. If it looks like there are more than one of these icons stacked up on top of each other, then they are capable of taking part in multi-party conferencing. Anyone showing a telephone symbol can use audio to chat, but will be unable to take part in video chats as they do not have a compatible camera connected.

Between your name at the top of the window and the contacts list that takes up the major part of the interface you'll see the status line, which most likely says Available. Clicking on it drops down a list of alternatives with whichever one you select being reflected in your contacts' own contact lists. A wide range of default options have already been entered, including one to post name of the current song playing in iTunes as your status, but by selecting either 'custom available' or 'custom away' you can write your own such as 'here, but busy'.

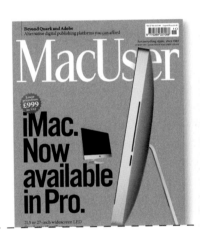

Mac App Store

The Mac App Store is set to follow in the footsteps of the iOS App Store, and for many will become their primary means of buying software for their computer. Here's how you can put it to use.

....

The days of walking (or driving) down to your local software shop and buying one of a limited number of copies of the latest release they happened to have in stock could well be numbered if Apple's plans for the future of software shopping come to fruition. With the App Store is has created a highly successful software outlet to which developers are flocking, thanks to the ease with which they can distribute their products and their consumers can download them.

The App Store arrived as an add-on to Mac OS X 10.6 Snow Leopard – specifically, version 10.6.6 – and offers an easy way to pay for, download and install software on your Mac, all in one step. It looks very much like the iTunes Store for buying iPad, iPhone and iPod touch apps, but rather than being devoted to iOS devices, it serves software designed for use on a desktop or laptop Mac running OS X 10.6 and later.

Unless you bought a new Mac with Lion (OS X 10.7) already installed, if you're running that operating system you will almost certainly have already encountered the App Store, as it is the only outlet through which Apple is selling future versions of its operating system. It is also selling much of its key software lineup exclusively through the App Store. Final Cut Pro X isn't available in the shops – only on the App Store – and although at the time of writing iLife and iWork

....

■ NAVIGATE THE APP STORE TOOLBAR

Navigation   Highlighted downloads   Filed apps   Your previous downloads   Available updates

Featured   Top Charts   Categories   Purchased   Updates

wunderlist

The OS X App Store makes it easy to find the hottest Mac software and download it in a single click, without entering your payment details each time you make a purchase. Use the sidebars to find popular applications, or search through the toolbar box, using app names or keywords.

were available both on the App Store and as boxed products from regular shops, the likelihood is that this will change with the next versions and they, too, will become App Store-only products.

■ APP STORE ACCOUNTS

Buying from the App Store is not only quick and easy; it is also safe, as it uses the credit card and contact details that you have already provided to Apple, and so these are not passed backwards and forwards over the web each time you make a purchase.

If you don't already have an account with Apple, launch the App Store and then, from the Store menu, click create an account. You will have to agree to Apple's terms and conditions before you can set up your account, and must provide a payment method in the form of a credit or debit

card that Apple can charge every time you make a purchase. Step through the setup screens to create your account.

If you already have an account with the iTunes Store then you can safely skip this part of the process, as the same account is also valid here. In this case, pick Sign In from the Store menu and enter your Apple ID and password.

You'll need to set up an account before you can download from the App Store, unless you already have an Apple ID from iTunes.

Top: Sort your search results to find the best applications in any field. Bottom: Don't know what to search for? Navigate through the categories instead to find related software.

Once you have logged in, you will be able to see any purchases you have made on other Macs, and install the same software on the Mac you are using right now without paying for it a second time. You will also be able to check for updates to your software and install them in much the same way that you installed the original apps.

SEARCHING FOR SOFTWARE

The App Store home screen provides a curated selection of apps that Apple thinks you may find interesting. It's dominated by a large carousel at the top of the screen, which cycles through the headline products. However, below this you'll find sections for new and noteworthy, hot sellers and staff favourites, while in the sidebar are the top-selling paid and free apps and those that have so far generated the highest revenue. These sidebar entries are a great place to find the most popular software – particularly in the free section – as each high position equals a popular rating.

As with the iTunes Store, a search box in the upper right corner allows you to pinpoint specific applications, by searching either on an app name if you know what it is, or a function. So if, for example, you want to find a new word processor, you might type 'word processor' or 'writing'. Likewise, to find a driving game you might type 'Asphalt 6' to skip straight to that game if you knew that was what you want to play, or instead enter 'racing' for a more generalised list of driving games. Experiment with other keywords until you turn up a list that matches what you're looking for.

Results can be sorted by relevance, popularity, release date, and customer rating, again allowing you to quickly pick out the most popular apps to match your query. When you're presented with a bewildering list of options, sorting by popularity lets you filter the dross.

If you prefer to browse rather than search, then the toolbar buttons below allow you to examine the top charts and categories. Of these, categories is by far the most useful, for while top charts mixes together apps from every area of the store, categories lets you drill down through specific sections, such as business, finance, games, or lifestyle. In each instance, example application names give you a taste of what you can expect to find in each category.

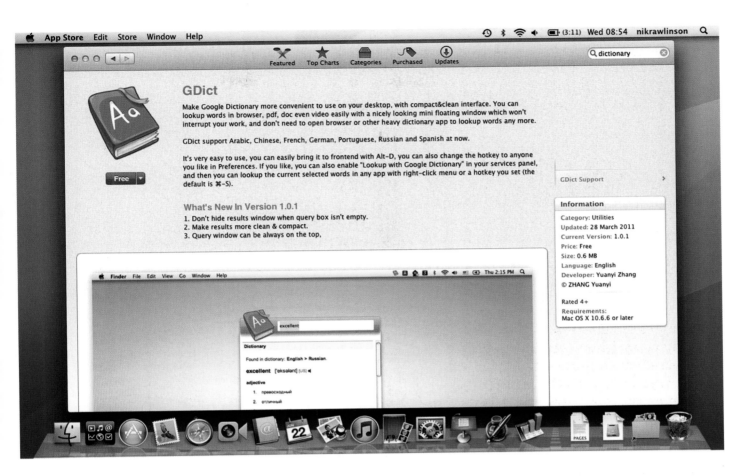

Above: Each application has its own dedicated page on the store where you can read more about what it does and what changes have been made in the most recent edition. Click the price or 'Free' button to download.

Below: Apps appear in Lanchpad in OS X Lion. In OS X 10.6 they install directly to the Dock. Either way, they're immediately ready for use.

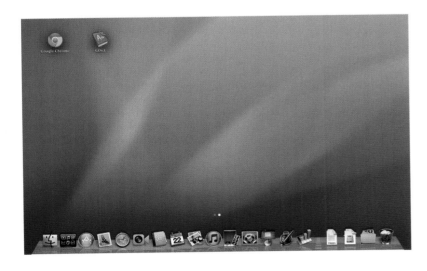

■ BUYING APPLICATIONS

Once you have found the software you need, click its title to view a full rundown of its features. Each app's page on the store also includes links to the developer's homepage, a short sales blurb, details of any changes made to this current version, and customer reviews and ratings. These latter points are a great way to help you decide whether or not to spend money on a charged-for application.

If you decide that you do want to buy the software, look for the button immediately below its icon. If it's a charged-for application, this will show its price. Otherwise, it will say free. Click the button, and on a paid app its text will change to 'Buy App'. On a free app, it will change to 'Install App'. Click the button once more to perform the relevant action. You will need to enter your password once more to authorise the installation. Once you have, the app will jump out of the store and land in the launchpad in OS X Lion. If you're running version 10.6, it will install to the Dock.

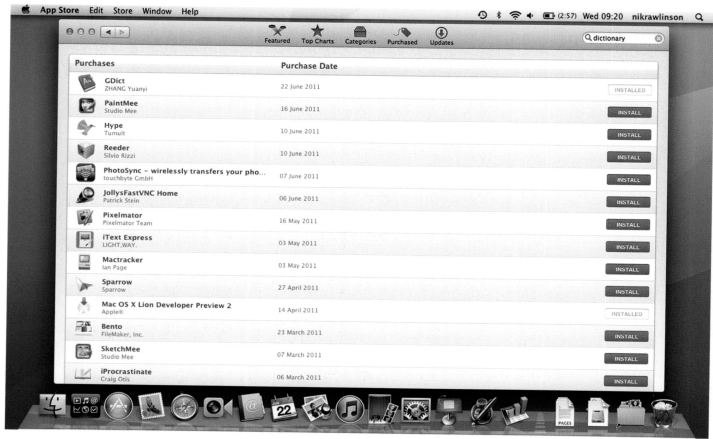

So long as they're all logged in to the same account, multiple Macs can install the same downloads from the App Store. Click the Purchased tab to see what has been downloaded through your account.

Returning to the Store, click Purchased in the toolbar and you'll see that the app you just downloaded now appears at the top of the list. To its right, the greyed out install button informs you that it is already present on the Mac you're using.

Should you visit this same section on another Mac, having logged into your account on the store using that machine, the install button wouldn't be greyed out, and clicking it would install a second copy of the app on that machine.

Whenever you purchase an app, Apple will send you a receipt. These are sent periodically rather than immediately, so it may take a couple of days to arrive, and when it does it may also include details of other apps you have bought since making that initial purchase. It will be sent to your registered email address. You won't receive receipts for apps you then install on other computers through the same account.

■ UPDATING YOUR APPLICATIONS

Software installed by any other means than through the app store must be manually updated, either by sourcing new optical media from which to install a later edition, or by downloading an update from the web and installing it over the top of your existing copy of the file.

The App Store, however, simplifies updates just as much as it does the process of making that initial purchase.

The final button on the toolbar is Updates. The App Store keeps an eye on which applications you have installed and whether or not they've been amended since you first downloaded them. Any that have changed will be listed on this tab, but to save you from having to check it manually every time you enter the store, a badge that sits on top of it will show you how many are available.

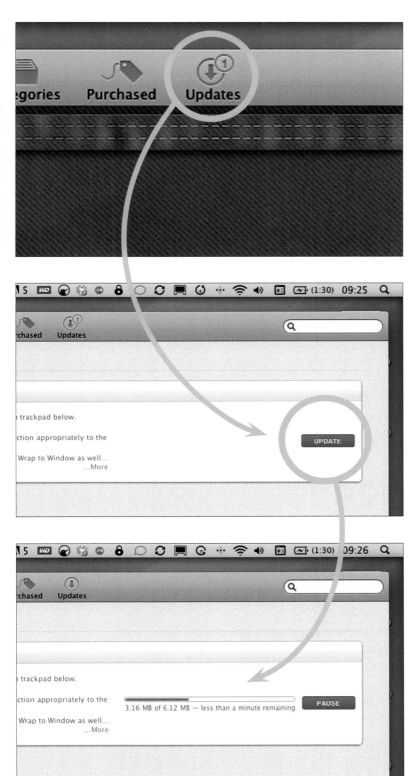

If there are none, the badge will not appear.

To install an update, click the button beside whichever app you want to upgrade and the App Store will automatically install the new version over the top of the original.

■ REDEEMING CODES

Apple allows third parties to give out codes for applications sold through the store. Codes relate to specific products, and so aren't like gift vouchers, which can be spent on any application at all. They are often used by developers who want to gift a copy of their application to a user, perhaps as compensation, as a competition prize, or so that they can test it on their behalf.

To redeem a code and download the associated software, click the Redeem link in the sidebar and enter the sequence exactly.

■ TROUBLESHOOTING THE APP STORE

The App Store is a fairly foolproof method for buying software, but should you find that an app does not correctly download, perhaps because your Internet connection was interrupted, then you can check for unfinished downloads from the Store menu. Enter your Apple ID and password, and the App Store will check your past purchases and find any that need attention. Should there be none, it will inform you that all of your apps have been downloaded.

If your Mac crashed while making a purchase, use the Store menu to check for downloads.

Above: A badge on the toolbar helpfully informs you of available updates as soon as the appear on the store. Click UPDATE to download them. A progress meter monitors the download.

Pages

Is it a word processor, or is it a layout tool? In truth, it's a bit of both. Pages is Apple's consumer application for writing, designing and publishing, both in print and online.

. . . .

On every new Mac you'll find a trial copy of iWork, and part of that is Pages, Apples word processor. It replaces the much admired equivalent that was in AppleWorks, but expands greatly on its feature set to offer basic page layout tools. It may not rival the kind of software used to design magazines and newspapers, but for home users who need to knock up a quick birthday card, poster or invitation it is both flexible and easy-to-use. Here, we'll take a look at Pages' key features and show you how to use its styling tools.

Pages is Apple's word processor. It's not quite a full replacement for Microsoft Word on the PC or Mac, but the two do share many common features, such as the ability to track changes, check your spelling and format documents. However, while Pages may be lacking some key word features – and by default uses its own file format – it boasts some impressive features that put it ahead of its competitor, such as a desktop publishing-style layout mode that performs many of the tasks of Microsoft Publisher.

Pages looks and works very much like an application from iLife. A large, simple toolbar at the top of the interface gives you access to its most common features, and an inspector palette (accessed by clicking the blue 'i' towards the right) lets you make changes to your document and pull in resources from iPhoto and iTunes.

It's a highly organised application, which works on the basis of applied styles. Styles are

. . . .

■ NAVIGATE THE PAGES TOOLBAR

Show/hide; full screen; outline

Document elements

Share on iWork.com

Open pallets

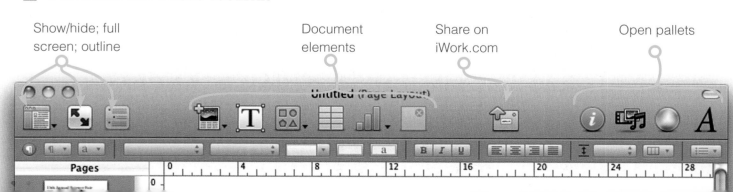

collections of attributes, such as text colour and size, font, alignment, spacing and so on. While you can change each of these individually – you can pick a new font using the drop down menu on the toolbar, for example – it's much more efficient to either tweak the styles or define your own.

You can see this in practice by opening a new Pages document (command-n) and clicking the circular blue icon on the far left of the toolbar. It looks like it has a back-to-front 'P' in it (actually, this is a paragraph marker called a pilcrow). This opens up the styles drawer. Now type a few words and then pick a new font from the toolbar.

Notice how the downward pointing arrow beside Normal in the drawer, which was once black, is now red to indicate you have made some changes. Click it and select Redefine style from selection. Your previously entered text will change to your new font; as will any other text styled up as Normal elsewhere in your document.

There's also a wide range of predefined layouts built in. Click File > New from Template Chooser...

and all of the available templates will be displayed for you to choose from.

These are divided by type. Some of them will be pre-populated with important information, such as your name and address, which is drawn from your own card in Address Book.

Once you have completed your document, you can obviously save or printed from the file menu. You can also share it using the iWork.com service. Be aware, though, that in the process of saving Pages uses its own file format by default, so if you want to share your documents with other people – especially those on a Windows PC – they may have some trouble reading them. The answer is to export them rather than save them. Choose Share > Export... and then click PDF, Word, RTF or plain text from the menu. Plain text is the most compatible of all, but you lose all of your formatting. To both retain your formatting and maximise compatibility, choose RTF (Rich Text Format). For Word-native files, pick Word, and for use on the web, pick PDF.

■ STYLE TYPES

Paragraph Styles

Paragraph styles format whole blocks of text in your document and can't be applied on a character-by-character or word-by-word basis. Click anywhere inside a paragraph and choose a paragraph style and that style will be applied to every word between the two paragraph breaks.

As well as font faces, character sizes and colours, paragraph styles can encompass line spacing and indents, making them the most versatile styles on offer, and one of the quickest ways of ensuring your document has a uniform look and feel from the very first word through to the final full stop. Use them liberally.

Character Styles

Character styles can be applied on top of paragraph styles to format smaller blocks of text. They don't automatically apply to whole blocks, but only to the parts of text on the page that you have selected at the time you apply them. As such, they don't encompass more advanced layout attributes, like line height and paragraph indent, as these are controlled solely by the applied paragraph styles.

List Styles

List styles are used solely to define how individual elements within a list are differentiated – for example, with bullets, dashes, shapes, numbers, letters or Roman numerals. Although a list can sit within a paragraph it will always start and end on a line of its own.

■ WORKING WITH PARAGRAPH STYLES

Pages will work however you prefer – either on a case by case basis where you style every element on the page individually, right down to single letters if you choose, or where you work with pre-defined styles. The latter, certainly, is its preferred modus operandi, and it's by far the most efficient way to work with your text. In particular, it lets you make speedy changes to set styles throughout your whole document by making an amendment to just one instance.

Here we have a long document that includes both headings and subheadings. The subheadings are styled in 18pt Palatino. *[1]*

We want to change that to make the subheadings more obvious, so we'll select just one of them – the heading Low Startup Costs in this instance – and change the style to 14pt Blair, which we have coloured blue. *[2]*

Pages has immediately spotted the change and warns us in the Paragraph Styles drawer by placing a red triangle beside the Subheading name *[3]*. If we move away from the current subheading onto another, the triangle would become black again, as currently no other subheading veers away from the defined style.

We want this new style to be applied to every other subheading in the document, so with the changed instance still selected we'll click the red triangle and pick Redefine Style from Selection, from the menu that pops up *[4]*. Instantly, Pages re-styles all of the other subheadings to match, as can be seen in step *[5]*, where the heading 'Long Opening Hours' now matches 'Low Startup Costs'.

Sometimes you'll want to create a style for alternative subheadings. You can do this through the red triangle menu, too, by adjusting the styling of the text you want to format and then picking Create New Paragraph Style from Selection. You'll have to give your new style a different name to the original so that you can tell them apart.

Wherever possible, avoid styling individual parts of your document without using styles, or at least applying those formatting changes to styles themselves. Once you get into the habit of working this way it becomes second nature, and you'll start doing the same in other apps, too.

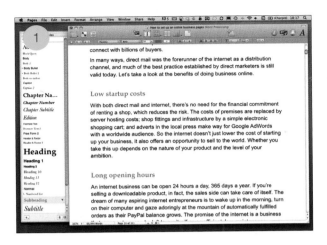

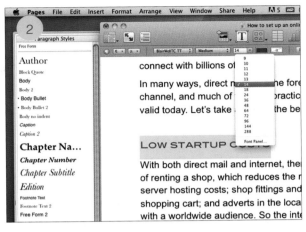

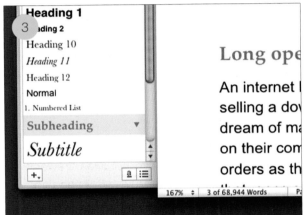

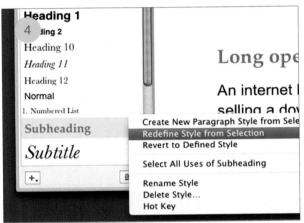

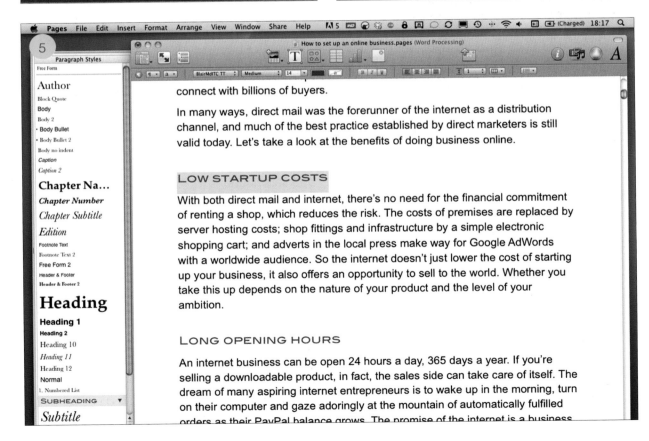

Numbers

Apple's radical rethink of the way we should all interact with and lay out a spreadsheet was a bit of a mind-bender when it first appeared, but now that it's bedded in we can't imagine working any other way.

What's so different about Numbers from Excel, the market-leading spreadsheet that forms part of Microsoft Office? Crucially, it's all down to the tables and sheets.

Apple took a brave step when it released the first version of Numbers in not only inventing its own file format, but using the flexibility and freedom this afforded it to rethink from scratch the concept of gridded tables on a page.

The result is a more flexible way of working, and a more attractive way of presenting your results.

The best looking spreadsheet application on any platform – bar none – is Numbers. It took a long time for Apple to add spreadsheet to its iWork office suite, but once it arrived it was well worth the wait. Thanks to a set of great layout tools, it produces the smoothest, most engaging charts, and lets you put more than one table on any sheet. This last feature is the ace in its hand, and it's not until you've used it and then switched back to something like Excel that you realise how innovative and useful it is.

The first time you start Numbers, you'll be presented with a blank spreadsheet. To the left is a column showing the number of sheets in the document, and the tables on each sheet, and below that the styles that can be applied to the tables. You'll see that there are grey cells running across the top and down the left-hand edge of the current active table.

■ Navigate the Numbers toolbar

Add sheets and tables   Data management   Add document elements   Share on iWork.com   Open pallets

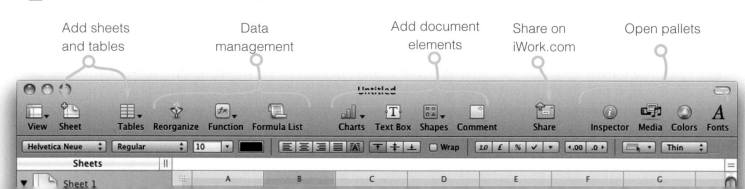

The easiest way to understand the relationship between sheets and tables is to right click on Table 1 in the sidebar and select delete. The cells will disappear, but you'll see that Sheet 1 stays active in the sidebar. Click on the Tables button in the toolbar and select Basic to insert a new table into the sheet. By default it will have 10 rows and four columns, but you can make it larger or smaller by dragging the fat corner handles at the bottom right. Click on Tables again and select Sums Checklist. A new table will appear in the same sheet, this time with check boxes that let you mark off different items in a list. Note how both tables can exist side-by-side and you can work on them both at once. You can't do this in Excel.

Add some details to columns B and C in your new spreadsheet, and then check a few boxes to the left. Note how the total at the bottom of column C doesn't start to rack up until you check boxes in column A. This is an example of the predefined functions Apple has built into Numbers.

Try moving your tables round by dragging the dimpled area above row 1 and to the left of column A. Notice how guidelines appear to help you line up with other elements on the sheet, making Numbers one of the best spreadsheet applications for laying out pages of data.

To add new tables on a separate page you need a new sheet. Right click in the top half of the sidebar and select New Sheet to create one.

Elsewhere, Numbers works in a similar way to Excel, and if you have any familiarity with Excel's formulas, you should have no problem making the switch. =SUM(D3:D9) would add together all of the cells between D3 and D9. =SQRT(C2) gives you the square root of the value in cell C2, while =AVERAGE(B1:B4) will give you the average of those same cells. A quick way to check the validity of your functions as you type them is to always use lowercase, and watch how the case changes as you type your opening bracket. Thus =average(will jump to upper case, showing you that the function is correct, while =avg(will remain in lower case, indicating a problem you need to resolve.

◼ UNDERSTANDING TABLES AND SHEETS

Spreadsheets are jacks of all trades, but that doesn't mean they're masters of none. Excel, Numbers and their ilk are just as good at tracking your financial health as a dedicated accounts package – it just takes a little more work.

Over the next four pages, we'll use Numbers to create a summary sheet to sit in front of a calculations table. This will give us an at-a-glance overview of our net worth, without us having to trawl through the calculations that makes it work every time we want an update.

We'll do this by referencing data in a series of working tables that sit on a completely different sheet to the results. Before you read on, then, open a new Numbers document and create two sheets, one called Summary and the other called Workings, with Summary at the top of the sidebar and Working below it.

Naming tables and sheets is a good habit to get into as it makes the process of cross-referencing data much easier to keep sorted in your mind. To remane a table or sheet, double-click its entry in the sidebar to edit their names. To do the same in Excel you would right-click the tabs at the bottom of your spreadsheet.

There is no reason why you couldn't use the cross-referencing techniques employed here on a whole range of spreadsheets in either Numbers or Excel to analyse a sports team's performance, grade pupil results in school tests or track changing weather patterns over several months. It's a highly flexible and easily adapted routine.

While a summary sheet of this type is undoubtedly helpful when illustrating your financial situation, the most important thing is to be realistic in your calculations and honest with yourself at all times, or else there's no point in conducting the exercise at all.

In the steps that follow we'll show you how to calculate the residual worth of your debtors' outstanding bills and how far you will have paid down your mortgage 12 months from now so you can budget properly for the year ahead. In doing so, you should always under-estimate anything that counts in your favour, and over-estimate possible bills and liabilities for true peace of mind.

01 Mortgage We'll start with the mortgage calculations. Our summary sheet will include a full breakdown of our financial health, including all assets and debts, so it's important to know how much remains to be paid on the purchase price of our house. The calculation for amount paid is a simple subtraction of the current mortgage value from the initial loan value. Calculate the percentage paid with =SUM(100/B3)*B6/100 and the cell type set to percent to give yourself an at-a-grance view of your current progress.

02 Shares Add a new table to track the value of a portfolio of shares. To work out what you would be left with if you sold all of your holdings, you need to calculate any fees levied by your broker, which would usually be charged for every company bought or sold. Multiply this by the number of stocks you hold and subtract it from your portfolio with this sum in cell B7: =SUM(B3-(SUM(B5*B4))). Remember to update the value of your shares over time using online sources.

03 Savings Savings are our liquid assets – cash in the bank. They are our most easily accessed financial instruments and could be called on at a moment's notice to pay off an unexpected bill or set against the mortgage. For simplicity we have ignored the pence in each account by setting the number of decimal places to zero and leaving Numbers to do the rounding.

04 Debtors Debtors are the people who owe you money. You can include their debts in your assets, but should apply the relevant tax rate. Here we're using the higher personal rate of 40%, but if you bill through a company and charge corporation tax it will likely be lower. The calculation in cell B10, for the post-tax value of those debts, is: =SUM(SUM(B3:B6)*(SUM(100-B8)/100))

05 Capital assets Now let's work out the value of our assets, the primary example being the house or flat on which we're paying that mortgage. Be careful here – it's tempting to overestimate the value of your property, but after a couple of years of financial turbulence most of us have seen the value of our capital assets fall.

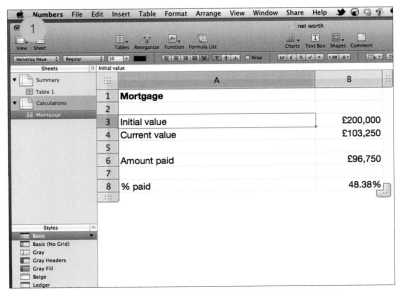

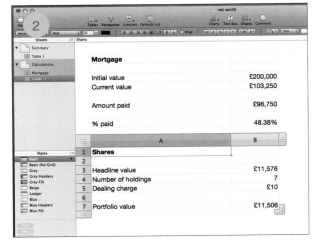

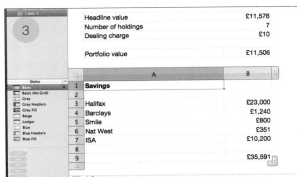

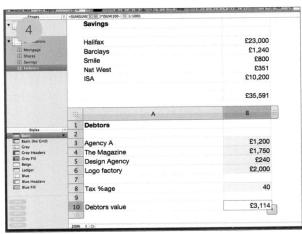

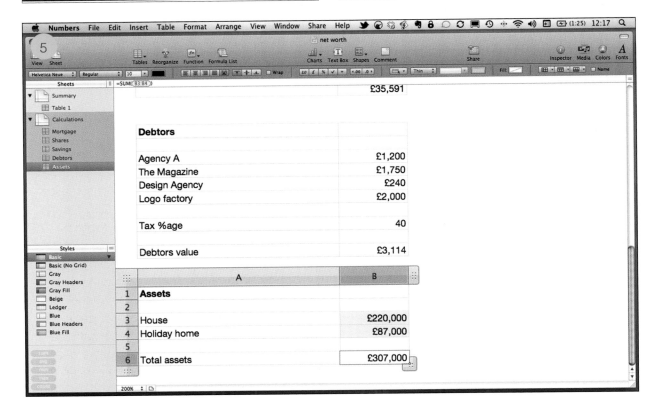

06 Get Organised That's all of our calculations in place. Now we need to organise them into a meaningful layout. This is an area in which Numbers excels, with guidelines appearing to show when the edges of tables or the cells within them line up with others on the page. We've arranged the tables into columns: assets on the left and debts on the right.

07 Payments We want our summary sheet to show us not only our current financial condition, but also what it might be in 12 months' time. To do this, we need to detail our monthly payments towards the mortgage and any loans or credit cards, with a simple sum adding them all up. This is our last table we need before building our summary sheet.

08 Summary Switch to the Summary sheet and add a plain table without headers. This single table will contain the full summary of our current financial state, so drag it out to fill the page and give yourself plenty of room for your sums. You can add rows between existing data while editing the a table by holding alt and tapping the cursor keys.

09 Tally your assets Create headers for your capital and liquid assets, stocks and debtors, with a total line below them. Click cell B3 to accept the total of your liquid assets and type =SUM(then click the Savings table in the sidebar, followed by the cell showing the total value of your savings. Note how the input box from the Summary table continues to float over the second spreadsheet, and the cell reference is preceded by the name of the sheet containing your selected cell ('Savings' in our case). Close the brace and press Return to copy the savings value to your summary sheet.

10 Subtract your liabilities Create a new column for your debts, including your mortgage and any loans, again drawing in the data from the relevant cells on your calculations tables by typing the first part of the sum itself in the cell and then clicking the relevant reference table in the sidebar. You can work out your net worth by subtracting these from your total assets.

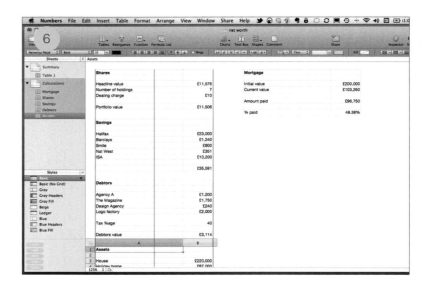

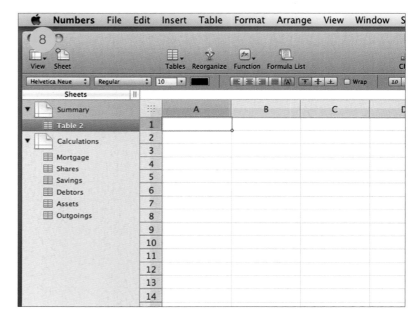

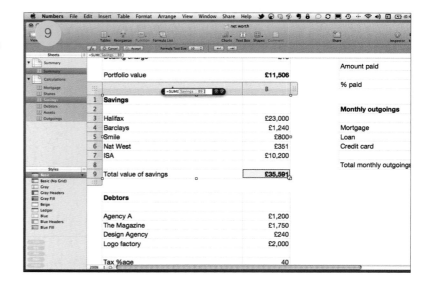

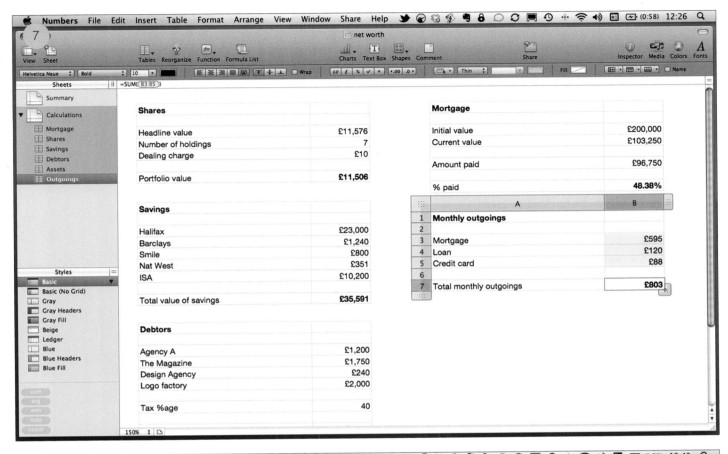

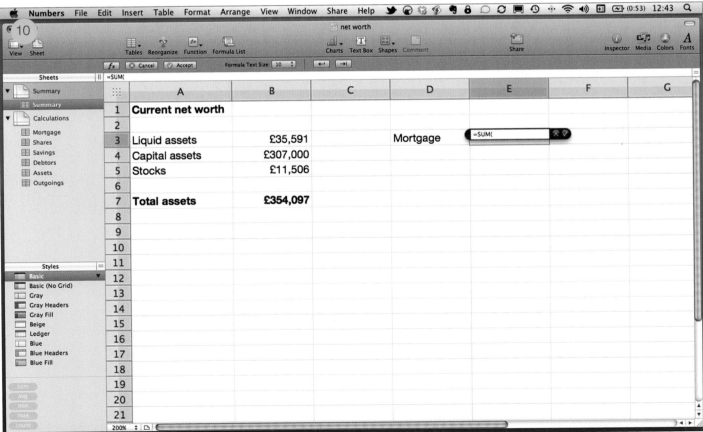

Keynote

Named after Steve Jobs' famous six-monthly addresses to the gadget press and consumers alike, Keynote is an accomplished, attractive and easy to use digital presentation tool.

. . . .

Ever since the demise of acetates and overhead projectors, the world of business presentations has been dominated by just one application: PowerPoint. Its name has become so attached to the practice that people now talk specifically about going to a 'PowerPoint' presentation, rather than simply a more general 'presentation'.

With the advent of Keynote on the Mac, it finally has some serious competition on this platform, leaving us wondering how long it will be before people talk more often about attending a Keynote.

If there is one thing for which Apple CEO Steve jobs is famous, it's his Keynote addresses every January and September. At these he steps on stage with a minimum of props, always wearing his trademark blue jeans and black polo neck jumper, and announces what products the company will be launching in the next six months. His only prompts are a series of impressively slick slides that pop-up behind him

For years, it was obvious that he was not using PowerPoint, Microsoft's industry-leading presentation software, so it came as no surprise when the company finally released Keynote, a rival Mac-only presentation package.

Keynote is an absolute gift for anyone lacking design experience. It ships with 36 predesigned themes, each of which can be created in one of five different screen sizes. The themes boast a wide variety of master slides, allowing you to drag

. . . .

■ NAVIGATE THE KEYNOTE TOOLBAR

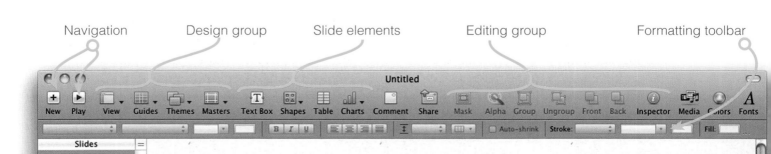

different designs onto pages you have already produced to change their layouts. If you change your mind about the theme altogether, you can even swap themes half way through, and Keynote will re-layout all of your slides to match.

Keynote takes the best of Pages and Numbers, giving you access to first class layout tools and powerful graphing features. It also integrates chunks of your iTunes and iPhoto libraries, allowing you to directly place media within your presentations, and can even incorporate QuickTime movies to create some truly compelling output. These are controlled by the inspector palette which, as in Pages and Numbers, is split into different areas, each of which focuses on a specific task, such as changing fonts, adding tables, adjusting the size of images and applying masks.

Beyond this, the most important button of all is the View menu button found on the toolbar. This lets you skip between slide creation and navigation modes, a light table on which you can organise and reorder your slides, and the central Presenter Notes view. Presenter notes are

additional points you make to help you through your presentation. They only come into play if you're running a presentation on two monitors, or a monitor and a projector. The slides will be shown or projected for your audience, while the presenter notes will be shown on your screen.

As with any presentation tool, though, the rule by which you should live when creating your slides is to keep them simple. Don't be tempted to put so much content on each one that you end up reading it out wholesale when you come to give your presentation, make sure your text is large enough to be seen from the very back row of your audience, and if you can ever use a picture instead of words, do so. Let it illustrate what you're saying while you speak by yourself.

You should also avoid using too many transitions. We would suggest sticking to just two wherever possible; a subtle motion from one slide to the next, and a more obvious choice, such as the rotating cube, to move between sections or groups of slides. Combine these with builds to introduce the parts of a single slide in succession and you will build an engaging presentation.

◼ UNDERSTANDING TRANSITIONS

Everything in Keynote is adjusted and controlled through the Inspector, which is called up by clicking the blue 'i' on the toolbar.

This floating interface has tabbed controls for both your slides themselves and the elements you have positioned on them. To change the way your presentation swaps out one slide for the next, use the second tab – the slide tab – and choose from the drop-down menu of transition types *[a]*.

The tab to the right of this controls the build in and build out, which respectively describe the way the various objects on your slide appear and disappear, thus allowing you to have individual points pop up one at a time, or a graph slowly grow in size *[b]*.

In each instance, you can pick from a variety of effects and change the speed at which they play back when you give your presentation for a truly polished end result.

◼ HOW TO APPLY MASKS TO IMAGES

Keynote doesn't have advanced image editing tools like Photoshop or Pixelmator, so it pays to get your photos and diagrams into shape before dropping them onto your slides.

However, it does have a very smart means of hiding extraneous parts of your images so that you can define the precise parts that appear, and the shape used to draw the frame in which it sits.

Start by dropping the image you want to use onto your slide. Don't worry for the moment about its shape, but do make it roughly the correct size, remembering to retain the proper proportions. *[1]*

Now use the Shape drop-down menu to choose the shape of the frame you would like to use to mask out your image. There is a wide range to choose from, including rectangles with subtle rounded corners. However, we are going to use a star. *[2]*

Position the star where you need it and adjust its size so that it achieves the final dimensions you want to use on your slide. Notice how Keynote pops up yellow guide lines to show the shape and size of the object, and inform you when it is lined up with other objects on the slide. *[3]*

With the shape correctly positioned, select both it and the underlying image by clicking them both with shift held down. You can see that both are selected here as we have a double set of grab handles; one for each object. *[4]*

Finally, click the Mask button on the toolbar. *[5]* Your image will be obscured, with only the part that sits directly behind your shape clearly visible.

Note that because we still have the shape selected, Keynote is showing is a knocked back preview of the whole image so that we can drag it to position the visible area within the star. We can also use the slider below it to resize the original image. Sliding to the right makes it larger, and so a smaller proportion will be visible within the mark; sliding to the left does the opposite.

To change the mask, either click the Edit Mask button, or select the masked object, click Unmask on the toolbar and delete the shape to reveal the full photo. You can then go back to the beginning and apply a new shape to the slide with which to mask the image.

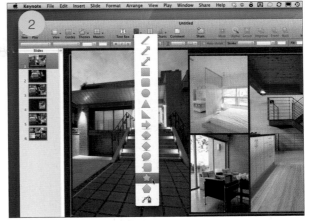

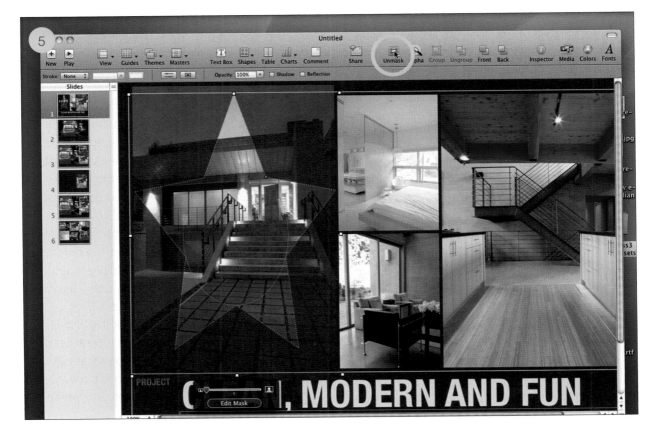

iPhoto

iPhoto is Apple's consumer-level photo management application. You may see it as 'training wheels' for Aperture, but don't let its family-friendly nature distract you from its surprisingly powerful tools.

. . . .

"*Whatever you want to do with your photos – whether it's simply organising them into logical folders or going as far as printing them out and binding them into professional books – iPhoto is here to help.*

Easy to use, yet powerful, iPhoto is an end-to-end photo management application for home users that's cleverly linked-in to online publishing and third-party printing services."

We've reached the point in consumer electronics when you're probably carrying a digital camera as part of your mobile phone, even if you've never purchased a dedicated digital camera. Over the years, even a casual snapper will build up a sizeable collection of photos of friends and family. It's important to keep them organised, but you could do that with folders. So why use iPhoto?

If you take lots of photos of many different people and places, iPhoto gives you the ability to attach keywords to each picture in the library so you can quickly find the one that you want at a later date. Make a habit of doing this from the start and it'll be easy to find the photos you want many years down the line. There's no need to pour through photo albums by hand, as you'd have to do with printed photos. Make good use of your Mac's ability to process information quickly and let it do the hard work of weeding out a handful of

. . . .

■ NAVIGATE THE IPHOTO TOOLBAR

Display controls

Film strip

Editing controls

Posting controls

iPhoto is a first-class photo management tool, which lets you not only rate and file your images, but also use them within products such as books and web sites (see image below). Here, we have tagged this image and positioned it on a map to show the location in which it was shot.

photos from hundreds or thousands of others, leaving you with a much easier job of pinpointing the exact photo that you want.

iPhoto's selection of editing tools is just right for the majority of us, allowing us to correct common flaws like redeye, tilted images were a camera wasn't held level, and incorrect white balance where a camera's automatic mode has failed to live up to expectations. The basic tools are complemented by a range of special effects and adjustment tools.

One of the standout features is the ability to make your own photo books, calendars and cards, and to have them printed and bound professionally. iPhoto provides a great deal of control over the look of each page with plenty of alternative layouts, cropping and scaling photos on the page, and captions to annotate events or other details for a photography portfolio. They

make wonderful gifts and are a superb creative outlet to make you proud of your handiwork.

iPhoto plugs in to the Mac's media browser so that you can access your photos from other applications within OS X. They even recognise your iPhoto albums, so the more work you do now on organising your photos in a logical manner, the more you will benefit in the long run.

HOW TO CATALOGUE YOUR PHOTOS

The best photos aren't shots of the beach, your holiday apartment or the rolling Yorkshire Dales, however pretty they may be. Anyone can take a picture like that, but only you can take pictures that really matter: shots of your family and friends.

These are the pictures that you will come back to time and again, and the ones that will bring back the happiest memories. When photos were developed from negatives, we had little choice but to keep whole packets of prints with the negative strips slipped into a pocket at the front. If your negatives got lost, then reprints would have to be sourced from the photos themselves, in which case the results were inferior.

That's no longer necessary. Now we can create as many copies as we like from our digital files, and with recent versions of iPhoto it's easier than ever to filter your collection down to just the photos of whoever you're looking for.

■ WHY CATALOGUE MY PHOTOS?

There are plenty of reasons to catalogue the people in your photos. Not only will a little work

Click Faces in the left-hand channel to view the identified photos in your library and click the Find Faces button to add new photos to the collection.

done now make it easier for you to find them in the future, but it also means you can quickly identify the people whose photos you want to use in the products you can create inside iPhoto, such as books, cards and calendars. These products mean so much more when they feature the people you know and love, and so make great gifts.

■ THE HISTORY OF FACES IN iPHOTO

Faces was introduced with iPhoto 09 and later found its way into Aperture 3, Apple's professional-grade photo editing suite. This clever feature can spot the features of a human face in any photo and isolate just that part of the image, making it easy for us to catalogue the people to whom they belong without having to create duplicates of each one.

When you have named a few faces, iPhoto will use the information you have entered to spot any other matching faces, thus quickly and easily building up a library of shots for each of the people in your photo stream. This database can be used in other Apple tools.

On the whole, Faces is very accurate, and the more people you identify, the better it will get at spotting and naming the important people in your life.

However, as we'll see here it can occasionally make a mistake, perhaps identifying the swoosh on a Coke can as a smile on a face, or your cat as a human because of the way the light falls on its features. On these occasions it's just as easy to tell it to ignore those shots and move on to the next one which, more than likely, will be someone you know. A few minutes spent working with Faces after every import will make your Library not only more useful, but also more meaningful.

ADD NEW FACES

Any faces that have already been identified are revealed when you click the Faces entry in iPhoto's sidebar. They're arranged as a series of Polaroids on a cork pinboard, with the name of each person written beneath the image.

Every time you import a new series of photos that includes shots of people, you should catalogue them into your Faces library. To do this, click the Find Faces graphic at the bottom of the Faces window (see grab, left).

IDENTIFY YOUR FRIENDS AND FAMILY

Above, iPhoto has picked out three photos from our library. The number of images displayed is determined by the size of the application window, so if you have a large monitor then it pays to stretch the window to the biggest possible size.

Because we have already identified some of the people in our library it is suggesting that the image in the middle is Richard Gooding, but it can't yet identify to the two to either side.

We'll add a name to the face on the left by clicking the 'unnamed' bubble and typing it in. As we start to type, iPhoto tries to second-guess what we're entering by pulling names from the iPhoto library and the OS X Address Book. We only need to type the R in this case to call up the correct name, as Richard Gooding is already found elsewhere in our iPhoto library. Pressing return confirms the choice, while tapping Tab confirms it and takes us on to the next face.

CONFIRMING GUESSES

It just so happens that iPhoto has picked out the correct name for the second face. Clicking on the tick beside the suggested name confirms it; pressing the cross lets us enter our own name in the same way we did with the first photo.

Once we have identified each of the faces in the pictures, clicking the Show More Faces button at the bottom of the interface calls up another pick of photos for identification. Step through your whole library in this way until you have catalogued each face in your collection.

■ DEALING WITH FALSE POSITIVES

In this selection (right), iPhoto thinks it can see a face in the crease of someone's jeans. Clearly this is incorrect, but it's easily removed from the Faces line-up by hovering over it and clicking the circled 'x' that appears in the upper left corner of the frame. When you do, the image stays in the line-up but is dimmed until you move on to another like-up by clicking the Show More Faces button again.

■ ADDING INDIVIDUAL FACES

If you don't want to spend half a day cataloguing every face in your library, you can add them as and when you come across them. Choose the photo you want to add to your Faces catalogue and double-click to open it. Now click the Info button at the bottom of the iPhoto window to call up all of the details associated with the image, including the shooting conditions and, if available, its location.

Below, we have a photo that features four identifiable faces, one of which – the lady in the background – just happened to be passing by. As

we don't know who she is we'll start by removing her from the catalogue.

When we hover our mouse over the image each face is outlined by a white bounding box. Moving our mouse over the lady's face puts a cross on her boundary box like the one the appeared on the jeans image in the previous step [1]. Clicking it removes her face from the list of possible matches in the Faces catalogue.

iPhoto has had a stab at naming the person on the right, but got it wrong. Nik Rawlinson is the face on the left. Clicking the 'x' beside this name

empties the name box, allowing us to type a replacement name [2].

By adding the correct names to the other two faces we can finish cataloguing the picture.

FOCUS ON JUST ONE PERSON

When you've given a name to a face in any of your photos, you can then use that picture in the Faces database to search for any other matches.

The name attached to each face in your library is accompanied by a small circled chevron. Clicking this will display all of the other images of that person that have so far been catalogued in your Library. Above, we have clicked the name of Richard Gooding from the image we catalogued in the previous step, opening a window on the ten pictures in which he has so far been confirmed.

As you can see from the bar at the bottom, though, iPhoto suspects he may appear in another four photos. We can check this by clicking Confirm Additional Faces... at the foot of the window [1].

Now that we have done, we can see that iPhoto was almost right. There are indeed several further pictures of this person in our Library, and some that are very clearly someone else [2]. Clicking the photos of Richard Gooding confirms that iPhoto's calculations were correct and adds the face to his entry in the Faces catalogue. Alt-clicking photos marks them as incorrect [3].

ADDING FACES MANUALLY

We have a rather unusual situation over the page: a photo that includes a person, but iPhoto doesn't realise that because they aren't looking at the camera, so it can't see their face. If we are to build the most comprehensive catalogue possible of everyone in our Library then we need to add this picture to the person's entry manually.

To start the process, we click the Info icon at the foot of the Faces interface, which calls up the now familiar sidebar showing shooting conditions and location, as well as an empty entry for Faces half way down the channel.

When we click Add a face... within this panel, iPhoto drops a bounding box onto the photo. Because it doesn't know where the face can be found, the box appears in the centre of the image, but by dragging it from the centre and resizing it using the handles on each corner we can identify the back of this subject's head and enter their name to add this photo to their entry in Faces.

By clicking the circled chevron that now appears beside the name we can see that the photo has been added to the relevant collection in our iPhoto Library, ready for use in products.

■ CHOOSE A NEW KEY PHOTO

Every person catalogued in Faces has their own entry in the Faces pinboard. Click the Faces entry in iPhoto's left-hand sidebar (or click away from it and back onto it if it is already selected) and you will see them lined up in columns and rows.

To the right, the photo used to denote Sal Norris is a poor choice as half of her face is obscured, and we know there are better alternatives in the library. We need to swap it out.

The photo that represents a particular person's stack is called the key photo. By rolling our mouse left and right over each face and iPhoto we can riffle through all of the catalogued photos associated with that person until we find a better choice. Any one of the displayed photos can be used as their default image.

When we find the image we're after, right-clicking (or ctrl-clicking) the stack calls up a context-sensitive menu from which we choose Make key photo. Now, when we switch back to the Faces overview, the old key photo has been swapped out for our more appropriate choice.

■ FACES OR PHOTOS

Double-clicking a face in your Faces catalogue shows all of the photos in which that person was featured, with a choice of two viewing modes.

If you're looking for a flattering shot of your subject, the best way to find it is to focus solely on the faces. If you want to show them in the most interesting scene, though, you'll want to view the whole of the photo in which they are featured.

You can toggle between these two modes by clicking the slider at the top of the Faces window. Note that whatever the shape or aspect ratio of the original image, close-up photos will always be shown in a regular, square box frame.

iMovie

Apple has a whole family of video editing tools for Mac users of all abilities. At the consumer end of the line-up is iMovie, its friendly, easy-to-use suite for putting together great-looking video compilations.

. . . .

" *The days when you could conceivably get away with sitting down your friends in front of the television – or even your Mac – and showing them hour after hour of unedited footage are long gone.*

iMovie makes it easy to knock your home videos into shape by removing the irrelevant, boring parts, and using transitions and effects to tell stories with whatever is left.

Like iPhoto and Aperture, iMovie is just part of a whole family of video editing products designed to take the developing user from beginner status to expert. The top-end product, Final Cut Pro X, is used in professional television and film editing studios. "

iMovie is a great application for editing movies, whether they've been recorded on DV camera, the FaceTime camera built into some Macs, a modern tapeless digital camera, or your iPhone or iPod. It handles the technical side of video while you concentrate on the creative part. It's far simpler to use than many professional applications, but don't be fooled into thinking this equates to poor results. With a little effort, you'll be able to publish superb video podcasts and professional-looking DVDs in no time at all.

When Apple released iMovie 08, its interface was a radical departure from what had come before, and some users were understandably concerned that it would no longer meet their needs. However, since then it has matured and developed, and it is easy to see now that the 08 edition was a transition.

iMovie in 11 lets you do more with your raw material in fewer steps than ever before. For those who want to apply effects, a new range of one-step options let you employ what would previously have been complex and difficult to achieve with just a single click of your mouse. New themes for sports and news enable schools, clubs and teams quickly to edit together screen reports that look as good as anything you've seen on TV. A new audio editor lets you make more refined cuts and tweaks to a soundtrack, and a fun movie trailers feature lets you drop sections of film into predefined placeholders and have iMovie edit them together into a well paced, cinema-rivalling production.

iMovie has also learned from the experience of other apps in Apple's portfolio, such as iPhoto, which has taught it how to recognise faces, and to accurately plot locations on the globe.

With iMovie, the baggage of professional applications is stripped away, to leave you with a clear view of your projects. Video, audio and other elements on the timeline are colour-coded so you can always see at a glance how much progress you have made on your project.

When it comes to finding footage, just roll the mouse cursor over a video and the preview is continuously updated in the viewer; it's a much faster way to work than dragging a play had around a timeline. iMovie is great for creating DVDs complete with chapter markers, and it's well worth the effort of adding them because the final result will look far more professional. When people receive your DVD they'll be impressed by filmmaking and DVD authoring skills, and they are unlikely to guess that it was produced software that cost little to download from the App Store.

iMovie is one of Apple's headline products, and in recent years it has broken free of the desktop, and now appears also on the iPhone and iPad. Here, it is able to directly edit footage shot on those devices so that it is ready for viewing or uploading to the web before you even come home. Apple's advances in building compact yet easy to use interfaces has paid enormous dividends with the result that iMovie's logical user interface is one of the best laid out, economical and easy to navigate of any you might expect to find in so accomplished an application.

■ WORKTHROUGH

Over the next three pages we'll walk you through the process of editing your first video, using the clip bin to import raw footage from your camera and then assembling it on the timeline by trimming the down clips to the most appropriate sections, and finally adding a soundtrack using a track from our iTunes library.

01 Import your footage The first step in editing a film in iMovie is to import your footage. Connect your camera and use the import tools to bring in the film you have shot. Footage is organised in a bin at the bottom of the screen and can be examined in more detail by running your mouse pointer over the film strips, at which point the current cursor position – the playhead – is previewed in the playback window at the top of the interface. When you have found the clip you want to use, you're ready to drag it into your project.

02 Place a clip Now that you have found the footage you want to use, click it once and drag it onto the timeline window at the top of the iMovie interface. Although you have used it once it's not locked in any way, as you can still place it as many other times as you want within the same project by repeating the operation.

03 Choose a theme We're now going to apply a transition to open the movie, but before we do we need to choose the theme we want to use. Click the transitions button in the lower-right pane of the iMovie interface and choose a new theme. We are using Photo Album as we want to use the album cover as our opener.

04 Apply the effect Effects are added in exactly the same way as footage. Here we are dragging the transition Photo Album 1 from the transitions pane onto the clip that is already in place on the timeline. This drops our clip into the pre-defined window on the front of the album.

05 Edit your effect At the moment the cover of the album bears the title 'My First Project'. That's not very descriptive, so we'll change it to something more meaningful. In this case, that will be Trip to Boulogne. Double-click the transition's yellow tag and type in the new text.

06 Trim your clip We can now start to think about the second clip we want to add to the movie, but before we do we need to trim the footage we have already placed on the timeline. The secret to effective movie making is to never leave a clip running for longer than is absolutely necessary, and to use multiple footage assets to build a story in parts. Be ruthless, then, when you roll your mouse over the clip and identify the most appropriate cutting point, then drag the handles at either end of the clip to isolate the start and end points of the section that best helps tell your story. Once you have made your selection, use the keyboard shortcut command-b to trim the clip.

07 Add a second clip With the cut made, drag your second clip onto the timeline and repeat the task of trimming it down to the appropriate length. Consider how you want to switch from one clip to the next and drag in a new transition from the transitions bin to sit between the two.

08 Reorganise the interface With a couple of clips in place our movie is starting to feel a bit cramped in that small window at the top of the interface. To give us more room to work on our movie, we'll click the double-headed circular arrow button to swap the timeline and clip bin.

09 Add some audio Finally we'll add a track from our iTunes library, which will run below the clips. Click the circled button above the timeline to change its view so that it runs as a single strip rather than being folded through multiple lines, and then click the music icon in the assets palette. Click the disclosure triangle to drop down the various audio sources available on your Mac and choose iTunes. Choose the track you want to use either by searching, using the box at the bottom of the panel, by scrolling through the list of available tracks, or navigating your existing playlists. When you've found a track you want to use, drag it on to the timeline. Repeat these steps until you complete your movie.

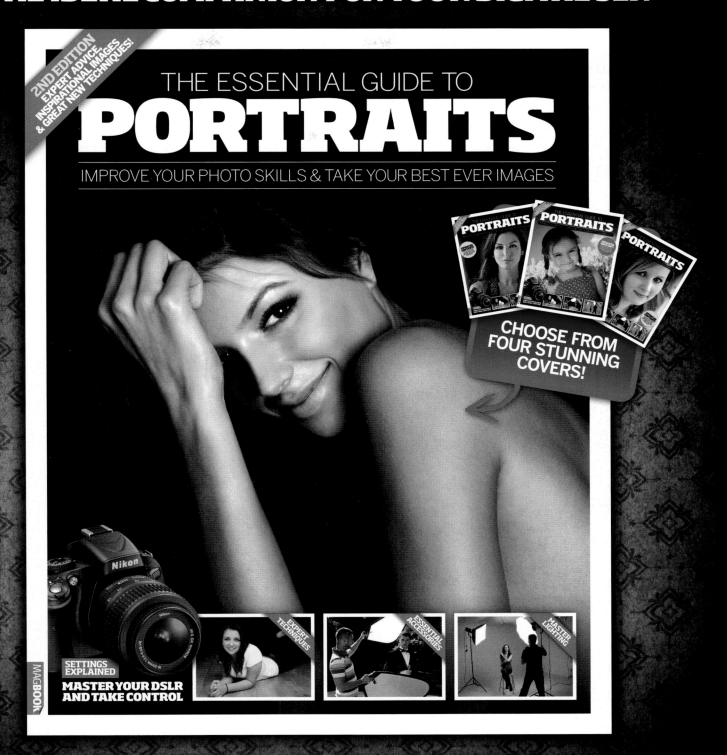

GarageBand

GarageBand might look like a very sophisticated toy, but scratch its surface and you find an advanced recording and editing tool just waiting to be exploited in the recording of your own songs.

· ·

GarageBand isn't about printing, publishing or organising, like the other applications that comprise iLife; instead, it's about learning, creating and having fun. Apple already has a high-end music production tool in the shape of Logic, so it was only natural that the company should want to appeal to consumers with an application that might introduce them to the idea of creating tunes and encourage an upgrade.

GarageBand is aimed at users of every ability – and none. If you have any musical talent already, you can plug in your guitar, midi keyboard or microphone and start recording a track using real instruments right away.

On the other hand, if you're musically clueless, can't sing and don't own any instruments, you can build tracks using a simple drag-and-drop process (see grab, right). Apple ships GarageBand with a large library of pre-recorded snippets that are designed to work together, with many matching tempos and lengths. They are organised into groups so that you can skip straight to drums, pianos, synthesisers and so on. Each sample can be auditioned with a single click and, if it matches the sounds of your song, you need only drag it into the workspace.

With several tracks at your disposal you can layer your samples to create complex compositions, and as you can download and install new loops over time, you should always find yourself with something fresh and up to the minute-sounding on the go.

The whole process is highly addictive, and it's easy to while away a couple of hours clicking, dragging, playing and rearranging your loops. The results more than justify this playtime, too, as your friends and family are sure to be impressed by the results.

The real power of GarageBand comes in its ability to sit at the hub of a home recording studio, though, recording live input, either to create a track from scratch, or to mix with loops from the library, so if you branch out into this kind of recording yo really will create something utterly unique, which can then be saved to your iTunes library, shared with friends or sent to other band members who can then add their own parts.

The GarageBand composition interface is simple yet effective. You need only drag and drop pre-recorded loops from the pre-installed library onto your score to build a track of your own.

GarageBand lessons are extremely well presented by engaging hosts and, if you plug in your own instrument you can have a fully hands-on experience by playing along.

If you're not yet at the stage where you could record your own parts of a song without reverting to the pre-recorded loops, then you have two further choices: lessons or 'Magic GarageBand'.

As a premium tool, lessons are largely add-ons, for which you'll have to pay a per-lesson supplement (although when you've bought a lesson you can, of course, 'attend' it as many times as you need to master everything that it contains). To get you started, Apple includes two lessons: one for budding pianists and another for those whose interest lies instead in the guitar.

The lessons are presented by engaging teachers who not only know their subjects well, but can also present them to camera with the skill of a TV-trained professional. If you plug in your own instrument you can also play along for a much more engaging experience.

Magic GarageBand, on the other hand, is a lot more fun and less highbrow. You start by selecting a genre, such as funk, rock or jazz, and

then picking which instruments you want to include in your virtual on-screen band, each of which starts to play automatically. It's not as rewarding as building your own tracks, even if you're only using the built-in loops, but it's fun to see what GarageBand comes up with each time.

GarageBand is a very versatile application for playing with just about any kind of audio. Indeed, it can even cut ringtones for your iPhone or, if you've always wanted a radio show of your own, record professional Podcasts.

Microsoft Office 2011

The lack of software compatible with Windows PCs is one of the most frequently cited reasons for not switching to the Mac. Yet with the continued updates to Microsoft Office for Mac, this argument now little bearing.

. . . .

Microsoft Office was originally a Mac application that later made the switch to the PC, so in some ways you could argue that it was not the Mac that was made compatible with PC, but the PC that was made compatible with the Mac.

The latest version for the Mac, at the time of writing, is Office 2011, and although it lacks some of the key features of the Windows edition it does boast excellent file compatibility, ensuring that Mac and Windows users can share documents with ease. That should calm the worries of the Mac's biggest detractors, and may yet be enough for some users to make the switch.

Yet there are some key differences, the biggest being the omission of Access, Microsoft's business and consumer database for Windows, from the Mac version. Fortunately, FileMaker, a wholly-owned Apple subsidiary, produces two excellent products to plug the gap: FileMaker Pro for business users, and Bento for home users.

■ THE LURE OF COMPATIBILITY

Word and Excel remain the world's most important word processor and spreadsheet. Their native file formats are used by a wide range of other apps. Other formats such as plain text, rich text and comma separated values are more widely used but you can't play an active role in document sharing if you can't read .doc and .xls. This is complicated slightly by the fact that Microsoft

changed file types recently when it introduced Office Open XML. However, that still doesn't mean that you have to invest in Word or Excel to keep up with the Joneses of the business world. Pages – part of iWork – can read and write Word XML documents and Numbers can read and write files for the latest version of Excel. Other applications such as Nisus Writer Express do an excellent although not quite perfect job of interpreting older Word files, offering you an inexpensive way into the format for simple documents.

■ MICROSOFT WORD

Microsoft is selling Word, in part, on the basis that it simplifies the creation of DTP-style documents. It ships with a wide range of templates on which you can change the default frame sizes, swap out images and re-style text. You can flow text into boxes where it moves from one box to the next as you edit it; you can drag images onto the page and, once they are there, resize them.

The 2008 and 2011 editions are far better at doing this than any previous versions, as they now boast a dedicated layout mode to complement the regular writing mode, so for home users there be little to choose from in this respect between Word and Pages (see grab, top right).

One feature missing from Pages is the notebook view that Microsoft introduced with Office 2004. Used to take notes with associated

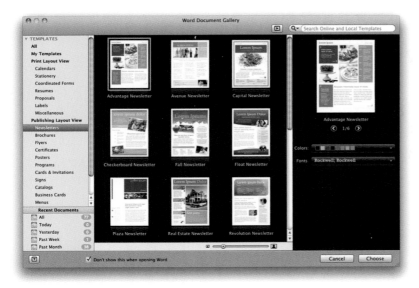

recordings, this has had a revamp in Word 2011 so you can now colour-code the pages it contains and create to-do items while taking notes. Word also has excellent outlining features, allowing you to quickly structure a document's outline, which you then flesh out later. For anything other than low-grade DTP or plain document writing, then, Word is the way to go.

■ MICROSOFT EXCEL

The world of business spreadsheets is ruled by Excel. Nothing else comes close. It took over from Lotus 1-2-3 on the PC a couple of decades ago, and has remained the dominant force ever since. If you want to use a Mac rather than a PC in a business environment, Office is a sensible move.

However, if most of your spreadsheets are destined to be printed and used as evidentiary documentation rather than shared digitally, we'd recommend also considering iWork's Numbers. Its

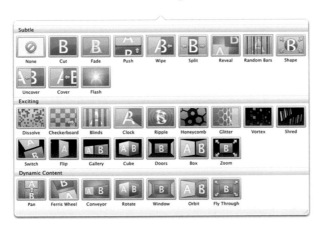

layout tools are first class, although with more recent Microsoft innovations such as Sparklines missing, compatibility isn't 100%.

■ MICROSOFT POWERPOINT

PowerPoint is the industry standard for giving presentations, so it was a shame that the Mac version lagged behind Apple's Keynote for so long. Microsoft has rectified that with this release, which boasts improved transitions and better slide designs (see grab, below left). However, as many users take their own computers to a presentation and plug them in before they speak, there is now little to differentiate between PowerPoint and Keynote since the latter became so well-established on the Mac and compatibility is now less of an issue.

PowerPoint 2011 sports a range of excellent themes that easily rival those found in Keynote, and while Keynote may once have been enough on its own to tempt many users to switch to iWork, this latest edition of PowerPoint deserves to tempt many back, and do much to retain those currently using Microsoft Office who might otherwise have been tempted to look elsewhere.

■ MICROSOFT OUTLOOK

Outlook is new to the Mac in Microsoft Office 2011. Previously, Microsoft had bundled an application called Entourage with Mac versions of Office, and although this could accurately claim to maintain good compatibility with the company's Exchange server technology, which dominates many business communications environments, it felt to many like a poor choice when compared to Outlook on the PC.

Microsoft clearly views Outlook as a primary business tool, however. It sells two different versions of Office for Mac, with the cheaper Home and Student Edition comprising Word, PowerPoint and Excel, and the more expensive Home and Business version adding Outlook into the mix. Home users, therefore, can make significant savings by using Apple's own Mail application, which is included as part of OS X.

Adobe Creative Suite

If one company other than Apple itself can be said to have ensured the
continued production of Macs, it's Adobe. As the owner of Photoshop and
InDesign, it is ensured a healthy stream of high-quality software for creatives.

. . . .

Of course, these applications are available on the PC, too, and Adobe sells more Windows editions of its software than it does for the Mac OS X, but the continued availability of Creative Suite is key to the continued existence of the Mac.

■ Photoshop

Photoshop is a powerful image manipulation tool with an extensive set of features that cover everything from adding a line of text to airbrushing out exes from photos. It can open an enormous range of file formats including many native camera file types, allowing you to import photos without first translating them using the software that came bundled with your camera. It also works with external peripherals, such as graphics tablets, and is extendable, allowing you to download or buy additional features from third-party publishers.

You can't deny that to get the most out of Photoshop you need to spend some time learning its features. However, there are some jobs for which it is not the best tool. Despite the fact that Creative Suite ships with a management application called Bridge, first-time users may find iPhoto better suited to storing and cataloguing their photo collections; particularly with the Events and Faces features in more recent editions.

It's not so hot on vector graphics, either. These are made up from specific coordinates, and the lines and curves drawn between them, which is

very different to photos, which are made up using a grid of coloured dots. Photoshop does offer some vector style drawing features, allowing you to draw shapes, lines and so on, but depending on your edition of Creative Suite you may also have a copy of Illustrator, which is built specifically to handle these types of files.

■ InDesign

It's a long time since the only choice in high-end desktop publishing was QuarkXPress. At one time that application was used to layout pretty much every newspaper, magazine, flyer and newsletter you read, but then Adobe came along with InDesign and things changed for good (above).

Photoshop is the leading image editing tool on both Windows and the Mac.

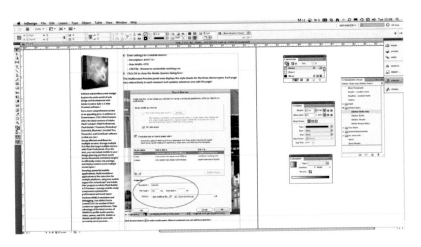

Over the years many users accused Quark of being slow to react to change and criticised its leading product's price tag, and although this has changed in recent years you can't deny that it must have contributed – in some part, at least – to the speed at which Adobe found an audience.

InDesign may be overkill for low-end home use, but if you do a lot of design work then you will find it a far more suitable application than Pages, which offers rudimentary layout tools for creating text boxes and positioning images.

Adobe also sells a companion application to InDesign called InCopy. This works in a similar way to a word processor, giving content creators a simple interface through which they can concentrate on writing the words without having to think about the look and feel of the page.

DREAMWEAVER

The majority of websites designed by professional web developers are built using Dreamweaver. It wasn't originally an Adobe application, but the company acquired when it bought rival developer Macromedia. Before Adobe's acquisition of its rival, the company sold its own tool, GoLive.

Dreamweaver lets you work in two ways: either code based were you type in all of the HTML underlying your pages, or design based, in which you draw boxes on your pages like you would in InDesign, then style up to your own requirements.

Dreamweaver understands a wide range of online languages, can connect to the most common database types to create interactive sites, and has excellent error checking tools to

make sure that the pages you create with it are compatible with the widest possible range of browsers. However, it is a very high level application, and its most powerful features are beyond some users. As such, first-time web designers would do better to check out an application like Realmac Software's Rapidweaver. Not only is this application inexpensive, but it is very well supported by an active user community, and it works on the basis of templates, allowing you to create new pages in no time at all, and change their look in even less time.

FLASH

One of the most important technologies on the Internet is Flash. It was the basis of YouTube's original incarnation where it was used to encode all of the videos in its library.

It's also the video mechanism that underpins the BBC's iPlayer, and it is the animation tool we must thank for those countless addictive online games that we waste many a Friday afternoon playing.

However, if Dreamweaver is a high-end application for professional users then Flash is in a different league entirely. It's easy to create new Flash files and position shapes on the page, and even to make them move around the screen, but to do anything... well, 'flash' with it you need to understand a complex coding language that can take months to learn to any competent degree.

While it is bundled with many versions of Creative Suite, and is therefore tempting to try, using it well takes some dedication.

PREMIERE

Adobe was once a big player in video on the Mac, and then along came Apple's own Final Cut, and Premiere disappeared from the platform. For a long time. But now it's back. On the PC it remains the leading application in its field, and on the Mac it's building itself a strong market once again. Like Flash, it's a high-end application that will appeal to fewer first-time users, who will naturally be drawn to iMovie, which ships as part of the iLife suite.

Best of the App Store

Developers have taken the App Store to heart, posting thousands of high quality Mac applications to Apple's online software shop. Picking through them all can be time-consuming, so here are some of the best.

....

" *The App Store is an integral part of OS X. Introduced in Snow Leopard – version 10.6.6 – it is a fully-integrated, quality-controlled outlet for buying software to install on your Mac. With your payment details already stored on Apple's servers there's no need to fiddle around with credit card details and delivery addresses, and as soon as you've completed your purchase, the app literally jumps out of the Store and down onto your Dock (on Snow Leopard) of Launchpad (Lion).*

By logging into the Store using the same Apple ID on all of your machines you can install the same software on every machine with a single click of your mouse, and with hassle-free upgrade nofications you'll always be running the most up-to-date and stable versions.

Apple has so much faith in its online App Store that it plans to deliver upgrades to its operating systems this way, starting with OS X Lion. "

The App Store has become one of the most important outlets for Mac software. It's a safe environment in which consumers can buy and download applications, and through which developers can sell their products without having to set up their own online stores. Apple takes a cut of the price of each app in return for handling the sale. This fee is included in the advertised prices, and paid by the developer.

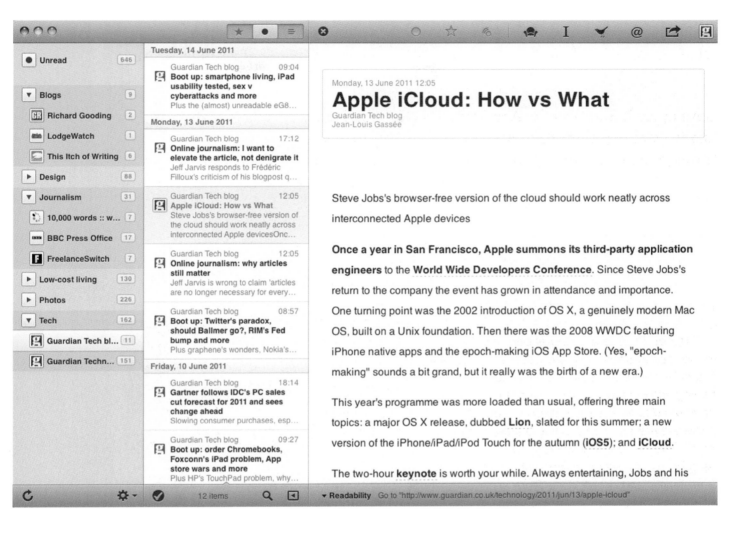

REEDER

£5.99

RSS has done much to simplify the way we consume information on the web. By subscribing to the feeds of the sites you visit most frequently you can actually visit them less often ... and still consume all the information that used to draw you to them in the first place.

The best online service for doing just this is Google Reader, which is free and highly efficient. If you don't want to keep checking in through your browser, though, check out this smart companion app – Reeder. It's completely independent, but uses your Google Reader account to sync, so that no matter how many Macs (or iPads and iPhones) you install it on they'll all still be showing the same state whenever you fire it up.

Subscriptions are organised in the channel, with the larger part of the app window given over to the body of each post itself. Organise them into groups and you can mark several as read at once, or combine their contents into one long list of posts. It really is the quickest way to keep on top of what you need to read.

There's no need to confine your reading to the Reeder environment itself, as clicking on a post's title opens it in an integrated browser, and thanks to smart gestures you can swipe back to the original feed entry when you're done. You can also mark particularly pertinent entries as favourites, or send them to third-party services like Twitter, Facebook or Instapaper for sharing with friends and colleagues, or simply keeping track of for your own future reference. If you ever use RSS feeds, you won't find a better reader than Reeder.

PIXELMATOR

£17.99

Many consider Photoshop the best image editing tool on any platform, and it's hard to disagree, but there are many who can't afford it, and even among those who can there are times when all you want is a light-weight editing tool.

Pixelmator is aimed at that second group of users. It's quick to load, easy to use, and has such a wide range of features and tools that you'll quickly come to realise what a bargain it is.

Its attractive interface is a collection of floating palettes that organise your tools, layers and settings. Your image sits among them, allowing you to position it wherever is most convenient for your way of working.

We particularly like the way that the current active tool is larger than its neighbours in the tool palette so you can see immediately what you're doing, and the way that all of its options are organised centrally on a palette of their own, so you've never unsure where you need to turn to

make changes. This is one aspect that makes Pixelmator so easy to learn.

For more creative types, it ships with over 130 different filters, while photographers will welcome the 15 colour correction tools that help pick up dull and lifeless photos without extensive manual editing, and the extensive set of cropping and retoucing tools that sit alongside them.

There's a dedicated save for web function that will intelligently compress your images so that they occupy the smallest possible disk space, allowing you to balance the trade off between bandwidth conservation and maintaining quality.

As well as being able to send your edited images to iPhoto or an email message, it can post them online to three popular image galleries – Flickr, Facebook and Picasa – so you can share them with friends without having to export them.

It doesn't have all of Photoshop's features and it probably won't meet all the needs of a professional photo retoucher or anyone using a Mac to put together high-end magazines and newspapers, but for a home user who doesn't need cataloguing tools, it's a lot more versatile than iPhoto, and a keenly-priced one at that.

BENTO

£29.99

One company above all others dominates the market for databases on the Mac: FileMaker. Best known for its epoymous FileMaker Pro database, in recent years it has been making great strides into the consumer market with Bento.

Bento is a far simpler database, which is quick to learn and hooks into key OS X features, such as the Address Book and iCal. It lets you pull in data from each of these for sorting, querying and reorganising in ways that are simply not possible in their native applications, also allowing you to design more attractive graphical layouts.

Bento isn't only about editing your existing data, though: it's a fully-featured database that will let you define your data sources from scratch, so would be perfectly at home in a small business where you need to keep track of customers, orders, or where you've filed certain documents.

All of your databases are stored in a single library within the application – much like your tracks in iTunes – so you can skip quickly and easily between the different tables in use.

Designing layouts is simplicity itself, as all you need do is drag the fields you want to use out of a list in the left-hand channel and onto your form, and decide whether you want to have them labelled. Each table can have several layouts attached to it, with each layout handling a different task. All in all, this makes for a very impressive and compact navigation system that provides multiple views of your data.

If you don't need enterprise-strength data management, Bento could well meet your needs.

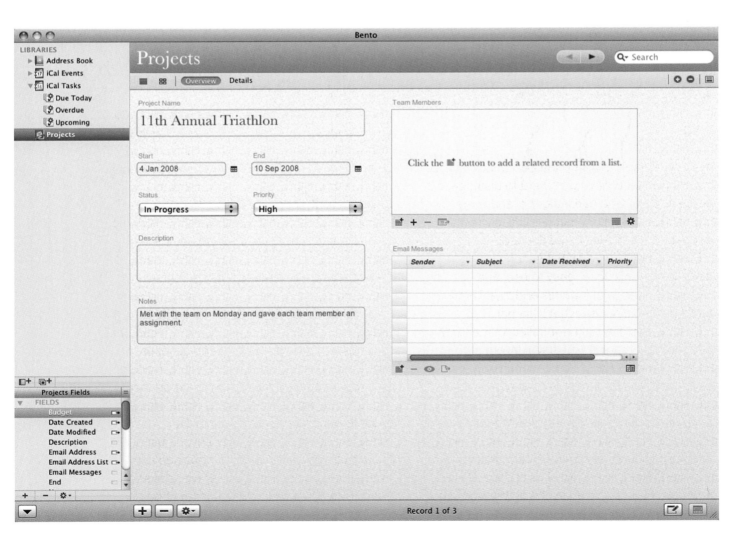

APERTURE

£44.99

Aperture was one of the App Store's launch products, and provided one of the launch's biggest surprises: the price. Previously it had cost well over £100, but suddenly it was marked down to less than £45, finally putting it within the reach of more ambitious home photographers.

Aperture is a professional-grade RAW editing application that works on the data taken straight from the sensor inside your camera rather than the converted Jpeg images output by low-end pocket snappers. This makes for far more flexible editing, enabling you to really explore the darker corners of your pictures and balance them with greater accuracy than you would if more of your data had been thrown away in the conversion.

Version 3 introduced new brushes that make it possible to paint on adjustments if you don't want to work on a picture-wide basis, and then change the strength of the adjustments. All adjustments,

whether made using a brush or the adjustments panel, are non-destructive, with Aperture saving any 'changes' merely as a file of XML data that it applies to each image every time it is loaded. In this way you have an infinite number of levels of undo, and you can spawn a copy of your original.

As well as being something of a safety net, working in this way is highly efficient. It means that Aperture doesn't need to write multiple copies of your images to disk, so your library doesn't occupy as much space as it would when you performed all of your work using some rival applications. It also means that you can direcly lift any adjustments you have already made to one image and paste them onto another, allowing you to quickly and easily apply a series of standard edits to a whole digital roll of film.

Support for Aperture is growing, with many third-party developers coding plug-ins and adjustments for the application, making it more versatile as it matures.

Always a great choice for the professional user, the price change means Aperture is now also a good choice for home snappers after more power.

BILLINGS

£23.99

Accounts applications and boring, unattractive and hard to master, right? Not any more. Billings has earned itself a devoted following on the Mac, and it's easy to see why. Not only is it easy to use, it's easy on the eye and powerful, too.

It works on the basis of projects and contacts: enter the names and addresses of the people for whom you'll be working, and then assign projects to each one. As they commission you to do some work for them, this becomes a project against their name. You can give it a start and end date, produce an estimate that your client can approve or reject, and then you get on with the work.

It'll track your progress, let you assign expenses and time how long you spend on each constituent part of the project. You can bill by time spent, a flat fee, or per unit, whether those units be images, words or some other element.

When you've completed and submitted the work, Billings will then sort out your invoicing. You can amaglamate several jobs on a single invoice to save you sending multiple separate sheets if that's how you prefer to work.

Invoices can be printed to paper or sent as PDF attachments for greener billing, and you can mark which have been paid so you know in an instant which are outstanding.

That's far from the end of the story, though, as Billings' reports give you an at-a-glance overview of your current financial situation. Need to know who should be chased? No problem – it's here. Wondering who your best customer is so you can needle them for some more work? Billings can tell you. Likewise, want to know who's worst at settling their accounts and should therefore be avoided in the future? The warning signs are there.

Considering how much time Billings can save you – time that can then be spent working and generating more income – the modest fee will be quickly recouped by both individuals and small or home businesses.

SPARROW

£5.99

Google Mail is one of the best webmail services currently available, with many large corporations using it as the backbone of their online communications. The ability to use it under your own domain name has proved to be a considerable draw, and even the US government is reported to be considering it as an alternative to traditional locally-hosted mail servers.

The trouble is, while it will happily work with a regular mail client such as OS X Mail or Microsoft Outlook, it lacks a lightweight client of its own. Sparrow, then, looks set to fill that gap, being lightweight, and working brilliantly with Gmail.

If you have any familiarity with the official Twitter client you'll notice that it bears more than a passing similarity. Messages are organised in a column, with a channel to the left giving you fast access to your incoming and outgoing emails, your favourites, trash and search results. We've extended the interface to give us a preview of our messages, but you can have these pop out in a separate pane if you prefer. Either way, they will be threaded so that you can track the flow of a conversation in a single window without having to pick your way through your inbox and sent folders to work out who was replying to whom.

If you're not convinced you need another email client, check out the free Sparrow Lite, which if you have only one account may already do all you need.

COURIER

£5.99

Take the hassle out of posting your images to social networking sites and online galleries by giving the job to your own personal courier.

We love the way this app works. Each of your chosen destinations – be they Facebook, Flickr or your own web space – is defined by a stamp, which you attach to an envelope. When you want to upload your images you drag them to the appropriate envelope and off they go, to wherever the stamp will take them. It's a neat idea, and the fact that you can put more than one stamp on each envelope means that you can send your images to several online destinations at once.

Courier will optionally geolocate your images, adding the necessary tags to position them on a map, and once they have been uploaded you can click them to view them, or to copy their online address so that it can be sent to friends or posted to Twitter or another social networking site.

As with other apps from Realmac Software, this one has a keen following, with third-party developers building add-ons to extend its features. Check out realmacsoftware.com to see what's available to date.

THINGS

£29.99

The secret to being efficient and effective is making lists. Not just strings of random words on scraps of paper, but proper organised sets of tasks with categories, deadlines and a way of checking them off.

It's up to you how many or few of its features you choose to use. At its most basic you could just tap your jobs into the list without setting dates, deadlines or tags, but its real power comes in helping you organise your working week.

Add deadlines to your jobs and it'll give you a countdown, showing you how many days you have left to do each one, which is due today and which are overdue. By organising them in order you will always know what is most urgent.

You can also give jobs priorities and levels of importance. Combine this with the deadlines and you'll know not only when something has to be done, but how important it is that you meet that deadline, which will help you decide which jobs you could put back to another day when it's clear you're not going to get everything done.

Perhaps the biggest motivator, though, is Things' column of check boxes in which you click as soon as you have completed a job. Do so and the job instantly disappears, shortening your to-do list and giving you an immense sense of satisfaction.

KINDLE

Free

Amazon's smart grey Kindle is perhaps the best known e-reader you can buy. Did you also know, though, that you can run a software version on your Mac, and that it's free?

You need an Amazon account to use it (this is also free), and once you're logged in you can buy digital books directly from the Amazon Kindle store and have them download to your Mac.

However, the really clever stuff happens if you already have another device running the Kindle app, such as an iPhone or iPad, or you have a hardware Kindle device. In this case, assuming you log in with the same user name on each device, you can synchronise your reading between them. So, if you have bought a book on Kindle for iPad you can also download it to Kindle for Mac at no extra charge and, thanks to Amazon's Whispersync technology, your reading position on both devices will be kept in line. The same goes for any hardware Kindles that, despite not being Apple devices, will share the data.

Amazon's Kindle catalogue is truly impressive, comprising 1.7 million books in the UK and 2.75 million in the US. Although many are digital copies of regular charged-for books, a lot are free, allowing you to catch up on your classics at no charge during your lunch break.

SKETCHMEE

£4.99

Sketch effects are far from rare. It seems that pretty much every graphics editing application has its own version, but the quality of their output varies enormously.

SketchMee is dedicated to performing just this task, transforming your photos into sketches, and nothing more.

Limiting though that may sound, it does mean that it's very good at it. Very good indeed, in fact.

The first step is to load your source image. Our tests prove that it's best if you use one with a good contrast between the light and dark areas, but it doesn't need to be of an especially high resolution, as SketchMee will output 16 megapixel files, whatever the resolution of the original – even if you crop it.

You can choose from two different sketching tools – pencil or chalk – and between colour and black, depending on the finished effect you want

to achieve. These are selected using drop-down menus to the side of your workspace.

The default results are excellent, and it really does look like someone has sketched out your image by hand, with an accurate appreciation of the way in which the strokes should be orientated to preserve the lines of your original image.

If you don't achieve the effect you were after in the first instance, then a set of secondary drop-down menus let you tweak the results, changing the fineness of the strokes, the texture of the paper and the lightness of the overall result. Switching between them is childs play, but if you don't have the confidence to fiddle with them yourself then you can switch between the ten presets by pressing command and a number key. The difference each one makes is remarkable.

Of course, over time you'll find your own favourites that you'll want to save for future use, in which case you can swap them out with the presets. SketchMee really is one of the most convenient, powerful and effective tools for transforming your photos into drawings with remarkable realism.

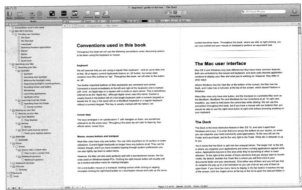

TRANSMIT

£20.49

If you want to publish online a good FTP (File Transfer Protocol) client is a must.

Transmit is something of an industry leader, and it's not hard to see why. It works happily with FTP, SFTP, WebDAV and Amazon S3 servers, and transfers files remarkably quickly. What we like best, though, is the way that it can mount folders on those remote servers as thought they were local to your Mac. They even appear in the Finder sidebar so that you can navigate them using regular OS X windows rather than Transmit itself, and copy files to them by dragging the files over their icons.

It handles synchronisation with aplomb, greatly saving time for anyone who needs to keep a selection of online and offline folders in line with one another, perhaps because they're working as part of a team and need to ensure they always have access to the most up to date versions of any files being written by colleagues.

Panic, which produces Transmit, claims on its App Store listing that 'this is the best file transfer client you'll ever buy', and we can't disagree on that front. If you've been struggling on with OS X's built in features for connecting to servers, or free alternatives, splash out on this competitively-priced app and see what you've been missing.

SCRIVENER

£26.99

Serious writers need serious writing tools. If you're tapping out a long, multi-chapter tome – perhaps a novel or dissertation – you could split up your various parts into separate documents, but there are two disadvantages to working this way. First, you don't get a true feel for the flow of your work as it's so fragmented, and second, you'll have to pick your way through each document in turn to work out your overall word count.

Scrivener keeps all of your separate documents together, organising them into folders in the sidebar. You can view them one by one, several at once, or all in one go so you get a better view of the flow of your work and can see how one section leads into the next. If you find it doesn't do that as smoothly as you'd like you only need drag the constituent parts into a new order to change them in the finished document.

When you have finished your writing, all that's left to do is compile your work into a single finished file, including all of your embedded images and styles. Scrivener gives you a choice of output formats to work with, including regular RTF and Word, alongside more specialised Final Draft script formats and ePub electronic books.

Scrivener is an industrial writing tool beloved of journalists and novelists, and the starting point for much of the book you're holding right now. If you want to get ahead in writing, investing in a copy could quickly repay itself in saved time and more successful project planning.

Networking your Mac

Your Mac already has all the features it needs to connect to a home or office network either wirelessly or by wired Ethernet. What are your best options for building that network, and how to you go about it?

. . . .

" *The average domestic broadband connection is faster now than ever before. Without a review of your local network set-up, though, you may well be missing the benefits this increased speed could deliver.*

BT Infinity promises speeds of up to 40Mbit/ sec; Virgin Media trumps it, racing ahead to 100Mbit/sec for just £35 a month. The question is, how best can you harness these blistering speeds in your home or small office?

The most efficient network will often be a mix of cabled and wireless connections, with printers, VoIP phones and the computers closest to the access point hooked up using cabled Ethernet. MacBooks, iPads and iPhones will likely use wifi, while further afield are those that sit beyond thick walls or in an end-of-garden office. Despite being out of reach of your wifi network, they can still share your broadband by passing data across the home or office electrical circuit. "

■ YOUR NETWORK CHOICES

At its most basic, your network may consist of a single ADSL modem with three or four Ethernet ports to which you connect your computers. Cable broadband users will need to add a router to their ISP-supplied modem. You can pick up a 4-port router that will work with both cable and ADSL modems for around £15, with play.com selling a Belkin 4-port Ethernet and 802.11g wireless router for cable modems for just £9.99, including VAT and delivery.

Apple's own networking products are sold under the AirPort brand, which it also uses to describe general wireless connections on its Macs (on the iPhone and iPad they're still called 'Wi-Fi'). There are three products in its line-up: AirPort Express (£83), with one 10/100Mbit Ethernet port for sharing printers and music; AirPort Extreme (£145), with four Gigabit Ethernet ports for building larger home and office networks and sharing drives and printers; and Time Capsule (1TB £239 / 2TB £396), which builds on AirPort Extreme's features to provide wireless backup for Macs running OS X 10.5 and later. AirPort Express can support a maximum of 10 simultaneous users, while AirPort Extreme and Time Capsule stretch to 50.

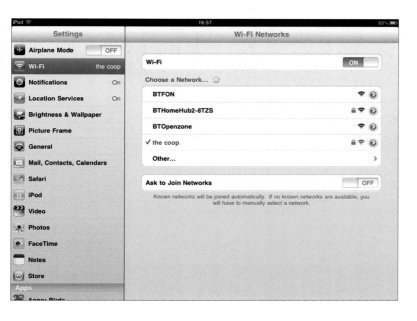

How do you buy a router?

Many ISPs include a free modem when you sign on the dotted line, so you may be reluctant to explore a paid-for alternative. Don't be fooled by such generosity, though. There are usually better choices to be had elsewhere, and some ISPs use the bundled modem as an excuse to tie you in to a longer contract. Plusnet, for example, throws in a wireless router for just the price of the postage if you sign up for 12 months, but it'll cost you £40 plus delivery if you'd rather avoid the contract. Forego the router altogether and for £33 you could instead buy TP-Link's fast TD-W8961ND.

Wherever possible, look for modems that conform to the 802.11n specification, which will pass data across your network wirelessly at up to 150Mbits/sec with a single antenna, and 300Mbits/sec with two using MIMO (multiple-input multiple-output). The use of more than one antenna also allows higher speeds to be maintained over longer distances.

Earlier standards – 802.11a, b and g – ran at 54Mbits/sec, 11Mbits/sec and 54MBits/sec – respectively, and although 802.11a is incompatible with 802.11b, Apple's AirPort base stations, and many of their rivals, support all four standards. Note, though, that if you mix clients conforming to the different standards on a single network you may notice a drop in performance.

Some routers connect specifically to 3G data networks, as used by the iPhone and iPad for mobile data, allowing you to share a single 3G connection between multiple devices when you're away from your office or your wired broadband is out of action. The iPhone 4 can perform a similar function by acting as a personal hotspot (mifi) to share your 3G connection with an iPad 2.

Connecting to your network wirelessly

Check the OS X Menu Bar for the wifi logo, which will show either four radiating beams if it's active, or an empty wedge, rather like you'd use in Trivial Pursuit, if it's turned off. If you have the wedge, click it and select Turn AirPort On from the drop-down menu, then select the network you want.

Each radiating beam will be either black or grey to indicate the strength of your connection.

iPad, iPhone and iPod touch users can connect to wireless networks through Settings > Wi-Fi. Tap the on-screen Wi-Fi switch to turn it on, and again choose the network you want from the list that appears. (See grab, above left).

Any network that requires a password is shown on both OS X and iOS devices with a padlock beside its strength icon, but even those that don't show this may be inaccessible if their administrators have enabled MAC (Media Access Control) address filtering, which checks the unique MAC address on each device that attempts to connect and only grants access if it appears on a list of authorised devices. See 'Wireless Security Choices', pxx.

In most cases you won't need to supply any further details as the router or access point will assign you an address on the network using DHCP (Dynamic Host Configuration Protocol). If you ever need to check your IP address, perhaps so that you can connect to your Mac using VNC or to diagnose conflicts, check System Preferences > Network. The address will be shown immediately below the connection status. On an iOS device, go to Settings > Wi-Fi and tap the blue arrow to the right of the active network name to reveal your IP and router addresses.

NETWORKING HOW-TO

■ WHY CAN'T I...?

Having trouble using FTP with your new router, joining online games or using VoIP? First stop: check your ports (they may be called virtual servers on some routers).

Ports, as the name suggests, are the virtual openings through which data can pass between your network and the wider world. Different data types use different ports. FTP uses port 21, HTTP (web pages) uses port 80, NNTP (Usenet) uses port 119, and so on. By closing off specific ports in your router through its configuration pages you can selectively block various traffic types from passing in either direction, thus increasing security or stopping children accessing services they shouldn't be using.

■ HOW DO I SHARE A PRINTER?

The simplest way to share a printer is to spend a little more on a unit with either an Ethernet port or wireless equivalent. Ensure it is Bonjour-compatible and it will appear in System Preferences' Print & Fax pane.

To share a printer without networking features, either connect it to an AirPort Express base station and use this to extend your existing network (see Setting Up AirPort Express), or connect it to a host Mac that will handle the incoming data. This needn't be a dedicated machine, so in a shared office it can be whichever Mac will be switched on for the longest amount of time each day.

Open the Sharing pane in System Preferences and click in the Printer Sharing check box to share the connected printer with other users on the same network.

■ HOW DO I MONITOR SHARED PRINTER USAGE?

Worried that someone on your network is printing the latest draft of their novel on your shared

printer? Open a new browser window and visit http://localhost:631 to access the print queue inside Mac OS X. You can perform various maintenance tasks from here and, perhaps more usefully, see a full list of completed print jobs. Click the Printers tab, the name of the printer in question and then the Show Completed Jobs button to call up a list of all printed documents, who printed them and when. Keep an eye on the 'Pages' column for any particularly sizeable documents.

■ HOW DO I CONNECT TO A LOCAL SERVER?

If you're working in an office you'll almost certainly need to connect to a server now and then. Likewise, home users may need access to network attached storage. To connect to a server, go to the Finder and press command-K, enter the IP address of the server and click Connect.

Servers also appear in the Finder sidebar.

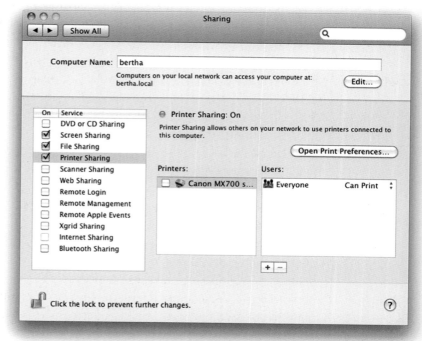

should then appear in the sidebar whenever you open a new Finder window.

If you would rather keep the sidebar short you can leave this unchecked and connect by pressing command-K again and entering either the remote Mac's IP address or its computer name.

Every Mac has a Drop Box (find yours at ~/Public/Drop Box) into which other users on the network can drop files for your attention. Without your password, though, they can't see its contents. Place the files you want to share in the remote Mac's Drop Box. If you need to access any other part of the Mac's system you'll need a password. Click its entry in your sidebar and then the 'Connect As...' button at the top of the Finder window to enter a user name and password.

Open a new window, and if the Shared section isn't visible in the sidebar open the Finder Preferences (command-,) and make sure the Connected servers box is checked. (see grab, right)

■ How do I share files with a Mac on my network?

Make sure File Sharing is enabled on the remote Mac (System Preferences > Sharing, check the box beside File Sharing), and that the Bonjour computers checkbox is ticked in Finder Preferences on your own Mac. The remote Mac

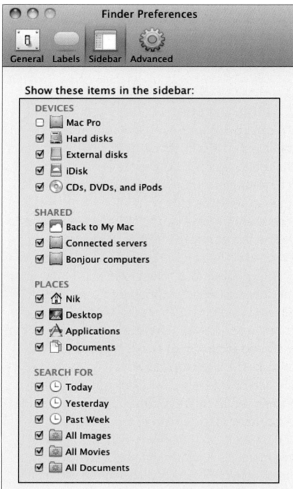

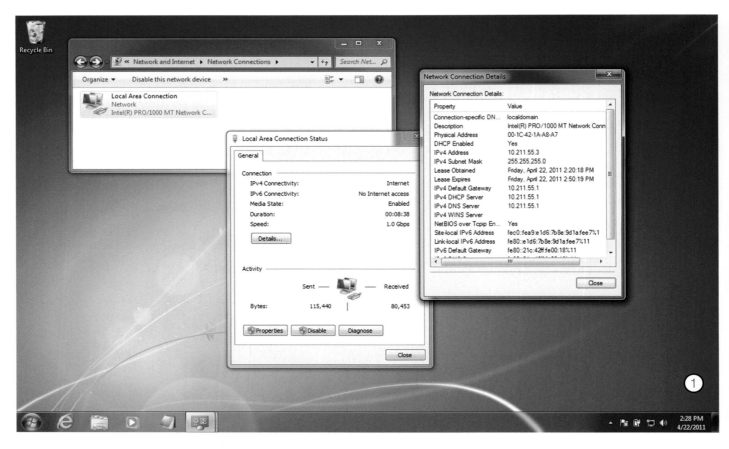

■ How do I share files with a PC

Look up the PC's IP address by clicking Windows' Start button and typing View Network Connections in the search box. Double-click the name of the active connection to bring up the status dialog, and here click Details. The fifth line of the Network Connection Details panel that appears shows the IP address of that PC on your network. *[1]*

Back on your Mac, press command-K to open the Connect to Server dialog and enter smb:// followed by the IP address of the PC. When asked, enter the user name and password for the Windows account *[2]* you want to use and then choose which volume should be mounted. *[3]*

Once connected, the PC will appear in the Shared section of the sidebar, and you'll be able to navigate its folders using the Finder. *[4]*

Accessing your Mac folders from the PC is a little more involved. On the Mac, go to System Preferences > Sharing and tick the box beside File Sharing. Next click the Options... button, and check the box beside Share files and folders using SMB (Windows), and the one beside the

account on the Mac whose files you want to share. You'll need to enter your Mac's user account password. *[5]*

Now check your account name (marked Full Name at System Preferences > Accounts) *[6]* and the user name on your home folder, as selected in the Finder sidebar here. *[7]*

Move to your Windows machine, click Start and in the search box enter Credential Manager. Click the link to add a Windows credential and add the IP address of your Mac, your Mac account name and its password. *[8]* OK out of this dialog to save your details, and you won't have to enter them every time you connect to the Mac from Windows.

Finally, click Start > Computer and click the Map network drive button on the toolbar. Choose a drive letter (here we have selected Y:) and enter the IP address of your Mac and the home folder name, as shown here. *[9]*. The Mac's user folder will be mounted as a drive under the Computer section of the Windows Explorer sidebar.

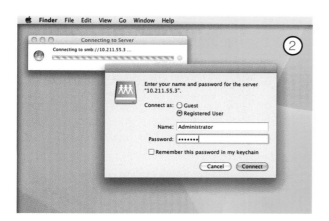

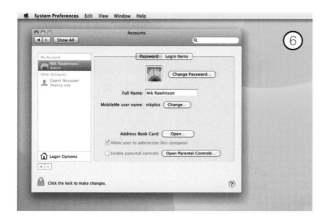

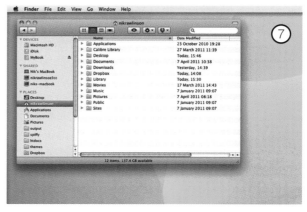

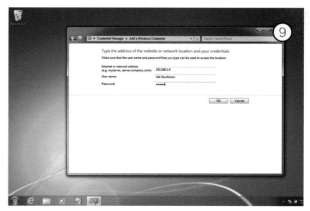

WIRELESS SECURITY OPTIONS

Failing to protect your wireless network can be a costly mistake. Moves from music rights-owners to hold you responsible for unauthorised downloads and file sharing on your connection look like being kicked into the long grass, but if someone should choose to download a couple of movies on your connection they could quickly exceed your bandwidth limit, and you still could find yourself paying fees for any excess usage. Worse, they might use an open connection to access your network and retrieve sensitive personal.

You should therefore ensure that your network is adequately protected. The following can be set in your router's administration pages, usually through the browser. The precise method will vary from router to router. Secondary wired routers on your network shouldn't require any further security settings to be applied, but if you're setting up secondary wireless networks that create a separate network connected to the first (rather than just extending the existing network) then consider these factors for each access point within your architecture.

■ EMPLOY A SECURITY ALGORITHM

There are three primary security algorithms used to protect 802.11-based wireless network, with each providing a greater degree of protection than its predecessor. Choose the highest level compatible with all of the devices on your network for the most comprehensive possible protection. Each demands the input of a 'key' of varying lengths that is used to encrypt and decrypt data as it passes between the client and base station.

WEP, Wired Equivalent Privacy, is the oldest of the protocols and has been deprecated and so shouldn't be used any more unless you know for certain that you have clients on your network that can't use either of the WPA algorithms (and even then you should consider swapping out those clients entirely for greater security).

WEP was eventually compromised and so the Wi-Fi Alliance developed WPA (Wifi Protected Access) and then WPA2 replacements. Any device that carries the wifi trademark must have WPA2 certification. If your router offers a range of security settings to choose from, you should therefore opt for WPA2 wherever possible, and consider upgrading incompatible client devices to preserve the integrity of your network.

■ DON'T BROADCAST YOUR SSID

Don't broadcast your network name (also known as SSID or Service Set Identifier), as this makes your network easier to find (if you don't believe us, click the wifi icon in your menu bar and the chances are you'll see your neighbours' networks appear). If you don't broadcast the name, anyone who wants to join your network wirelessly will have to enter the network name themselves – with the correct capitalisation – and usually specify what security policy is in place. Unless they already know what your network is called, or they can guess it because they know some other information about yourself, they'll find this almost impossible to do. Some routers, including AirPort

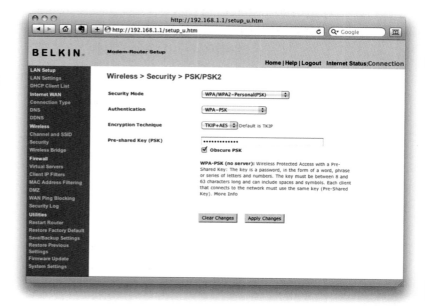

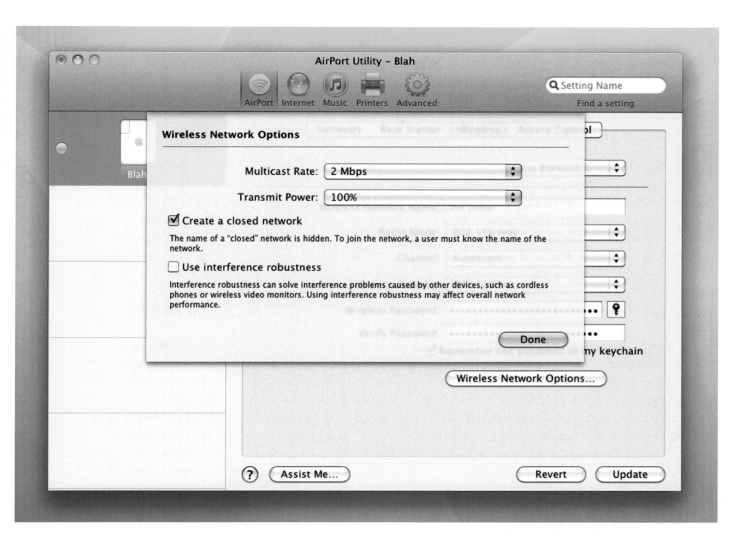

Express, offer not to hide the SSID, but to create a 'closed' network, which is the same thing. (See grab, above)

To join a network that's hiding its SSID, click the network strength icon in the menu bar and choose Join Other Network..., or open Network in System Preferences and choose the same from the Network Name pull-down menu. On the iPad and iPhone, open Settings, tap Wi-Fi and then choose Other... in the Choose a Network... box and enter its name.

■ DISABLE DHCP

Make it more difficult for would-be intruders to get on your network by disabling the automatic distribution of addresses. Not only will interlopers

have to find themselves an available address by manually entering it, but they'll also have to know the address of your router and the subnet mask.

To manually enter the necessary network details on a Mac, open the Network pane in System Preferences and, with the network selected, click the Advanced... button. Click the TCP/IP tab and, from the 'Configure IPv4' pull-down menu, select Manually. Enter your IP address, the router address and the network subnet mask in the marked boxes. On the iPad and iPhone, tap the blue circle to the right of the network name in Settings, followed by the Static button. This clears out the address boxes, which you can now tap on to enter your IP address, router address and the subnet mask. In both cases, if you need to specify a DNS address,

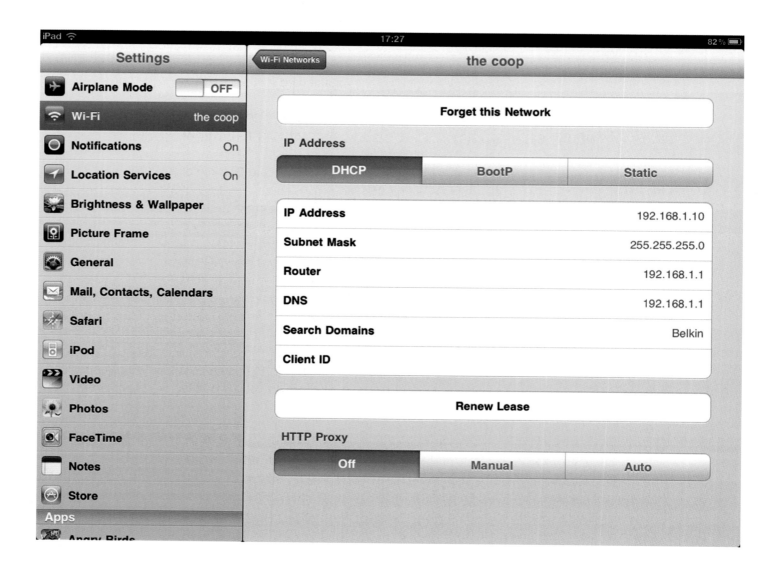

enter your router address again.

Disabling DHCP is a simple security fix, it but does limit flexibility in that if you want to grant network access to visitors you'll have to walk them through entering your router and subnet mask details, then assign them an IP address that isn't already in use on your network.

■ MAC ADDRESS FILTERING

Taking this one step further, enable MAC address filtering. Every wireless device has a unique MAC address that identifies it. You can find the MAC address of your Mac by opening the Network pane in System Preferences, picking AirPort in the sidebar and then clicking Advanced... The MAC

address is the group of 12 hexadecimal digits (six groups of two) on the Ethernet tab. On an iPad or iPhone, open Settings > General > About, where it's called Wi-Fi Address.

Enable MAC address filtering on your router and enter the MAC addresses as they are in each of these places (including the colons) for each of the devices you want to allow on your network. All other devices, which haven't been authorised, will be locked out.

There are two downsides to MAC address filtering. The first is that many routers restrict the number of addresses you can add to the list of authorised clients. This won't be a problem for most home users, but when you start to add networked printers, VoIP phones, games consoles

and, if it offers that option, through the router admin pages themselves to keep yourself protected against known vulnerabilities.

■ CAN I CONTROL ANOTHER MAC ACROSS THE NETWORK?

Yes. Download Chicken of the VNC (sourceforge. net/projects/cotvnc) and it will pass your keyboard and mouse commands to the remote Mac while passing back its display output to your own screen.

Chicken of the VNC is free, but there are paid-for alternatives, with offer a more versatile range of features, including intelligent screen scaling and an enhanced range of connection protocols for different security types.

You can also use VNC to control a PC in the same way, and use a VNC client such as Mocha to control a networked Mac or PC from your iPad or iPhone.

■ SHOULD I ACCEPT THE USB ROUTER I'VE BEEN OFFERED?

We wouldn't recommend it. USB routers require a driver; Ethernet routers don't, so you should avoid this additional layer of complexity if at all possible. An Ethernet router is virtually guaranteed to work with your Mac, whereas the chances of a USB router's drivers being compatible are slim.

Don't confuse a USB router, to which your Mac connects using a USB cable, with the USB Ethernet adaptor used by the MacBook Air, which neither needs a driver nor acts as a router.

and more than a handful of Macs or PCs you could find yourself running short. The second is the admin involved in authorising new clients. While you can assign an IP address to a device from the device itself, MAC authorisation must be done on the router or modem, usually via a browser, from either a wired connection or a device that has already been authorised.

■ CHANGE THE ROUTER PASSWORD

Every router has some form of password protection, but unless you change it from the factory default it's not much better than useless. Various sites publish exhaustive lists of the defaults for every make and model you could name, which would make it easy for anyone with malicious intent to change your settings, locking you out and giving them access to whatever they want.

■ KEEP YOUR FIRMWARE UP TO DATE

Routers are little computers in their own right, and each has an embedded OS. Check regularly for firmware updates, both through the vendor's site

SETTING UP AIRPORT EXPRESS

Apple's AirPort Express is discrete enough to plug into the wall without any trailing leads and add wifi to a regular wired network. The real power, though, comes in setting it up to stream media around your home from your iTunes library. Set-up involves answering some set questions, and deciding what changes you want it to make to your network layout.

[1] Open AirPort Utility and select the AirPort Express you want to set up. We have two on our network. 'Blah' is the base station plugged into our router that provides wifi around the house. The one we want to set up currently bears its default name – Base Station 02904b.

[2] Each AirPort Express needs a unique name, and although you could leave it set to the default it's much easier to diagnose problems and send iTunes output to specific places if you give it something more meaningful. Choose a password, too, mixing letters, numbers and symbols.

[3] There are three ways to set up your AirPort Express, depending on your existing network architecture. If your existing wifi network extends as far as this base station's eventual home, pick option one to give it a boost in that location. You will only see one entry in the list of available wifi networks. If you are using Power Line Networking to take your network to a part of your home that's out of the reach of your existing wifi network, or you want to share a wired connection in a hotel room, conference centre and so on, pick option two. If you just want to use the AirPort Express to connect speakers to the output jack, or share a printer on your network, and can plug in the device using its integrated Ethernet socket, pick option three.

[4] We're adding this unit to our existing network to extend its range, so don't want the base station to differentiate itself from the existing network. If we wanted to create a secondary network, perhaps with lesser access, we would use it to create a new wireless network, which would have a different name to the original.

[5] As we're extending an existing network, we need to specify which one and enter the required password before we can access it. To all intents and purposes the base station here is acting as a regular client on the network.

[6] AirPort Utility will show a summary of the settings it's going to apply. Assuming they're correct, click Update and they'll be written to the device. It will reboot and, all being well, you'll see a confirmation, with details of what your new base station's rights.

AirPort Express (left) plugs directly into a power socket and can be used to extend your existing wifi network, add wireless to a wired network, share a printer, and share your iTunes media courtesy of an integrated 3.5mm audio jack.

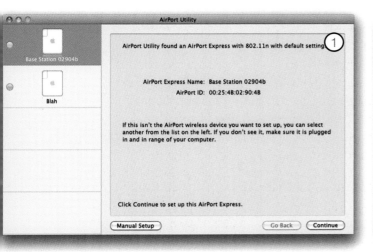

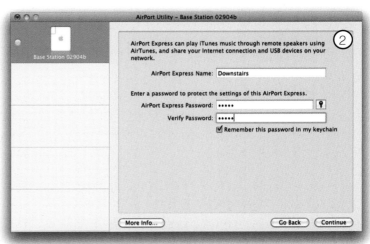

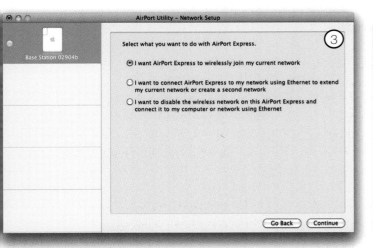

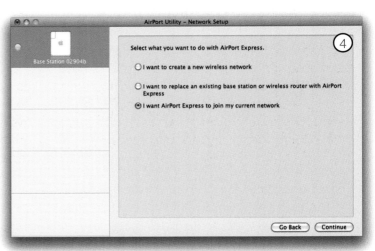

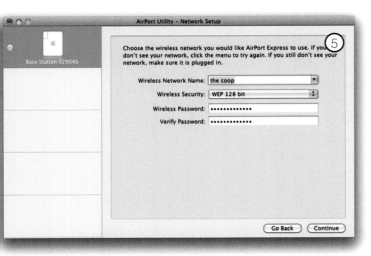

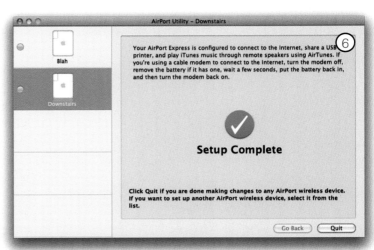

POWER LINE NETWORKING

If your house has thick walls or your office is a shed at the bottom of the garden, there's a fair chance that wifi won't work for you. Poor propagation or the simple fact that your client devices are too far away from your router will prevent them latching on to your home network. Signing up for a second broadband account on a separate phone line would solve the problem of getting them online, but it would be expensive and wouldn't let you share files between the various machines on your network without using third-party web-based services like SugarSync and Dropbox.

You need to turn to Power Line Networking, which uses add-on boxes to pass your network data over your home or office electrical cabling. Each kit requires a minimum of two boxes, which plug directly into your wall sockets and configure themselves without any further user input. Each plug has an Ethernet socket. Connect one to your router and each of the other plugs on your network can be used either to connect a Mac as though it was connected directly to the router, or a wireless access point like AirPort Express, to easily extend the reach of your wireless network.

Networking this way is often more secure than using a wireless access point as no data is passed over the air and, to all intents and purposes, each client on your network is directly cabled back to the router. They work through extension sockets, but the data doesn't pass beyond your fuse box so even if you live in a block of flats your neighbours won't be able to watch you do your online banking.

▇ DEVOLO DLAN 200 AV WIRELESS

Rating 5
Verdict A breeze to set up, and extremely versatile, the Devolo dLAN 200 AV Wireless N is our recommended choice for powerline networking.

This powerline twinset has two neat tricks up its sleeve that its rivals are missing. The first is the simple addition of three Ethernet ports on the downstream plug, which makes it well suited to use in a small or home office where several devices, such as a Mac, printer and VoIP phone will be clustered together. Now they can all share a single connection without the use of a router.

The other trick? 802.11n wireless networking built into the downstream plug. A button on its front turns the wireless features on and off, with a wifi light indicating data transfer. The network is secured by a 16-letter code printed on the reverse of the downstream unit, and we had no problems connecting each of our Macs to the new network.

The bundled CD includes Windows, Linux and Mac software for adding further downstream devices to your network, and configuring the wireless features. The wifi 'software' actually opens a webpage hosted in the devices itself from which you can change the network name and password, hide the SSID and see which ports are in use. Security options run to WPA / WPA2, WEP and no encryption at all, the latter two choices being marked as not recommended. There's no MAC address filtering.

■ SOLWISE PL-500AV

■ D-LINK DHP-P307AV

Rating 4
Verdict Great build quality and a neat power pass-through feature, but a lack of Mac utilities disappoints.

If points were awarded for looks alone, D-Link would win hands down. These plugs not only look good; they feel well-built, too. They are particularly large, though, both vertically and horizontally. We had trouble using our regular power socket, which sits below a radiator, and so had to use a power strip instead. Even there we could only accommodate them in between two regular plugs – not the bulky adaptors for our router and broadband modem.

    This can be explained in part by the fact that the P307AV features a pass-though socket on each plug, through which you can power your modem at one end of the link and your Mac at the other. There's also a smart 'green' feature that puts the units into power saving mode after five minutes of network inactivity.

    The P307AV's quality of service features automatically prioritise high-demand data packets in order to enhance HD video, online gaming and VoIP applications. The driver disc is a Windows-only affair, but a dedicated button on the side of each plug lets you set up network encryption without using the software utilities.

Rating 4
Verdict The smart choice for anyone who needs to build a fast network on a budget... but no Mac set-up utility.

The Solwise PL-500AV is so wide as to encroach on the neighbouring socket space in each plug and adaptor in our home (like Netgear, Solwise recommends against using an adaptor strip as surge protection measures could degrade performance). This wouldn't be so bad if it had a pass-through socket, but without one its bulk means it's effectively occupying two sockets.

    Although rated at 500Mbit/sec, they are designed to work well with an existing 200Mbit/sec homeplug network, which explains why they are sold as individual plugs, rather than a pair. The price at which they're advertised is usually for one plug, but even if you were to double it so that you could build a 500Mbit network from scratch, you'd still pay a lot less than you would for many rivals. You don't get the pass-through socket of the D-Link or the excellent software of the Devolo, but you could buy another plug with the change to expand your network yet further.

    This value for money is Solwise's trump card here, as otherwise the plugs are fairly unremarkable, with just an encryption button and three indicators set into the casing. Yet, if you're after a no-frills, fast powerline network, you needn't look any further.

Choice add-ons

Mac OS X is complete in and of itself. Most of what you'd want to do, you already can, thanks to a base installation of essential applications. With a little bit of downloading, though, you can make it do much more.

. . . .

Mac OS X ships with a first class email client, a complete calendaring application and a basic word processor in the shape of TextEdit (which is much improved thanks to the addition of drop-down formatting menus in the edition that ships as part of OS X Lion).

But it's missing some key features which, when added in, round out the Mac-using experience. There's no integrated spreadsheet to go with that word processor, and there's no very easy way to send richly-laid-out emails with images and overlaid text. Here we've picked out two applications – the free, open source LibreOffice [1] and Mail Designer – that plug those gaps.

Likewise, while FaceTime is perfect for video-conferencing with other Mac users and friends who have an iPhone, iPad and recent iPod touch, it doesn't let you talk to your Windows-using friends. Fortunately Skype [2] lets you do just that, and although version 5 may have piled on the virtual pounds since its last iteration, it's still free, and remains one of the best-value ways to make international calls with your Mac.

Elsewehere in this section, we've highlighted Money [3], a personal finance application that will help you manage your money more easily and efficiently than even the best hand-crafted spreadsheet. Plus, if you're looking to beef up your hardware without digging around inside your Mac, check out the cool speakers and desktop stand at the end of the section.

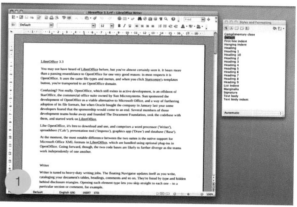

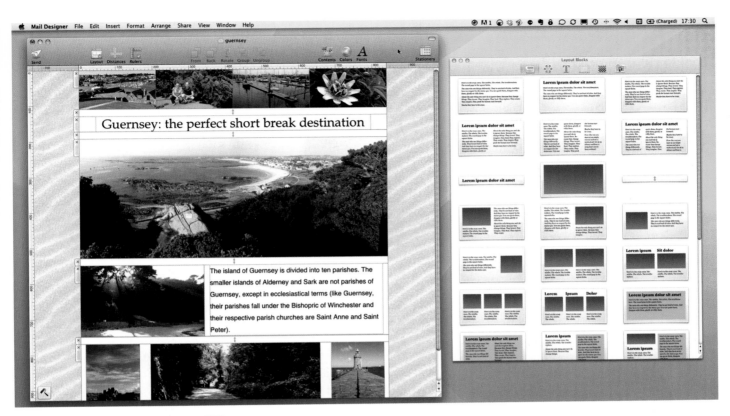

MAIL DESIGNER

WWW.EQUINUX.COM

HTML emails were once difficult to do well, but Mail Designer reduces the whole process to the simple task of dragging and dropping.

It ships with 45 templates to get you started, and has 142 action graphics like 'new' flashes, discount rosettes and page curls. You can overlay both these and your own images with text objects, and group your elements or change the stacking.

All images are embedded within the email, so there's no need to host them online and your email will always be displayed as it should, even if your recipients' clients block external images.

Text placed on an image is flattened to become part of the image itself, allowing you to use more adventurous fonts than you might in the rest of your email. Individual text and picture boxes can be resized within each placeholder, and any neighbouring boxes will dynamically resize to preserve your chosen overall message width.

Activating the Distances tool overlays your design with dynamic guides, which mark out the edges of objects within your email and show how far they sit from their neighbours and the edges of your layout.

We were disappointed that Mail Designer couldn't handle linked text boxes. We understand that this is because it would be difficult to render multi-column text accurately using CSS without knowing exactly which email client will be receiving your messages. However, as part of the rendering process involves processing and flattening graphics, this would have been the ideal time for Mail Designer to also split linked boxes.

This small point aside, Mail Designer is a joy to use. The option to start with a blank canvas and save your work as an outline for future re-use makes it an invaluable business asset. Its simple tools and the option to start with a template, on the other hand, also make it ideal for home users writing a club or family newsletter. It will change HTML emails for the better, and truly is a tool you didn't know you were waiting for, until you get it. It's the perfect OS X Mail add-on.

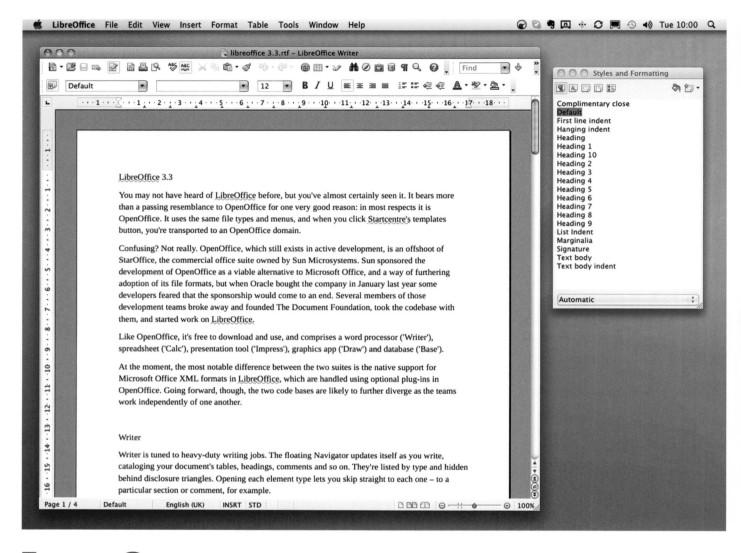

LIBREOFFICE 3.3

LIBREOFFICE.ORG

OpenOffice, is an offshoot of StarOffice, the commercial office suite owned by Sun Microsystems. Sun sponsored the development of OpenOffice as a viable alternative to Microsoft Office and a way of furthering the adoption of its file formats, but when Oracle bought the company in January 2010 some developers feared that the sponsorship would come to an end. Several members of those development teams broke away and founded The Document Foundation, took the codebase with them, and started work on LibreOffice.

Like OpenOffice, it's free to download and use, and comprises a word processor, spreadsheet, presentation tool and database. There's also a vector graphics tool called Draw.

At the moment, the most notable difference between the two suites is the native support for Microsoft Office XML formats in LibreOffice, which OpenOffice handles using plug-ins. LibreOffice also natively handles SVG graphics across all applications. Going forward the two code bases are likely to diverge as the teams work independently of one another.

WRITER

Writer is tuned to heavy-duty writing. A smart Navigator window updates as you write, cataloging your document's tables, headings, comments and so on. They're grouped by type and hidden behind disclosure triangles. Open a group and you can skip straight to its contents – to a particular heading, graphic or comment, for example.

Compatibility with Word 2011 was good in our tests, but not perfect. Comments made in Writer to a Word .docx file didn't carry across. Comments made to a document in Word that was then re-opened in Writer made the transition, but they were stripped of their attribution, so it wasn't clear who had made them.

Footnotes and endnotes, too, performed differently depending on the direction of travel. From Writer to Word they carried across, but lost their attributing numbers, so while you could see the anchor points in the body text there were no matching digits beside the notes themselves.

We experienced a persistent glitch with the word count, which would always show the previous count when re-opened. To update it each time we had to delete something from our text (usually the most recent space or punctuation) and ask it to count again. This is a clumsy solution.

Above left: The word processor is a heavy-duty tool, able to handle long documents and demonstrating good, although not perfect, compatibility with Word 2011 files.

Right: The document navigator makes it easy to isolate specific parts of yor document by using the disclosure triangles to reveal content types.

There's a reading view that takes away your cursor and toolbars, but switching to it and switching back lost our formatting in the editing view – not such a problem when you've applied a single style throughout your document, but a headache to remedy if you've specified headings and body styles throughout.

CALC

Calc largely flew through our tests. We imported an Excel document of seven sheets, each comprising 175 columns by 122 rows. The data

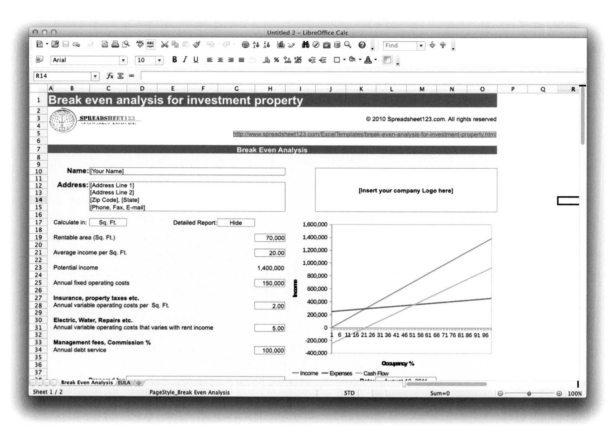

A wide variety of free-to-download templates such as this investment analysis is available from the OpenOffice document repository to get you up and running in no time at all.

included digits, text and date formats, and a mixture of typed integers and formulae. Calc took it all in its stride. Our frozen cells remained frozen in Calc and font / colour-based conditional formatting was carried across, with the various instances listed in the styles palette. This would have been more useful had they been given useful names – it's not easy to differentiate Excel_CondFormat_1_8_1 from Excel_CondFormat_2_7_1.

We pushed Calc further by moving on to a more complex internal form for expenses, programmed to handle multiple currencies. As well as formulae and entered data, it introduced drop-down menus within the cells themselves to select departmental data. All of this was proprietary to the company itself, yet it rendered perfectly in Calc.

Understandably, some of Excel 2011's more esoteric features didn't carry across. Sparklines were missing from our imported document – as they would be in Excel 2008 and earlier – and more advanced conditional formatting such as

colour scales and data bars degraded gracefully: they were missing, but at least they didn't throw up an error.

■ IMPRESS

PowerPoint has long enjoyed an enviable position as the go-to application for PC presentations, and for a long time that was equally true on the Mac. Then Apple unveiled Keynote and PowerPoint took a beating. It was the kick Microsoft needed, and PowerPoint 2011 made up the lost ground.

Just as PowerPoint underwhelmed when stood beside Keynote, so Impress trails PowerPoint. Quite literally, in fact. Our test file – a PowerPoint document of 19 slides – ran more slowly in Impress on a Quad-core Mac Pro with two 2.8GHz Intel Xeon processors than it did in PowerPoint on a MacBook Pro with a single 2.4GHz Core 2 Duo.

Links in a PowerPoint document remained active in Impress but lost their underlines, some transitions didn't carry across, and text became jagged in some places.

However, Impress does have some neat features. There's a handy underlying grid to help with laying out on-slide elements, the drawing toolbar makes short work of adding vector graphics and an interactivity panel provides an easy way to run applications or macros with an in-presentation mouse click.

◼ BASE

Base is a showcase for LibreOffice's tightly-woven components. Create a new database and you can register it within the suite itself, at which point its data is available to each of the other apps through their Data Sources panels. These contains both tables and queries, and let you embed variable data within your documents, such as addresses in mail merge fields or sources in a bibliography.

Queries and tables can be built graphically, and more experienced users will appreciate the SQL view. The productivity benefits this delivers if you have familiarity with SQL will be akin to switching from mouse to keyboard shortcuts in any other application.

A generous selection of templates is available online, ready to be downloaded for free.

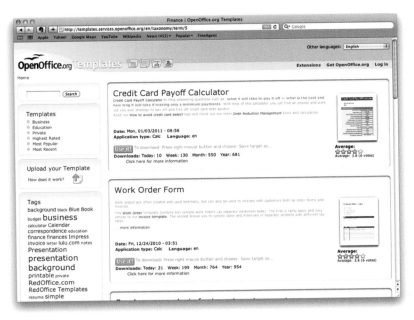

◼ THE SUITE

LibreOffice isn't much of a looker. There's nothing OS X about its menus or toolbars, and no matter how many different document types you have open, they're all represented in the OS X app switcher by a single LibreOffice icon, even if they're a mix of text files, spreadsheets and slides. This becomes more of an issue when dialogues from one app stop you working in another. Pause half way through setting up a new Impress presentation, for example, and you won't be able to do anything in Writer because it sees Impress' dialogue box as a prompt needing attention, despite the fact that most users, us included, consider it a different application.

There's no integration with the OS X media browser, so no easy route to your iTunes or iPhoto Libraries. LibreOffice does have a store of its own assets, though, with backgrounds, bullets and sound clips ready to embed, and you can import your own assets by dragging from the Finder.

In directly comparing LibreOffice to Microsoft Office, its most obvious threat, the free suite has come off poorly, yet we want to like LibreOffice. We've long admired the power of OpenOffice and the collaborative environment that lets it persist, but the sad truth is that even beyond Office there are better options for pure Mac-based outfits.

The free Bean (bean-osx.com) has quickly gained a well-earned reputation as a first-class word processor for Mac OS X. It isn't as well-specified as LibreOffice Writer and misses many of Writer's most impressive features – commenting and footnotes being two prime examples – but it does support .docx files so for anyone who wants to work with lengthy yet fairly simple documents it meets the bill.

LibreOffice is a good, highly competent office suite. It's powerful, extensible and broadly meets so-called industry 'standards', and if you're working in a mixed environment then its cross-platform editions make it a smart choice. Despite the years of development under the OpenOffice banner, though, it still needs further work.

MONEY 4

WWW.JUMSOFT.COM

Good though Numbers might be, no spreadsheet can entirely supplant a dedicated app when it comes to home accounts. Money 4 totts up your income and expenses to provide an up-to-the-minute picture of your financial health.

New in version four – beside a revamped interface – is a document-based file structure. This bundles multiple account into a single file, which can be opened, closed and swapped, allowing multiple users on a single Mac to use the same installation. Each file can be password protected.

It supports just shy of 150 currencies, and downloads the current rate of exchange for each

one. Tax calculation is turned off by default, but enabling it lets you set as many rates as you need, and you can synchronise your scheduled transactions with iCal to avoid any nasty surprises. It'll even set up a new calendar for you.

You're not restricted to working with bank accounts, either. Money will track the full gamut of financial instruments, including credit cards, loans, the value of a capital asset – such as your house – and even unbanked cash.

Everything is summarised on the Overview screen, and corralled according to your own parameters in so-called Smart Accounts. These work like iTunes' Smart Playlists, drawing up a list

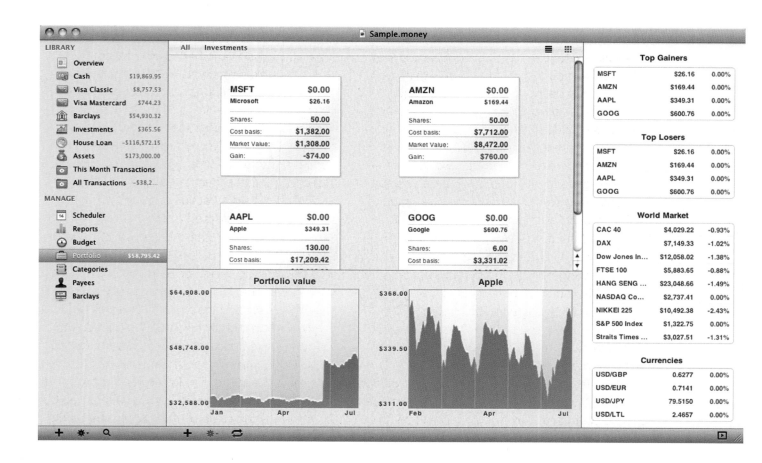

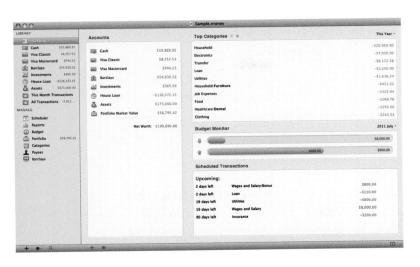

Above: The smart overview pane gives you an at-a-glance snapshot of your current financial health, drawing together all of the various data from the different parts of the application. Whether it's good news or bad, at least you'll never be unaware of where you stand.

Left: The portfolio is both attractive and useful, but the inability to specify share prices to more than two decimal places could be problematic.

of data that match particular variables, including transaction category, payee, amount and status.

The longer you use it, the simpler it gets, as it adapts to your needs. Start typing a category name when entering a new transaction and the list of suggestions updates on the fly. If the one you want doesn't already exist it'll be created there and then so it's ready to use the next time around. The same goes for the tags used to file and sort your data. Regular transactions can be set up to recur and used as the basis of a budget – simply click the Add button beside each one and it'll be added to your forecasts, with the option to set a maximum budget to which you should stick. Exceed this and up pops a warning triangle.

But it isn't all good news. We couldn't import transactions downloaded from Barclays in either Quickbooks or Microsoft Money format. Neither could we import them using Money's neat WebBank feature. This opens up a Webkit window inside the Money interface through which you can log in to your bank. Download the data from this view and Money intercepts the file and imports it

directly, cutting out the intermediate step and saving you time which, where finances are concerned, is good.

Well, that's the idea, anyway. In the end we had to enter all of our transactions by hand as even importing a CSV file was only partially successful. The dates and values were accurately brought in, but the transaction details weren't, so we couldn't say what each referred to.

It's impossible to test the import feature with every bank, so your mileage may well vary, but if this feature is important then it's worth downloading the trial from the Jumsoft site first, rather than heading straight for the App Store.

It's also worth bearing in mind that we could import our downloaded data in multiple formats when we downgraded to Money 3, although some of the fields were still misfiled. The payee column was blank, but at least what should have been there appeared in another column called Comments, from which we could copy it.

Anyone considering an upgrade from Money 3 should be aware that its invoicing feature has disappeared in the upgrade and that while the previous version let you enter share quotes accurate to three decimal places in your portfolio, Money 4 truncates them to just two, so you can't accurately record a fraction of a penny. This will apparently be addressed in a future update.

It's a mixed report, then. There's much to like in Money 4, and the workflow has been extremely well thought-out. It has achieved the goal of making personal financial management painless, data input swift and the whole process easy.

However, in directly comparing Money 3 with Money 4 we're concerned by some changes that feel like they were implemented solely to meet an unforgiving deadline. The loss of its invoicing feature may indicate a subtle change of focus, but the same can't be said of the portfolio. Try before you buy.

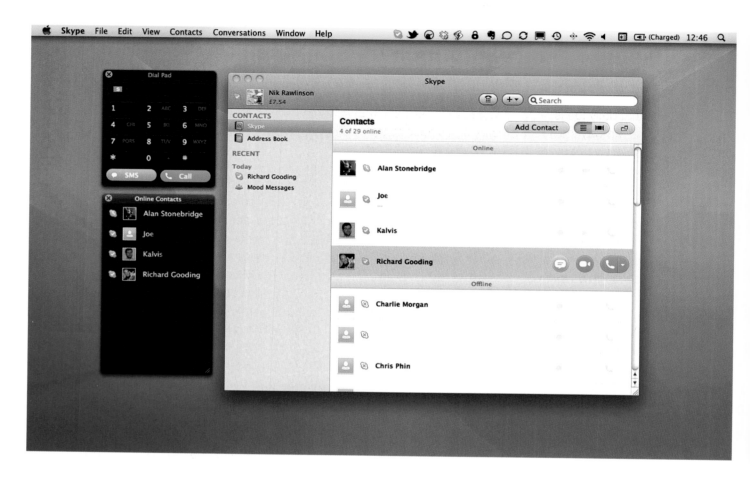

SKYPE 5

WWW.SKYPE.COM

Bigger isn't always better. Somebody ought to tell Skype. With the arrival of Skype 5 – its eponymous video, text and voice messaging tool – the once-compact app now consumes so much of your screen that you'll want to keep it shrunk to the Dock, whatever your resolution.

We can't deny that it looks good. The extra pixels have been used to give the interface a significant spit and polish, but neither can we claim that it's anything more than window dressing. The avatar view, in which your contacts scroll past as though they were albums in CoverFlow, is certainly pretty, but offers no more information than the traditional list view. Even that is larger than it need be, with oversized buttons for interacting with your contacts, each of which is padded with at least as much blank space again.

We soon resorted to the iLife-like head up display (HUD) to display our online contacts and the matching HUD dial pad, closing the primary window altogether. These are smart touches, but in breaking out the app's component parts into floating panels, Skype has delivered a less unified experience, which feels like style over substance.

Design issues aside, Skype 5 for Mac is a worthy upgrade. Full screen video calls are back, and group video calling is now available as part of a Skype Premium package (one-on-one video calls are still free). Occasional users may have a tough time justifying the rather steep £3.44 (£2.99 ex VAT) day pass for conference video when the monthly subscription costs only £5.74 (£4.99 ex VAT), but when compared to the cost of travelling and the lost productivity that journeys entail even

When you don't need to use the full interface you can switch to Skype's integrated HUDs.

that daily fee is highly competitive. There's a free seven-day trial for new users if you need to try before you buy, and Skype Premium also offers one-on-one customer support, although only in English.

Group video calls can be shared between three to ten participants and rely on a broadband connection maintaining at least 512kbits/sec downstream and 128kbits/sec upstream – although Skype recommends a more lofty 4Mbits down / 512Mbits up for best results.

For remote teams working from different offices, video conferencing will be a significant draw, in which case Skype Manager will come into its own. Again a monthly subscription feature, Manager is a web-based tool for assigning accounts, handling voicemail and call forwarding and, of

Skype offers widely-used cross-platform video conferencing features that allow Mac users to talk with friends and family on Windows-based PCs.

course, video conferences. All payments are handled by an authorised manager who can credit users' accounts, letting those users get on with their work while one authorised manager keeps an eye on spending.

Skype-to-Skype voice conference calls remain free, and you can add in non-Skype subscribers with regular phones if you have a subscription or positive credit balance. Skype also remains a viable alternative to iChat for file- and cross-platform screen sharing, enabling you to show your screen to other users or, with their permission, view theirs to help them diagnose problems.

It's clear with Skype 5 that a concerted effort has been made to beef up the VoIP tool's business credentials, and we're glad to see that it hasn't been to the detriment of its consumer appeal. It remains the best choice for casual online voice chat thanks, in large part, to the way in which it will grow with your needs, doing little more than iChat in the first instance, but offering bolt-in landline calling, incoming numbers and more as your needs develop. Its competitive international call rates, too, remain a significant draw.

Our concerns about the inflated interface persist, even after several days use, but we've learned to turn a blind eye: we close the application window altogether and set our status through the Menu Bar icon. We can't see our contacts but they, at least, can see us.

PALO ALTO AUDIO CUBIK

■ WWW.PALOALTOAUDIO.COM

Whatever your Mac, you can always improve on its native speakers. Palo Alto Audio's Cubik set features two 2.5in metal cone full-range Danish designed speakers that promise to deliver unbelievable bass and crisp highlights.

The cases look great, so you can enjoy these speakers even when they're switched off. Each has a metal stand to keep it stable and lift it from your desk so that it doesn't deaden vibrations.

Each is a fully digital unit, with the set connecting via a mini USB 2.0 cable for streaming from your Mac. Around 1lb in weight, they're 6.5 x 2.8 x 3.3in, so won't rob you of excess desk space, making them the ideal choice for anyone for whom their Mac is more than a work device. If you're one of the many Mac users who use their machine for watching movies, these specs are sure to be tempting.

MOSHI MINI DISPLAYPORT TO HDMI ADAPTER

■ WWW.MOSHIMONDE.COM

Want to connect your Mac to your TV and enjoy your iTunes downloads in comfort, on a larger screen? Check out Moshi's Mini DisplayPort to HDMI adapter, which supports full HD at 1080P resolution and multi-channel digital audio via HDMI passthrough on compatible Macs.

The full list of compatible machines goes back to the 27in iMacs of the late 2009, with a full list of supported devices maintained on the Moshi Monde website.

It's perfect for connecting your MacBook, iMac, Mac mini or Pro to any HDMI-compatible output device and, with a smart aluminium casing that reduces electro-magnetic interference, it won't spoil those clean lines, either.

HENGE DOCKS

WWW.HENGEDOCKS.COM

Why has nobody thought of this before? We all know that Apple's notebook computers can hold their own again the best mid-range desktop computers (and, depending on your spec, some high-end rivals, too), so it makes sense for anyone who does most of their work at a desk rather than perched on

their lap to buy a monitor and keyboard and use it as though it was just that... a desktop Mac.

The only trouble is, Apple doesn't produce a docking station, which means you're left on your own to solve the problem of what you should do with your machine while it's plugged in.

Well, now that problem's been solved, courtesy of the smart people over at Henge Docks, who create third-party docking stations for Apple notebook computers.

As well as looking smart, the idea really is very simple. You pick the appropriate dock for your size of MacBook or MacBook Pro, with the 13in, 15in and 17in models all well catered for, and then slot your machine into the top, where it's held securely in an upright position. It looks like a very slim, very smart Mac Pro.

There's a full range of connectors in the bottom of the slot that automatically fit into the matching connectors on the side of your MacBook, so you can still use all of your regular peripherals and, if you want to use your Mac as a home entertainment centre, plug in your TV to watch downloaded shows and movies courtesy of the optional Mini DisplayPort to HDMI and DVI connectors.

Windows on the Mac

Whatever the reason you chose to buy a Mac and run OS X, there are still times when you may need to run Windows applications – or Windows itself – for compatibility with colleagues. What's the best way to do just that...?

. . . .

" *Nobody needs to run Windows on their Mac. What you might need is to run some Windows applications, in which case the question is how best to do it. The answer, it may surprise you, needn't touch on Windows.*

Whatever spin Apple and Microsoft give them, Windows and Mac OS X are little more than containers for the applications that run our lives. They file our data, sketch out an on-screen interface and help our third party apps talk to our hardware.

So, assuming you can't achieve all you need on a Mac – perhaps you need to test sites in Internet Explorer, or edit an Access database – how should you run the Windows tools you need?

You could buy a PC but that would be wasteful. Every machine built and sold consumes resources today and ends up in landfill years down the line. Software is far less eco-unfriendly, and cheaper, too, helping you run those apps on your Mac.

Over the next 10 pages we'll show you how to do just that. We've examined the five primary means of installing Windows software on your existing machine, and not all involve touching Windows itself. "

■ THE OPTIONS

One of the most appealing side effects of Apple's switch to Intel was the ease with which we can now run multiple operating systems side by side, with each using the Mac's underlying architecture.

It's a long time since emulation was a serious option for running Windows applications – or indeed Windows itself – on the Mac. Virtual PC for Mac, which once ruled the roost, was bought by Microsoft and bundled with versions of Office 2004. It's since been discontinued, and if you're running it today then the most up to date version is pushing three years old. Microsoft still ships a feature called Virtual PC as part of Windows 7, but the Mac version is no longer a suitable option for running Windows under Mac OS X. It was written for PowerPC processors and Mac OS X 10.2.8 to 10.3, both of which are now considered very old technology.

That leaves us with three options: virtualisation, emulation or skipping out of Mac OS X altogether.

■ VIRTUALISATION

Virtualisation, as its name suggests, creates a series of virtual machines running on top of your computer's physical hardware, with each 'machine' being an installation of an operating system that you can switch between at will or run side by side. It is the closest current technology to

With plenty of alternatives to choose from, the companies behind these virtualisation tools have done all they can to make their apps easy to install, as can be seen in this grab from VMWare Fusion.

that seen in the old Virtual PC for Mac. At its heart is an additional software layer on top of OS X.

Called a hypervisor, this software layer passes the demands of the guest operating system – Windows, Linux or a third alternative – to your Mac's underlying hardware, which does all of the legwork and then passes back the results. This happens in real time, and with a modern Mac you can expect performance that comes close to matching a PC of equivalent specification.

There are three options for virtualisation on the Mac: the commercial VMWare Fusion and Parallels Desktop for Mac, and the GNU-licensed Oracle VirtualBox.

▨ EMULATION

Each of the virtualisation options above presents the full Windows environment, with all the benefits and pitfalls that entails, including the requirement that you familiarise yourself with Windows' way of working. One alternative – CrossOver Mac – dispenses with the need of a second operating system altogether, wrapping native Windows

applications in a layer that makes them executable on the Mac.

This is a considerable money saver, as not only are you not required to buy a PC, but neither need you source a licensed copy of Windows. The downside is that if you want to run software for any platform other than Windows then you'll have to look elsewhere.

Boot Camp partitions your hard drive and installs Windows in its own dedicated section.

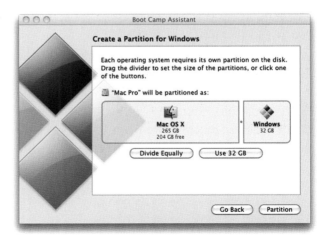

CrossOver lets you install Windows applications directly, without the use of Windows itself.

With security in mind, Fusion and Parallels let you save the state of your Windows virtual machine.

■ Beyond Mac OS X

Apple's own solution to the issue of running Windows applications on the Mac is Boot Camp, first introduced in April 2006 as a means of installing Windows XP on Intel-based Macs. Initially a free download from apple.com, it's since been rolled into Mac OS X 10.5 and 10.6, and now supports Windows as far as version 7.

By dispensing with the OS X environment altogether, Boot Camp devotes the full resources of your Mac to Windows, so will deliver the best possible performance, but has one major downside: it's an either / or solution – you can't run Windows and Mac OS X side by side as switching from one to the other requires a reboot.

■ The cost of Windows

None of these products includes a copy of Windows, which needs to be bought separately for all except CrossOver Mac. The current edition, Windows 7, comes in Home, Professional and Ultimate editions. Home (£149.99) performs the core Windows functions and will run all compatible Windows software; Professional (£219.99) adds domain tools and more extensive backup features; Ultimate (£229.99) adds BitLocker data encryption to guard against lost devices spilling your secrets.

■ Security

As Mac users we rarely have to consider ongoing security concerns beyond installing updates for the operating system and applications as they appear in Software Updater. Few of us run anti-virus software, simply because we don't yet need to. Installing Windows can change all that.

That Windows exhibits a far wide range of security vulnerabilities than Mac OS X is well publicised, and inviting it onto your machine invites them, too, particularly if you have chosen to share any of your Mac OS X folders with your Windows installation. So, the question is, how do you protect yourself?

Parallels Desktop 6 includes a 90 day trial of Kaspersky Internet Security. This is a well-regarded security suite that keeps watch not only for virus and Trojan incursions, but also spyware, adware, rootkits and a raft of vulnerabilities that will be unfamiliar to Mac users. When your 90 day trial expires it'll cost you $39.99 a year to continue.

VMWare Fusion includes a complimentary 12-month subscription to McAfee VirusScan Plus (AntiVirus Plus 2011 costs £44.99 when this expires), but VirtualBox and Boot Camp ship without any third-party security tools in place.

CrossOver Mac runs Clamav in the background to protect Windows applications within your Mac environment.

NATIVE WINDOWS SECURITY TOOLS

Windows doesn't come with its own anti-virus software installed by default, but there are a number of measures you can install for free as soon as your virtual machine is up and running.

SmartScreen Filter works with Internet Explorer to compare the websites you're visiting with a list of known malicious hosts maintained by Microsoft. Microsoft claims that no personally identifiable information is passed from your computer to its servers, which is good. What's less good is that it's an IE-only technology, so if you want to use Safari on both your Mac and virtualised PC you won't be covered.

Microsoft's own Security Essentials covers most bases, protecting you against viruses, spyware and other malicious software and is a free download from microsoft.com/security_essentials. It will protect up to 10 machines on one location, so is well suited to small businesses.

Security Essentials will only run on an activated copy of Windows, so don't install it if you're using its 30-day grace period to decide which virtualisation product is right for you.

TIME MACHINE

Virtual Machines present a unique problem for Time Machine. Each is contained in a single large file of several gigabytes, which can grow over time as you use it. Because Time Machine treats these like a regular file rather than a separate computer it would back them up on the hour every hour for as long as you were using them, as they would be changing all the time. This would quickly deplete the available space on your backup volume.

Regular backups should therefore be performed from within the virtual machine itself and only periodic backups from within the Mac OS X environment.

Fusion, VirtualBox and Parallels Desktop provide a means of creating these periodic backups as snapshots, each of which stores a frozen image of your machine as it stands, complete with files, folders and applications. Should anything disastrous later happen, such as

a malware infection or a failed software installation, you can then roll back to a known good state by choosing an earlier snapshot.

Add your virtual machine files to Time Machine's ignore tab through System Preferences > Time Machine > Options to prevent it backing up your virtualised machine's altered state.

Boot Camp works in a different way, partitioning your hard drive and installing each file individually, as Windows would. You can therefore safely allow Time Machine to back up this partition as it will only make incremental copies of the individual changed files, rather than the whole OS.

NETWORKING

Each of the virtual machines reviewed in the pages that follows, plus Apple's own Boot Camp and CodeWeavers' CrossOver, uses your Mac's existing network connection – whether wired or wireless – to connect to the Internet, saving you from fiddling with Windows' own network settings to get things up and running.

We had no problems with this in any of the applications we tested here, except for Internet Explorer 8 on CrossOver. However, as this is not officially supported by CodeWeavers – only the CrossOver user community – we fixed it by rolling back to the officially supported IE7.

KEYBOARD CONUNDRUM

Mac and Windows keyboards have several subtle differences, the most obvious among them being the existence of a Start key on Windows devices, and Command on the Mac. They also work in quite different ways, with the alt key used more often for keyboard shortcuts on Windows, and Command more common on the Mac.

Fortunately virtualisation products perform a certain amount of translation, and you can perform tasks like capturing screen grabs from the parent application's menus. However, Boot Camp users may find investing in a cheap Windows keyboard beneficial, as it gives you access to bespoke buttons, like PrintScn, which copies the content of your display, that don't have direct Mac equivalents.

WINDOWS FEATURES

Both Fusion and Parallels Desktop support Windows 7's Aero graphics, and not just inside the Windows environment. Drop down Fusion's Menubar icon, which gives you direct access to your Windows applications, and you'll notice that it features a smeared glass background through which your Mac desktop will be visible. Likewise, switch to Parallels' Coherence mode to run Windows apps in OS X without their Windows surroundings and they'll exhibit Aero-style semi-transparent title bars. Fusion's windows do this, too, where they overlap other Windows applications, but in our tests reverted to regular opaque borders where they overlapped only Mac OS X areas on the screen.

CrossOver Mac doesn't apply the full Windows look and feel to its applications as it runs on top of the X11 windowing environment, but the application content of the windows themselves does, of course, look like whichever version of Windows you have chosen to impersonate.

ACCESS WINDOWS FILES FROM OS X

MacFUSE is a technology that allows you to mount Windows virtual disks in Mac OS X so you can work with your Windows files without having to start your virtualisation software. It's also the technology that underpins Transmit 4's ability to mount remote file systems in the Finder sidebar.

It is an optional install for VMWare Fusion, and can be downloaded for free from http://code.google.com/p/macfuse/

ACTIVATION

Unlike Mac OS X, which can actually, although not legally, be installed on as many Macs as you like, each installation of Windows must be activated. This ties it to the hardware on which it is installed, of which Microsoft keeps a record to ensure that it's not installed on more than the authorised number of machines.

If you are trialling several virtualisation products to see which best meets your needs, make sure you uncheck the option to activate Windows when you are online, which appears when you enter the product license key. You will then be given 30 days' grace before activation becomes mandatory, which should be enough for you to decide with which virtualisation product you want to associate it.

GAMES

Despite now enjoying a wider choice of games than ever before, the Mac still lags behind Windows. This, in turn, relies on Direct3D and OpenGL support, which varies depending on your emulator.

VirtualBox describes its support for OpenGL for Windows 2000 and later and Direct3D for XP and later as 'experimental'. Further, as it relies on replacing some core Windows files there are certain safeguards in place to protect your virtual machine. It must be manually enabled within the machine's settings, and can only be installed under Windows when running in Safe Mode.

Things are more straightforward with Fusion and Parallels Desktop, which both have built-in support for DirectX 9 and OpenGL 2.1.

CrossOver Mac supports a wide range of games, including and its support of DirectX9 is rated as bronze (as opposed to the better silver or gold), but serious gamers should consider the £25.99 dedicated CrossOver Games, which uses a highly refined version of the Wine layer to deliver better frame rates for more responsive gaming.

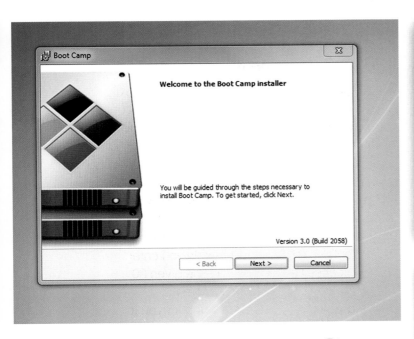

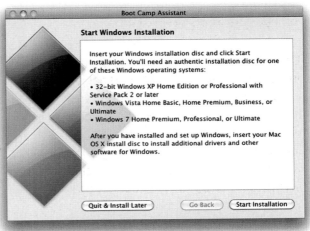

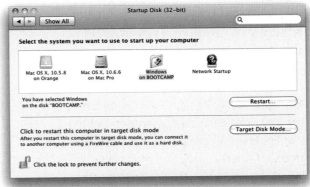

APPLE BOOT CAMP

Price Free
Contact Apple + apple.com/uk
Needs Intel Mac + Mac OS X 10.5 or later
Pros Devotes full system resources to Windows
Cons Inflexible + Installation may be daunting
Verdict The most cost-effective choice for anyone who doesn't need to switch between OSes regularly

Installing Windows under Boot Camp is a three-stage process. Your launch point is Boot Camp Assistant (in the Utilities folder), which partitions your drive and then reboots using your Windows installation DVD. The installer will handle formatting your drive, but as it's up to you to pick the one you want to use for your Windows installation you'll have to be careful to make sure you pick the one called Boot Camp. Choosing your Mac OS X partition could see you lose everything on your Mac, so making a backup before you start is a must.

The Windows installer didn't recognise our Magic Trackpad, but plugging in a mouse let us progress, and the installation completed in six minutes. The third step is to install the Boot Camp drivers from your Mac OS X installation disk, which support the Mac's native hardware –

including the FaceTime or iSight camera – and add a Boot Camp pane to the Control Panel so you can change its settings.

Boot Camp makes your Mac OS X partition available, so you can navigate your existing folders and open files created on the Mac, but without the correct permissions you can't write to that partition. This is an excellent security feature that will do much to keep your files safe from malicious attack, but is frustrating if you regularly need to work on the same files under both operating systems. Setting up a shared partition on a server or NAS drive greatly simplifies the task of writing and sharing files between the two operating systems in this instance.

Switching between Mac OS X and Windows requires a reboot. Hold alt (option) as your Mac starts up and you'll be given a choice of drives from which to restart.

Boot Camp doesn't have the flexibility of a true virtualisation tool like Fusion, VirtualBox or Parallels Desktop for Mac, but for anyone who is happy to work in one OS at a time it's a powerful, fast and free way to run Windows on your Mac.

VMWARE FUSION 3

Price £62.04
Contact VMWare + vmware.com/uk
Needs Intel Mac + 1GB Ram (2GB recommended) + 700MB disk space for Fusion plus 5GB for each virtual machine + Mac OS X 10.5.8 or 10.6 or later
Pros Menu bar Start Menu keeps Dock clear + Bonjour-based Migration Assistant
Cons None to speak of
Verdict Just pipped to the post by Parallels, but it was an extremely close race

We tested Fusion after installing Windows 7 under Boot Camp – a fact that didn't pass it by. It spotted the Boot Camp installation and offered to use it without us installing a new copy. We said yes, it applied some tweaks, and five minutes later we were running Windows in a window, surrounded by Fusion. It didn't give us the option to convert a Parallels machine to Fusion format, but the free-to-download vCenter Converter is available on VMWare's site for performing the conversion under Windows.

Fusion integrates well with Mac OS X, adding a Fusion icon to the Menubar through which you can directly launch any of the applications installed inside an active virtual machine. They're also indexed by Spotlight, along with your Windows files. You can map common Mac folders to Windows, with a shortcut to your Mac partition appearing on the Windows desktop.

Your installed operating systems are organised in a virtual machine library that acts not only as a jumping off point for each one, but as a way of monitoring what each is doing. It's resizable, so you can keep it in the corner of a window to track the progress of a task in Windows while doing your regular work in a Mac app.

VMWare's free Migration Assistant uses Bonjour to look for PCs on your network and transfer their apps, files and settings across your network to a virtual machine on your Mac. This is a boon for switchers who can then immediately recycle their old PC and use their virtualised machine in a manner that is already familiar.

Fusion didn't recognise our monitor's native resolution as Boot Camp and Parallels did, but it supported it without problem when we specified it through Windows Control Panel. Neither did it automatically install VMWare Fusion Tools, to which we only had access after rebooting the virtual machine, at which point we could install the necessary drivers to enable our host machine's full features and, more importantly, Unity mode, which allows you to run Windows applications in Mac OS X without seeing Windows itself.

Fusion is infinitely customisable, even after you've installed your Virtual Machines. Each can be tweaked to use more or fewer processor cores, a greater or lesser proportion of your memory, and your graphics card's 3D features.

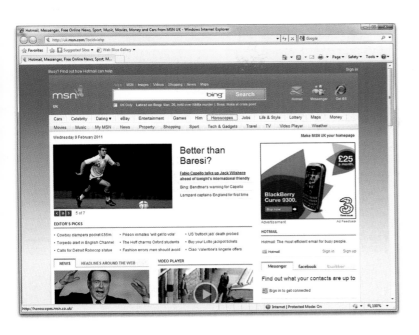

Parallels' smart Menu Bar icon gives you direct access to Windows' Start Menu, allowing you to switch between apps from outside of the Windows environment.

PARALLELS DESKTOP FOR MAC 6

Price £64.99
Contact Parallels + parallels.com/uk
Needs Intel Mac + 1GB Ram + 500MB of space on boot drive for Parallels plus 15GB per virtual machine + OS X 10.5.8 or later or 10.6.3 or later
Pros Conversion of existing, competing virtual machines + Easy set-up + Excellent Mac / Windows integration
Cons Multiple app folders in the Dock may become confusing unless removed
Verdict The best example in this test of a close to perfect blending of Windows and Mac OS X

Parallels spotted our Fusion virtual machine and offered to convert it into a machine that it could use itself. This was done without damaging the original, as a copy was made in the Parallels folder inside our Documents folder. It also offered to do the same with our Boot Camp partition, but only after we'd set up a new virtual machine.

There are three modes of working: full screen, windowed and coherence. Coherence puts an icon in the Menubar for accessing the Start menu and managing devices, while a folder to the right of the Dock's divider (where it becomes a permanent resident) gives you access to your

Windows applications, even with the virtual machine powered down. This can get confusing if you have more than one instance of a particular operating system as you'll spawn a folder for each. In this case you'll probably want to drag them out of the Dock.

With everything set to default, Parallels is happy for you to access your Mac folders from within Windows, but this can be changed on a case-by-case basis for each virtual machine. So, too, can the option to map common Mac folders to their Windows equivalents, such as movies, music, downloads, documents and pictures. Opt to share your music folder and you can access your iTunes library from the Windows virtual machine without re-ripping your CDs.

Like Fusion, Parallels didn't install its own tools until we told it to do so, and thus Coherence mode was out of reach. Unlike Fusion, though, it did manage to find the necessary installer without us rebooting the virtual machine.

If you have a foot very firmly in both camps – Mac and Windows – then Parallels will likely suit you the best of all the options here. The distinction between the two environments is further eroded with every release, to the point where our Mac applications appeared on the Windows Start Menu within our Parallels virtual machine.

ORACLE VIRTUALBOX

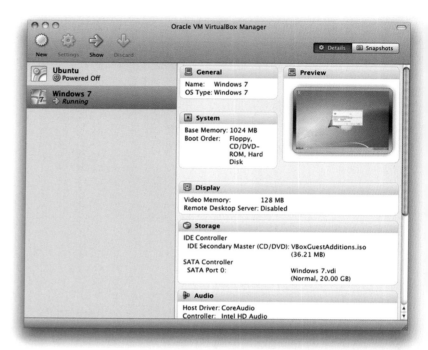

Price Free

Contact VirtualBox + virtualbox.org

Needs Intel processor + 512MB Ram + 30MB for VirtualBox, plus space for each virtual machine

Pros Free

Cons OpenGL and Direct3D features remain 'experimental'

Verdict A slick, efficient means of running Windows on the Mac, and the only one that can give Boot Camp a run in the value for money stakes.

VirtualBox has much to recommend it, but none more tempting than the price: it's free.

Originally developed by Sun Microsystems it's now a part of the Oracle portfolio, and it offers many of the same features as Fusion and Parallels Desktop, including its own equivalent of Coherence and Unity to run Windows applications without the surrounding Windows interface, called Seamless Mode. In contrast to Parallels and Fusion, though, this carries across the Windows Task Bar, which runs across the bottom of the screen behind the OS X Dock.

It's possible to share Mac folders with the Windows installation, either as read-only folders or with full access. They're seen as network shares, rather than integrated into the local file system,

Like its rivals, VirtualBox lets you run Windows applications in OS X, and can keep the Windows Task Bar visible for easy access.

but can be set to auto-mount, at which point they're given their own drive letter. Despite sharing our Music folder in this way, the only way we could get Windows in VirtualBox to see our iTunes library was to manually add a .itl extension to the iTunes Library file within Mac OS X.

VirtualBox didn't install its add-on utilities by default – we had to manually install them later to take advantage of all of its features, including Seamless mode – and it couldn't determine our screen resolution, in this instance refusing to render any other aspect ratio than 4:3 until we'd gone into and out of full screen mode twice.

It didn't make any of our existing virtual machines available for conversion, or spot our Boot Camp partition, but installing Windows from original media caused no problems, and the process was a carbon copy of the non-simplified methods for both Parallels and Fusion.

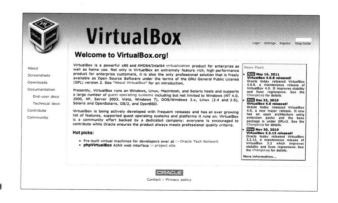

Search for apps and CrossOver Mac will install them for you without any further configuration.

CodeWeavers CrossOver Mac

Price Standard £25.99 + Professional £44.99
Contact CodeWeavers + codeweavers.com
Needs Intel processor + Mac OS X 10.4.4 or later + 512M of RAM + 100MB of available disk space
Pros Doesn't need Windows
Cons Selective application compatibility + Less attractive interface
Verdict An excellent, cost-conscious choice, so long as your required applications appear on its supported list.

CrossOver Mac takes a radically different approach to running Windows applications: it doesn't need Windows. It uses the Wine (WINdows Emulator) compatibility layer to provide all of the hooks that Windows applications need to run on Mac OS X's Unix underpinnings. The installer is complete in itself, but it's much improved by the quartz-wm component, which it retrieves from your OS X installation DVD, and when complete it leaves you with another installer.

This is CrossOver Mac's only public face, and it's used to set up your chosen Windows applications. At present there are 68 officially-supported apps, including Microsoft Office 97 to 2007, Lotus Notes, Visio 2000 to 2003 and Quicken. All of the business big-hitters are catered for, but if you want to run anything more esoteric or less mainstream then you'll have to turn to the 130 'community supported' applications. These include Photoshop 7 to CS2, Internet Explorer 8 and Visio 2007.

You'll need your installation disc to run a commercial application, but the Installer will download free apps, such as IE, mIRC or Word Viewer 2007 as part of the installation process, and all you then need do is click through the dialogues. Each app is installed in an Accessories folder and indexed by Spotlight.

Free applications can be installed directly from CodeWeavers' website. Unsupported apps can be proposed and, if sufficient voices cast votes for the same one, it will be bumped up the list.

You can choose the version of Windows you want to emulate (2000, XP or Vista), although not all are compatible with every app, and because they're actually run within the X11 environment they don't always look as good in CrossOver Mac as they do in a native Windows environment.

At just £26 for the standard edition and £45 for professional, CrossOver Mac is excellent value as the cheapest means of running Windows apps on your Mac, due to the fact that it doesn't require Windows. Make sure you check the list of supported applications at codeweavers.com.

Browser alternatives

Safari may be the default browser on OS X and have a dedicated slot on the Dock from the first day you switch on your Mac, but there are plenty of reasons to consider switching to one of these excellent alternative options.

. . . .

Everyone has their favourite browser, and most of us are fiercely loyal, claiming the 'other browsers' don't work they way we want. From how they handle tabs to the number of compatible add-ons, the subtle but significant differences between each one are enough to keep us fiercely loyal to our chosen window on the web.

What's more surprising, though, is the number of people willing to dump their operating system's default browser for a third-party alternative. Browser usage is notoriously difficult to measure, but as of February 2011, Net Applications gave Safari a share of 6.36%. Firefox had 21.74%; Chrome, 10.39% and Opera 3.47%. Microsoft's Internet Explorer remained top dog with a 56.77% share. W3Schools, though, put IE's figure at just 26.5%, Firefox at 42.4% and Safari at 4.1%.

So what's tempting so many switchers?

■ TABS

Safari and Camino hang their tabs from the bottom of the address bar, illogically separating the bar from the pages themselves. Chrome, Flock, Netscape, Camino and Opera and put the tabs above the bar, making it an integral part of the page to which it refers. OmniWeb carves its own path; while it still calls them tabs it actually uses thumbnails, organised in a slide-out drawer. It also lets you save workspaces, which are collections of tabs that are grouped together and switched between on a group-by-group basis. This is similar to the groups in Firefox's Panorama mode, which opens collections of tabs whenever you click any one of the pages in the group.

Firefox's App tabs deserve a mention. They let you keep online applications resident in your tab line-up, without using the full width of a regular tab. It's a great saver of both space and time.

Tabs up or tabs down? Apple and Google can't agree on the way to display tabs with Safari (top) dropping down and Chrome (bottom) popping up.

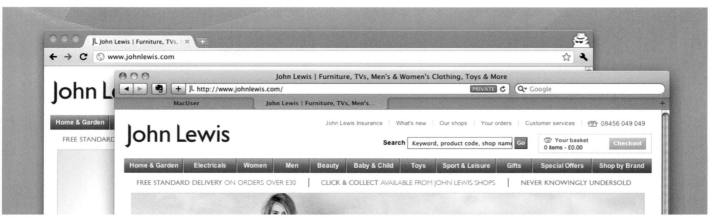

Hide your browsing history with Incognito mode from Chrome (top) and Private Browsing from Safari (bottom). Apple sold the idea of Private Browsing on the fact that it would hide shopping habits for gift buyers who share their Mac with other users in the same house.

PRIVATE BROWSING

Apple suggested we might use Safari Private Browsing when gift shopping for a partner on a shared Mac (check for the word 'Private' in the address bar). We consider it more likely that most users employ it when they're browsing questionable content they'd rather not find recorded in their history or cookies. Chrome's Incognito browsing (check for the private eye at the top of the application window) and Flock's Stealth Mode perform parallel functions, and so will be equally appealing choices for anyone who regularly does 'online shopping' for loved ones.

HTML5

A lot of developers are staking their futures on HTML5. The next-generation language of the web, it includes many native features like video and audio playback, text formatting and graphics rendering that are currently only possible with the help of plug-ins and players like Flash, Quicktime and Silverlight. There's no set suite for checking browser compatibility here, so we have used html5test.com, which tests whether each browser can interpret a variety of HTML5 tags and assigns it a score out of 400. A larger number represents a better performance in each instance. Over time, as their rendering engines are updated, we should expect these scores to improve.

GENERAL COMPATIBILITY

A more wide-ranging test is Acid3, which tests not only document object model, but also CSS3 compliance. Again this will become more important over time with the broader adoption of CSS3 alongside HTML5, since HTML5 doesn't make any provision for formatting inside validated pages themselves. We ran each browser through the tests at acid3.acidtests.org, which assigns them a score out of 100. Higher scores are better in each instance.

TEST RESULTS

HTML5 Performance	
Chrome 10	288
Firefox 4	256
Opera 11	234
Safari 5	228
OmniWeb 5.10	139

CSS3 Acid test results	
Chrome 10	100
OmniWeb 5.10	100
Opera 11	100
Safari 5	100
Firefox 4	97

FIREFOX 4

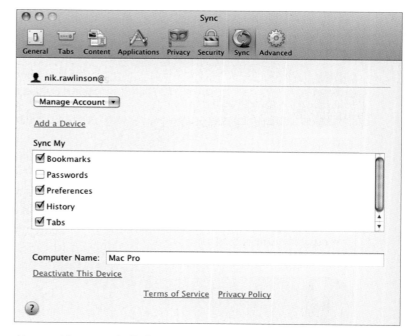

Rating 5
Download from mozilla.com/firefox
Pros Quarantined plug-ins + Panorama + App tab
Cons None
Verdict If you're looking to switch from Safari, look to Firefox – particularly if you work in a multi-platform environment

Mozilla has come up with a smart idea for Firefox 4: App tabs. Recognising the fact that more of us are using online apps to run our lives – Hotmail, Freshbooks, Twitter and so on – it lets you pin them to the tab bar in a smaller than usual tab bearing only the site's favicon. This way you can keep several application tabs open the whole time you're online without having to scroll along a bar that extends beyond the browser window to find them.

You can also gather tabs into logical groups and hide or show whole groups at a time. Called Panorama, this feature lets you draw out a number of virtual boxes into which you drop your active tabs. Clicking any tab in one of the boxes opens all of those tabs in the browser window, with the one you clicked frontmost. Switch back to Panorama and click another tab from a different box and all of the active tabs will be swapped out for those in the new box.

As of version 4, Firefox now quarantines plug-ins by default, so that if they crash they don't

Above: It's not only Safari that can sync its bookmarks across multiple Macs. While Safari requires a MobileMe account, though, Firefox lets you set up your own Weave server, which some users will find is not only cheaper, but gives them peace of mind as they won't be passing data through a third-party.

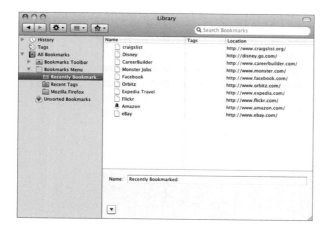

bring down the whole browser. Flash, Quicktime and Silverlight are all quarantined out of the box, but you can add your own choices to the list if you find yourself running an unstable add-on.

The version 4 release candidate scored 255 on the HTML5 test, putting it comfortably ahead of the current revision of Safari 5 and slightly ahead of Opera.

Firefox Sync, like Opera Live, shares not only your bookmarks but also your settings, passwords and even history between multiple Mac and PC installations. By default this data is passed through Mozilla's own servers, but if you'd rather play safe you can set up your own, using the Weave server add-on.

Firefox is just part of a large collection of tools including the Thunderbird email client and Sunbird calendaring application. The PC, Mac and Linux editions of each is developed in parallel, which is reason enough for mixed-platform workplaces to serious consider switching not only to Firefox, but its companion apps, too.

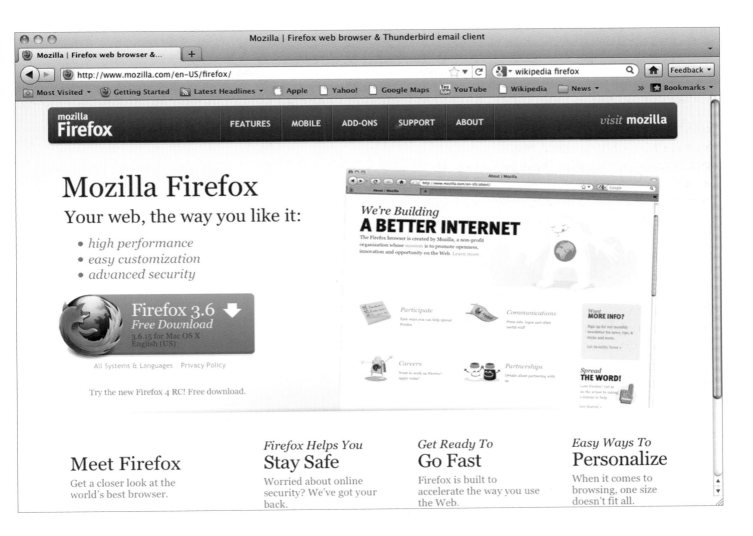

Below: Panorama lets you organise tabs into groups. Here, we have given each group a name and resized them to fit the application window, with those we're most interested in given more space. Clicking a page inside any group opens up all of the group's tabs in the browser window.

Below: App tabs are shrunk-down handles for those pages that you want to keep open all day, without having them take up a lot of space in the tab bar. Although they show only each site's favicon, resting your mouse on them calls up the page title.

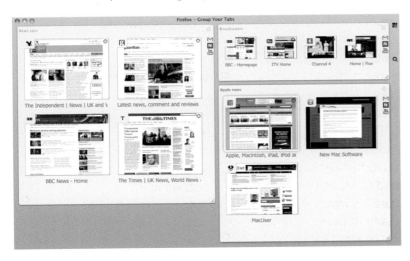

Opera 11

Rating 5
Download from opera.com
Pros Widgets sit outside the browser window +
Unity simplifies complex network sharing tasks
Cons None
Verdict Opera's platform-like approach to
organising incoming information makes this so
much more than a simple browser

Opera should probably be considered a platform,
rather than a simple browser. Its use of extensions
and plug-ins could make it the focus of your
whole working day. These run inside the browser
and add email clients, RSS aggregators and so
on. Allied to these are Widgets, which sit outside
of the browser and keep running after Opera
quits. Broadly analogous to OS X Widgets, they're
a neat way to keep various reference tools handy
without having to switch to the Dashboard.

Without some nifty organisation, so many
add-ons and extras could become
unmanageable, so Opera has implemented a
smart panel that's hidden by default but which,
when revealed, keeps your mail accounts,
widgets and so on in order. They can be
synchronised across multiple installations – on
both Mac and PC – through Opera Link.

The panel pops out from the left-hand margin,
and again focuses ever more of your attention,
and your working hours, on your browser. It will be
particularly attractive to those who would rather
not have to access their web through a website,
but still prefer not to use a separate application to
handle their email.

More ambitious users will likely supplement this
with Unite, an integrated lightweight server for
browser-based collaboration. This lets you share
files between computers wherever they happen to
be. There's already an impressive list of
compatible tools to use with it, including
messaging, photo hosting and media sharing
features, the last of which lets you access your
home music library remotely. This remote music

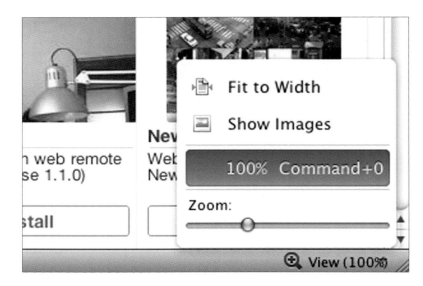

A pop-up menu in the Opera status bar gives you
speedy access to the zoom slider and the option
to turn off images, which will speed up the rate at
which your browser pages load.

sharing ability could come to rival iTunes Match
for some users – and particularly those who have
not bought any of their music through the iTunes
Store, or spent time re-naming tracks in a way that
makes more sense to them, thus making them
unrecognisable to the matching service.

A lot of thought has gone into how Opera can
help you work faster. One result is gestures – hold
down your right mouse button and push it away
from you to stop a page loading; pull it closer to
open a link in a new tab, and move left or right to
navigate your history stream. There's also a Quick
Preferences panel, which saves you a trip to the
full Preferences menu if you only want to tweak
the way it handles your cookies, pop-ups and
plug-ins.

A more ambitious server-side tool, Turbo,
compresses and optimises web content – chiefly
images – to speed the download and rendering of
pages. Particularly useful on slow or congested
broadband lines, this can be set to on, off, or
auto. Choose the third of those options and Opera
will determine for itself when it would make the
biggest difference.

Opera is one of the most impressive browsers
available for any platform, and in version 11 we
have seen its features blossom. It's now less a
browser, and more an environment in its own right

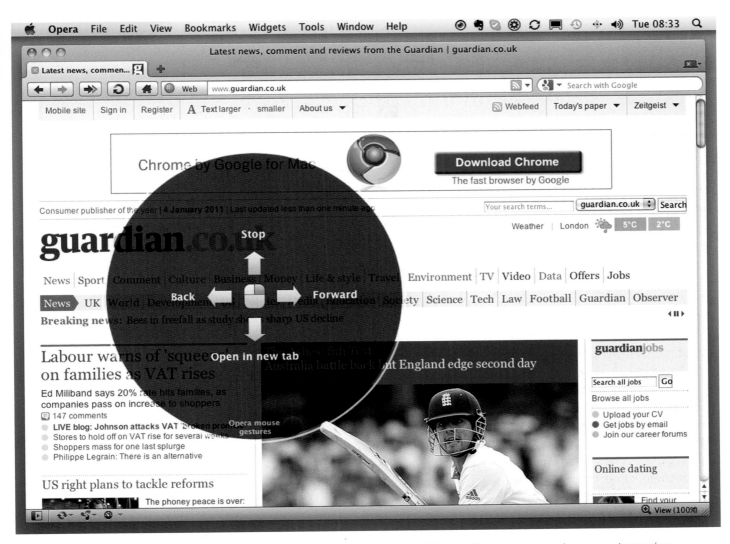

Below: Opera Unite is an under-the-hood web server that helps you to share data stored on your Mac with other computers, both locally on your home network, and over the Internet.

Above: Gestures speed up your browsing. Holding down the right mouse button pops up an overlaid graphic explaining what each movement achieves.

Below: Apps build in the Opera codebase greatly expand the browser's feature set.

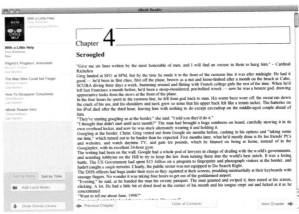

CHROME 10

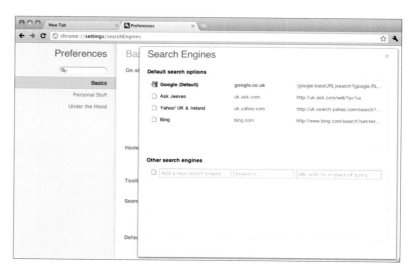

Rating 4
Download from google.com/chrome
Pros Fast + Neat integrated search feature
Cons Many add-on apps are third-party links
Verdict It's easy to see why Chrome has become so popular so quickly, but others offer better-integrated non-browsing features

If Google had its way we'd eschew installed software in favour of web apps. Chrome is its way of maintaining some control over how we run our lives, providing it with a stable, reliable platform against which it can develop its own applications – Gmail, Docs, Calendar and so on.

Apps take centre stage on new windows in version 10, alongside a link to the Chrome Web Store, which has been a background feature since version 8. The more 'apps' you install, though, the more you realise they're links to third-party sites, and all you've actually done is fill the home screen with some pretty links.

Chrome was the first mainstream browser to position the tab handles above the address bar. This is a more logical position than Safari's tabs-under design, as each page is given its own address bar, which doesn't change until you load a new page. In Safari, with just one address bar shared between all pages, its contents change when you click a new tab.

The Customize and Control button gives you speedy access to a range of tools that might otherwise be included on a toolbar, including page zoom and a full-screen view that takes away all of the extraneous browser elements, including the tabs, address bar and application window.

Google's primary money maker is search, so it's initially a surprise to see that there's no search box on the toolbar. That's because the address bar doubles up as a search input, with the first entry in the dropdown list being an option to search Google. You can change this to Ask Jeeves, Yahoo or Bing, and add your own search engines manually by supplying their URLs and the query

Chrome is from Google, but there's no reason why you have to use its own services. You can switch the browser's default search engine to Ask Jeeves, Yahoo! or Bing, and even add your own search options manually. There's no reason why you should only be able to specify search engines: you could use the function to search the archives of a bespoke news site or online store.

string. This is impressive. So is the fact that Google detected we were working from the UK and had set our default google.co.uk.

It beat Safari 5's score at html5test.com, scoring 288 out of a possible 400 when tested for compatibility with new HTML5 tags. This is good when compared directly with its peers. With HTML5 allowing sites to make use of local storage on your Mac to take web apps offline (clearing a webmail backlog during your commute, for example) it's perhaps not surprising that the Mac version of Chrome 10 doesn't support Google's own solution, Gears, which is now available only for Firefox 1.5 to 3.6, and Safari

The interface is stripped down, with just the address bar, tabs and page on display. A spanner button spins out a toolbar through which you can zoom the page, start new tabs and manage your bookmarks. There's also a neat full page feature, which takes away everything but the page body, so is great for web video. Moving your mouse to the top of the screen slides the bar back into view.

Chrome looks stripped back, but appearances can be deceptive. This is a powerful, fast browser, and highly recommended.

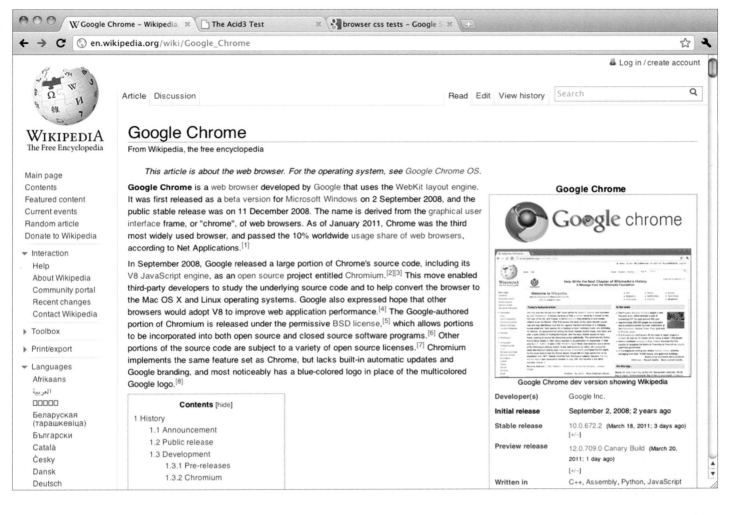

Google would like to see us live more of our lives online. Its Chrome App Store is a collection of links to third-party browser-based apps that are added to your Chrome homepage with a couple of clicks of your mouse.

Most browsers have separate input bars for URLs and searches. Chrome removes this distinction, with the address bar pushing you towards searching for your entered text if you haven't typed a URL

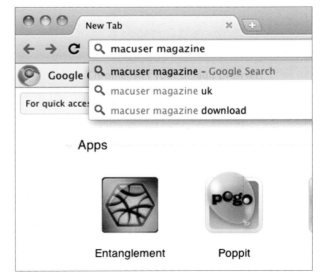

OMNIWEB 5.10

Rating 4

Download omnigroup.com/applications/omniweb

Pros Thumbnail tabs + Sessions and Workspaces + Per-domain preference settings

Cons Disappointing HTML5 test results

Verdict Some logical diversions from the norm make OmniWeb an excellent alternative to Safari for those who don't get on with traditional tabs

OmniWeb departs from the norm. Command-t opens a new tab, but rather than presenting a window with a clickable strip at the top it spawns a live thumbnail in a slide-out drawer. You can shrink these thumbnails down to a text-based list, but by sticking with the default you'll immediately see the state of each, and by resizing the drawer you'll fit more small windows or fewer large ones on screen.

The application window is aware of its surroundings, snapping to the edge of the screen as you resize it. It's a small point, but this makes it very easy to neaten things up when you have several apps running at once. Once you've it positioned the way you like, save a session. This not only stores your open tabs and history list, but also the location of your browser windows, so you can pick up where you left off the next time.

The Workspaces feature lets you run several browser instances at once, each with different active pages, and switch between them at will. It works in a similar manner to Panorama in Firefox 4, and with the addition of a snapshots tool you can save a workspace's current state and restore it later on if you go wandering through your links and lose where you started.

Like Camino it makes it easy to block ads, stop image animations looping and allow exceptions to both of these for specific domains. This can be set through the application preferences, with further variables set on a site-by-site basis, by visiting the site in question and toggling the site preferences inspector, which even lets you set the default text zoom, font style and image handling

Rather than tabs, OmniWeb has a neat channel in which it organises thumbnails of your pages.

for that site in isolation to all others.

OmniWeb 5.10 scored a disappointing 139 at html5test.com, which puts it low in the list among this collection of browsers. However, its unique, neat features are sufficient in number to ensure that it's not ruled out on the basis of this score alone.

The bookmarks manager looks like a web page. It's very powerful, allowing you to add keywords, and it even shows when a bookmarked page has been updated. This is particularly useful for anyone who prefers not to use a feed aggregator, or for sites that don't publish an RSS feed, as it saves you from making repeated visits.

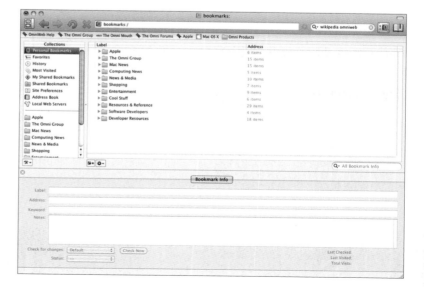

SAFARI 5

Rating 4
Download from apple.com/safari
Pros Rapidly-growing Extensions library + Reader pane
Cons No UK-specific search option
Verdict The Mac's default browser gets better with every release, but it's facing increasingly stiff competition

Safari appears now on no less than three platforms, spanning Windows, iOS and OS X. Despite that its having a tough time mounting a credible challenge against either Internet Explorer or Firefox outside of Apple's own OS.

Version 5 introduced Reader, which manifests itself as a small button in the address bar. It identifies the body copy on a web page, stripping out the surrounding clutter and ads to present the content in a panel that improves readability.

Also new are Safari Extensions. Bundles of CSS3, HTML5 and JavaScript, these are browser add-ons that perform specific tasks like searching particular sites or posting to social networks. Apple maintains a gallery of add-ons online.

Safari 5's support of HTML5 is good, but not excellent, which is surprising considering Apple's stance on the HTML5 vs Flash debate. By barring Flash from the App Store it's kept it off the iPad and iPhone, forcing developers to build web-based applications using HTML5. Safari scored 228 out of a possible 400 in the tests at html5test. com, putting it behind each of its major competitors. Beta builds of Safari 5.1 are scoring a more respectable 273.

Its history tracking is excellent, using CoverFlow to display thumbnails of the pages you've visited and searching not only on their addresses but the page titles, too. The address bar is context sensitive, so if you start typing an address it will pull out matching addresses from the history, and if you type a regular word, like 'news' it will use it to instead search the titles.

The default search tool remains Google, but you can switch to Bing or Yahoo, and have predictive results from any one of them appear in the search box drop-down. There's no option to specify any other browser.

Safari has excellent debug tools, which let you extensively tweak the way it runs, mimic alternative browsers for incompatible sites and diagnose page loading problems, helping developers identify sticking points in their code.

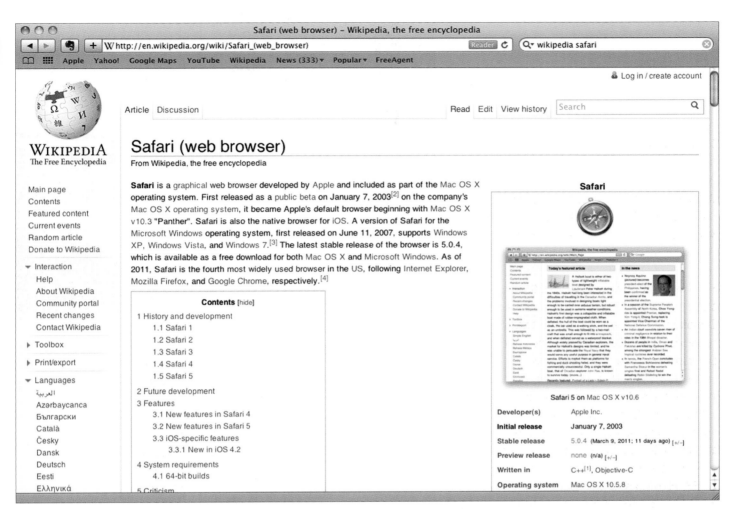

Left: Reader view dims the page and pulls out the primary content for distraction-free reading.

Below: Bookmarks and history lists are organised in a graphical carousel for each recognition.

Top, opposite page: Hot Sites shows a gallery of your most-visited pages.

Below: Safari 5 is extendable using HTML5 and JavaScript. If you can't, or don't want to write your own extensions, Apple maintains links to an extensive Gallery of Extensions, ready for downloading from its own website.

How to...

How to set up a printer

Printing is one of the most common tasks that any computer is asked to perform, yet setting up a printer and getting it to work flawlessly every time is still a frustrating business. Follow our guide to get your printer working first time.

. . . .

The easiest way to connect a printer and print to it is to use a USB port on your Mac. However, if you want to share the printer with other Macs or PCs it's not the best option. You can share a printer directly connected to a Mac with other machines, but only so long as the host Mac is running.

Instead, connect it to your network directly, either with an Ethernet cable, or by wifi. Decide on this before you buy it.

Something else you'll have to consider is the type of material you'll be printing. If you'll be churning out text documents a laser printer is the best option. If you want a printer to render photos on quality paper, choose an inkjet.

You should also consider consumables. Ink is expensive and it's tempting to consider buying generic ink cartridges or to have your old cartridges refilled at high street outlets. Although many generic inks are very good these days and produce decent prints, printers are complex beasts and the communication between printer and ink cartridge is essential to the smooth running of the printer. For this reason, ink cartridges on inkjet printers have a microchip fitted to them. Buying generic ink may require swapping the chip on each tank, which is a fiddly and messy business. Remember too, when buying a laser printer, to take into account the average cost per print and the lifespan of the drum. There is a surprising variation in both between manufacturers.

STEP 01 USB Printer Install the ink cartridges This process will vary depending on the printer you have, so be careful to read the Quick Start Guide. Plug the printer into the mains before you start so that the print head can be moved to the correct position. In most cases, the slots for the cartridges will be colour-coded, making it easy to see where each one goes.

STEP 02 USB Printer Connect the USB cable With the printer switched off, connect one end of the USB cable (which you may have to buy yourself) to the printer and the other end to your Mac. Now switch the printer on and wait for it to run through its set-up routine. Once it's done, check whether Mac OS X already has drivers for it installed by opening System Preferences.

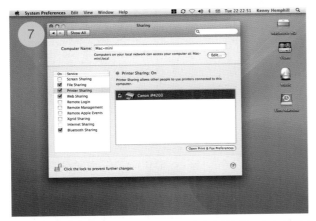

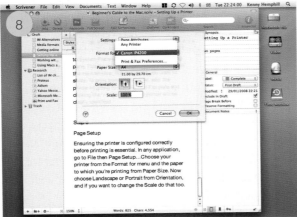

STEP 03 Installing Drivers In System Preferences, click on Print and Fax. If your printer shows up in the list on the left of the window, you need do nothing more. If not, and it's a USB printer, you need to install the drivers.

STEP 04 Configure USB Printer Now go back to Print and Fax in System Preferences. You should now see your printer listed. As it's the only printer connected to your Mac, it will automatically be the default printer. Select the default paper size, this is the paper that will be printed to if you hit Print from an application and don't change any options.

STEP 05 Adding a Network Printer Network laser printer drivers tend to be more generic than USB printers so there's more chance that your Mac will have the right one installed. Connect the printer to your network router and go to System Preferences/Print and Fax again. Press the '+' button and wait for your Mac to find it.

STEP 06 Adding a wireless printer Printing over a wifi network is a little more complicated as manufacturers use different methods to install and set-up printers. Getting a wireless printer up and running can be a frustrating business, even for experienced users, so consider before you buy whether you really need wireless, or whether you could share a USB printer using an AirPort unit.

STEP 07 Sharing a Printer To share a printer connected to a single Mac, go to System Preferences and click on the Sharing pane. Tick the box next to Printer Sharing and in the main window, tick the printer you want to share. To print from another Mac, add the printer by going to the Print and Fax pane and clicking on the '+' sign: the shared printer will be clearly identified.

STEP 08 Page Setup Ensuring the printer is configured correctly before printing is essential. In any application, go to File then Page Setup... Choose your printer from the 'Format for' menu and the paper to which you're printing from Paper Size. Now choose Landscape or Portrait from Orientation, and if you want to change the Scale do that too.

Beginners' Terminal

Mac OS X has an intuitive graphical interface, underpinned by a robust text-based command mode, which you can access using the Terminal application. Learn the basics with this guide and you can harness the full power of your OS.

. . . .

■ FIRST STEPS

Start by launching Terminal and looking at the last line. In the grab on the previous page, this shows the following: Keith-Martins-PowerBook:~ keith$

This tells you four things: the sharing name of the computer you're currently logged into (as shown in the Sharing pane in System Preferences), the directory you're currently looking at, the user name currently in use (this is your normal login user name), and what kind of user you are (the $ indicates a normal user, a hash character means a root user, which you won't be). Most of this isn't of immediate use, but the current directory information can be handy.

Rather than use Terminal to launch into running serious processes just yet, start by using it to look around your disk. The tilde indicator means your home folder, but you can get a full Unix-style path showing where you are if you type pwd (short for 'print working directory) and press return. Here, this returns /Users/keith; we're in the 'keith' folder inside the 'Users' folder on our hard disk. Remember: case can be important, at least for everything other than the initial commands (such as pwd) themselves.

■ WHAT IS TERMINAL

Terminal is a strange application. It has essentially no interface to speak of, just a text entry window. You use it by typing commands, not by clicking buttons. Unlike graphical user interfaces, everything you do in Terminal and everything it shows you is done using plain Ascii text. In fact, it's anathema to most Mac users, so why use it at all?

Well, because it lets you tinker beneath the hood, do things that might otherwise be tedious or time-consuming, and generally take control of your Mac in ways that were never possible before. Using Terminal doesn't mean you're working around flaws and blank spots in the Mac OS, it's simply a way to gain even further control of your machine. Rather than patching up gaps, Terminal comes in addition to the broad feature set of Mac OS X, extending the abilities of anyone who cares to learn its secrets. Of course, it's also a way to impress those who look down their noses at the Mac; it shows a face of the Mac that many people didn't know existed.

Using Terminal to perform some basic tricks isn't hard – but there's a problem. Terminal doesn't exactly lend itself to casual exploration without external reference information, and most of the websites that document how to do things with it tend to assume a certain existing level of experience. Manuals for all the commands on tap are built in, but you first have to know the command and then learn how to comprehend them.

One key point to understand is how instructions in Terminal are phrased. The basic construction is the name of the process you want to run followed by the instruction you want it to carry out and, sometimes, further parameters to fine-tune or extend the instruction. Unix applications are generally relatively sparse things compared to the feature-packed software you're more used to dealing with. Because of this, power users will often link commands together so that the results of one operation are automatically processed by the next.

One example of putting Terminal to good use is by deleting files or folders that refuse to be trashed in the normal manner. Another is monitoring one of Mac OS X's many logs to see specific activity and track down possible problems. Yes, these can be done with regular Mac OS X applications if you can find them online, but those simply use the same command-line instructions behind the scenes. Then there are the many things that aren't so easy to do with normal desktop applications. One complex search job that was needed some months ago involved finding words that contained just the letters a to g from a dictionary list of more than 100,000 items. Traditional methods were fiddly and would have taken hours, but a one-line grep command (admittedly fairly opaque to the uninitiated) took a second or two to complete the task.

Take a look through the following pages to get a feel for it and try out some of the suggested commands. Then put it to one side for a while and come back and read it again another day when things have sunk in a little. No, we don't expect anyone to live their Mac lives by sitting in Terminal typing commands. But if you take some time to learn its ways, you'll find you have a powerful new set of skills to call on. Even more importantly, you'll have learned that Terminal isn't arcane voodoo, it's simply a tool.

LIST COMMAND

Now type ls and press return. This lists (hence 'ls')

the contents of the current directory. The ls command has many additional parameters you can include to control exactly what's listed. Typing ls -a tells ls that you want to see all items including invisible ones. The result will be longer than what you get with ls on its own; all those items with dots at the beginning of their names are invisible in the Finder. Now try ls -l to see the item list shown in 'long' detailed format instead. Using -t sorts by modification date, -S sorts by size, and -r reverses the sort. Put them together and you get multiple operations performed at once; ls -ltr lists in long format sorted by modification date and reversed so older items come first. You don't have to just list the contents of the folder you're in at the moment; try adding a path to a different place on your Mac to list that folder instead. For example, type ls /Applications to see things in your Applications folder. But using cd to change the current working directory can make life simpler at times.

Use it with the following options to achieve these outcomes:

ls	-a	List all items including invisible ones
	-A	Lists all items except for the . and .. directory links
	-G	Use colourised output for list
	-l	Show a directory's contents in long (detailed) format
	-R	List all subdirectories recursively (can produce huge lists)
	-sk	List sizes of files in kilobytes
	-t	Show the list sorted according to most recently modified
	-T	Show full time information for each item
	-u	Show the list sorted according to last access time
	-1	Use single rather than multiple columns

CHANGE DIRECTORY COMMAND

The cd command changes the current working directory, like navigating around in a window in the Finder. The instructions on where to go can be relative to where you are now or complete. As you start in your home folder, type cd /Documents to go into your Documents folder, then use ls on its own to see the new listing.

cd	.	Start the path description from the current level
	..	Move up a level
	/	Start from the top of the startup volume
	/Volumes/diskname	
		Start from the top of a different volume
	~	Shorthand for starting from the current user's home

If you want to sort the results that ls gives with more control, you'll need to turn to the separate sort application, a tool that takes data and returns it sorted into whatever order you require. The trick here is knowing how to pass this tool the data you want to sort. To sort the output of processes such as ls, you need to 'pipe' the results of the first operation to the second. When you type ls, instead of leaving it to pour the results to the Terminal window, type the vertical bar character, known as the pipe, followed by sort (or whatever tool you'd like to work on the results). Here's an example:

ls | sort -k 2.1

This lists the contents of the current directory and passes that to the sort application, which is then told to sort using a custom 'key' (2.1 means the first character of the second word of each line) rather than the beginning of each line as normal.

To sort a text file, type its path after the sort command (or just drag and drop the file into the Terminal window to have the path typed for you). Press return and you'll see the results in the window. To write a sort to a file rather than to the window, add another path to a file. If necessary, a new document will be made when this is run.

sort	-b	*Ignore leading spaces when sorting*
	-d	*Sort in 'phone directory' mode*
	-f	*Fold upper and lower-case letters together when sorting*
	-k wordnum.charnum	
		Start the sort using characters other than first in each line
	-n	*Sort in numeric mode*
	-m	*Merge files by sorting as a group.*
		See 'man sort' for details
	-M	*Sort in month mode, using three-letter month abbreviations*
	-o outputfile	
		Puts the sort result directly into the specified output file
	-r	*Reverse the order of the sort*

■ COPY AND MORE COMMANDS

Renaming files is done with the mv command, effectively 'moving' the original file or folder to a new one. (As with regular Finder use, 'moving' something to a different volume copies it, leaving the original in place, so effectively spawns a second copy in the process.) Type *mv* followed by the file to move and the destination to move it to. To copy something within a single volume so the

original is left where it is, use the *cp* command instead.

You can use either of these commands to rescue music from an iPod if you've had a disaster with your iTunes library. Connect the iPod and make sure it's mounted in the Finder, then type *cp /Volumes/YOURIPODNAME/iPod_Control/Music/* ~/Music/* and press return. (Replace YOURIPODNAME with the name of your iPod, remembering to 'escape' spaces as instructed in the Paths information below.) This command copies everything that's within the invisible 'Music' folder inside the also-invisible '*iPod_Control*' folder across to the Music folder in your home, ready to drop into iTunes. The asterisk is a wildcard character that literally means 'any character or characters'. See Wildcards, below right, for more information.

cp, mv		
	-f	*Remove matching files in the destination without asking*
	-i	*Ask for confirmation before overwriting an existing file*
	-n	*Don't overwrite existing files*
	-p	*Preserve item details - modification time, access time, etc*
	-v	*Copy in verbose mode, showing each item as it is handled*

■ REMOVE COMMAND

The Unix 'remove' command, *rm*, is one to approach with caution. However, it, and its cousin *rmdir*, can be extremely handy when you want to delete something that's being a bit stubborn about going. This command can delete items that the Finder refuses to trash.

Don't use wildcards with the *rm* command until you're reasonably experienced, and even then only with caution; you could easily delete more than you mean to. To delete a file in the current working directory, just type *rm* followed by its name. Alternatively, use relative or absolute paths to the file. The *rm* command can't delete folders without help; the *-d* and *-R* parameters help here. Typing *rm* followed by the path to a file and then pressing return will normally delete the item, even if other methods have failed. This won't delete a folder (directory) without help, however, so you'll need to add a parameter to the bare command (before the item path) to persuade it to cooperate. The basic *-d* parameter will delete empty directories as well as files, but any folders with things inside are left alone.

Instead, use -R, which goes through nested folders, deleting anything it finds, and then deletes the newly empty folders.

rm	-d	Attempt to remove directories as well as files
	-f	Remove files without prompts, regardless of file permissions
	-i	Ask for confirmation before removing each file
	-P	Overwrite files securely before deleting
	-R	Remove the file hierarchy for each file delete request
	-v	Delete in verbose mode, showing each item as it is removed

■ WILDCARDS

When you're trying to refer to files by name you can use a wildcard – the asterisk character – to refer to one or more characters in a name without having to type them specifically. For example, to move every file on the desktop which ends with .png into a 'PNGs' folder in your Pictures folder, type *mv ~/Desktop/*.png ~/Pictures/PNGs/* and press return. Using a wildcard as the only thing in a path after a slash character will include everything from that point onwards, including whatever's in any subsequent folders. Be very careful with this, especially if using this with the *rm* command.

■ PATHS

Getting the path right is one of the most important keys to using Terminal successfully with your files and folders. This is where the built-in clue about the current working directory comes in handy. You can normally refer to a file without listing the full 'folder/folder/file' pathname to it if it's in the current directory; where the Terminal window is focused right now. Otherwise, use the path to it from the top of the disk.

~	Shorthand for the current user's home directory
/	Indicates the top level of the system volume
.	Starts from your current location as shown in the Terminal prompt
..	Move up a level from where you are
\	Precedes a character that isn't legal in Unix

The home-orientated path can start with */Users/ username* or simply ~, the tilde character. The full path from the top of your hard disk is either */* (for the system volume) or */Volumes/diskname* for other volumes. Finally, a dot means the path starts from wherever you're currently focused, and a

double dot takes you up a level – type *cd ..* to get back out of the Documents folder. When working with path names you'll find that Terminal can't cope with certain characters without help. The most obvious example is the space character. Spaces are used to separate parts of commands and their parameters, so referring to something with a space in its name will cause hiccups. To get around this, you'll need to 'escape' those characters by adding a backslash character first. Other characters that need to be escaped include parentheses and most punctuation. A folder called 'My (old) Work?' would be 'My\ \(old\)\ Work\?' in Terminal. Drag and drop files and folders into Terminal to see how their names are escaped for you. In most cases, you can use this trick to avoid actually working those things out yourself. Don't forget to include filename suffixes as well when referring to documents. If your Finder preferences aren't set to show these, we suggest you change this. Go to Finder > Preferences, click Advanced, and check the 'Show all file extensions' checkbox.

■ LEARNING WITH MAN

Learning to browse the built-in manuals is a very useful task. This is done with yet another command-line application, this one called man, short for manual. It may take a little while to go through everything that can be done – and even longer to figure some of it out – but this is the proverbial horse's mouth for command-line application information.

Note that often the instructions that come back are highly verbose, so don't forget that you can scroll Terminal, just like any other window.

Type *man* followed by the application name – for example, *man ls* – and you'll be presented with a list of all the different possible commands you can send. Press the spacebar or the down arrow key to move down through the contents, and hit the up arrow key to step back. It's worth noting that you can't type commands in the same window while you're doing this, so open a new one to try things out while browsing the man pages. Use man to learn more about other Unix commands, even if you're not likely to use them yourself.

Parental Controls

You can't always supervise your child's computer use, so you should at least put some precautionary measures in place. Here's how to do just that using the settings built into OS X.

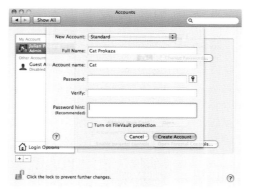

STEP 01 Set up a limited user You need two user accounts to use Parental Controls – an Administrator, plus one or more Standard accounts. If your children don't use separate Standard accounts for their Mac access, though, now is the time to make the change – go to System Preferences > System > Accounts and create as many Standard accounts as you need.

STEP 02 Turn on Parental Controls You can jump to Parental Controls from Accounts preferences by selecting the account you want to manage and clicking the Open Parental Controls button. Alternatively, go to System Preferences > System > Parental Controls for direct access. Select the account you want to manage and click the Enable Parental Controls buttons.

STEP 03 Apply limits Parental Controls' System tab provides the greatest control over how OS X is used. The Use Simple Finder option is ideal for very young children – it changes the Desktop to a simplified layout with a minimal Dock, limits access to the Finder and blocks access to all but the bare essentials of the OS.

STEP 04 Restrict app access If Simple Finder is too restrictive, stick with the standard Finder and instead use the 'Only allow selected applications' option, together with the application checklist to restrict access to only the software you deem suitable. There are options to prevent changes to printer settings, the user password and Dock, as well as disabling CD burning.

Much is made of the hazards that children may face on the web, and increased parental responsibility is often put forward as the common-sense solution for anyone who has concerns. Allowing young children uncontrolled access to a computer is a very bad idea, and a child of any age using the Internet for the first time should only do so under careful guidance.

Constant computer supervision just isn't practical for many parents, of course, but there are technological measures that can be taken to ensure that Internet – and general computer – use only takes place under controlled conditions. Many of these measures are already built into Mac OS X and simply need to be set up to suit.

Mac OS X's Parental Controls can only be used with Standard user accounts – something that your children should already have in order to limit their access to the operating system and third-party applications. The controls are split into four main areas, which can be used to restrict access to websites and installed applications. There's also a logging feature that allows you to see what your children have been up to.

Placing parental controls on any computer involves more than just ticking a few boxes and forgetting about it. Clever kids can find their way around many restrictions, and you'll need to apply some lateral thinking to cater for all – or, at least, most – eventualities.

If you don't patch up all the holes, your child might be able to bypass lenient restrictions, and install and run replacements for Apple Mail and iChat directly from the Desktop. Limiting application use to a fixed selection is one way around this problem, but both email and instant messaging can be used via websites such as Meebo, too, so you'll need to give plenty of thought to the websites you want to block in order to close the loopholes your child might exploit.

One final word of warning – no parental control software is ever completely foolproof, and nor is it a substitute for talking about responsible and safe computer use with your child. Deploying overly draconian computer controls can also drive your child to use someone else's computer – one that may have no parental controls or adult supervision in place.

STEP 05 Block risky sites OS X includes a filter that works with any web browser, not just Safari. Found on the Content tab, the filter offers three levels of website filtering and, by default, unrestricted web access is allowed. Mac OS X can attempt to automatically identify unsuitable websites, based on opt-in ratings.

STEP 06 Don't talk to strangers If you don't want to block email and instant messaging access, but do want control over who your child can communicate with, the Mail & Chat tab will let you put some restrictions in place. These are based on a whitelist of allowed email addresses for both Mail and iChat.

STEP 07 Healthy time limits The final Parental Controls tab lets you place time limits on computer use. You can set different limits for weekdays and weekends, along with 'bedtime' settings that block access completely, but you can't allow three hours of spreadsheet use and 30 minutes of game-playing each day, for example.

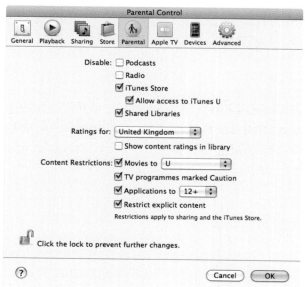

STEP 08 Check what the kids have been up to It's a good idea to keep an eye on the Parental Controls' Logs. The time spent using allowed applications and websites can provide some useful insight into your child's computer use, and the controls may need fine-tuning in the light of this information. Allowed websites can also be blocked – and vice versa – from this tab, but bear in mind that the web logs will also include sites opened as the result of embedded media and ads.

STEP 09 Block parts of the iTunes Store Blocking access to websites with age-inappropriate material is pointless if that same material can be accessed by other means. If you don't want to block iTunes, but are concerned about what it provides access to, use its Parental Control settings (iTunes > Preferences). These disable certain iTunes features, and content accessed via shared libraries and the iTunes Store can also be restricted. Existing content in iTunes for this account is unaffected.

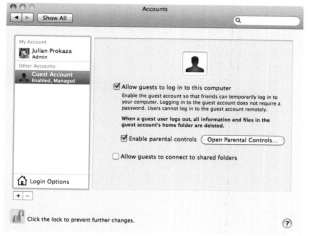

STEP 10 iPhone controls The iPhone also has built-in parental controls, but lacks the fine control found in Mac OS X. Accessed via Settings > General > Restrictions, they allow certain built-in iPhone apps and functions to be disabled, and age ratings can be applied to movies, TV shows and applications. These latter three options also apply to content already stored on the iPhone (unlike with iTunes), but stored content affected by ratings changes isn't removed, just hidden from view.

STEP 11 Lock down the guest account A Standard user account with Parental Controls applied is also useful as a generic account for use by friends and non-resident family members, but Mac OS X also has dedicated support for such times. The Guest account (System Preferences > System > Accounts) creates a Standard account with no password, but with the added benefit that any files created by this account are deleted when the user logs out. Parental Controls can be applied to the Guest account, too, making it a watertight way to grant safe access to your Mac.

Facebook in iChat

By using Facebook chat in iChat you can have the best of both worlds. You can use features such as automatic replies when you're away from your Mac and save chats to your Mac in case you forget to add arrangements for nights out to your iPhone.

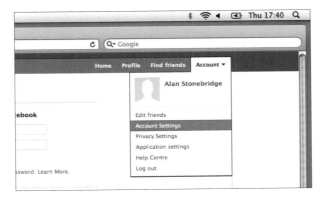

STEP 01 Verify your account To set a Facebook username, you'll need to verify your identity by using your mobile phone. Log into the Facebook website and click Account > Account Settings. Next to Username, click change and you'll be asked to verify your account by sending an SMS to your mobile phone. When the text arrives, enter the code and press Confirm.

STEP 02 Choose your unique username Next, choose a username. Before you commit to your chosen name, make sure you're happy with it. Once it has been set, you can't change it. After you've done this, people will be able to reach your Facebook profile by browsing to facebook.com/username, substituting your username after the forward slash.

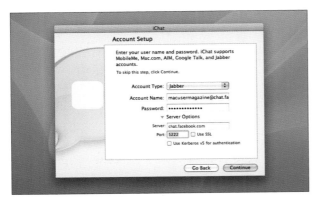

STEP 03 Add a Facebook account in iChat Open iChat. If you haven't used it before, the Account Setup pane will appear. Otherwise, open its preferences (Command+comma) and, under Accounts, click the '+' at the bottom left. Set the new account's type to Jabber. Enter username@chat.facebook.com as the account name, substituting the username you chose earlier. Enter the same password you use to log in to Facebook.

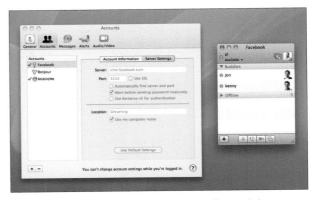

STEP 04 Connect to the chat server Expand the server options and enter chat.facebook.com as the server, and 5222 as the port. Leave SSL and Kerberos authentication unchecked and press Done. iChat will log in, remember to change the account description to say Facebook.

Keychain Access

The Mac OS X Keychain greatly simplifies the task of managing your Mac and the various apps its runs and sites it visits. How does it work, though, and how can you explore its contents to get the most out of it and diagnose – and solve – problems?

. . . .

◼ WHAT IS A KEYCHAIN?

Just as every user of your Mac has their own account with private space for documents, music, photos and personal preferences for applications, they also have a keychain that keeps their private passwords for servers and websites in one place.

More specifically, it's known as the login keychain, and it's normally protected with the same password as your user account. When you log in, the keychain is unlocked and ready to use, although applications don't have free access to its contents unless you grant them unrestricted access. You've probably seen this before; a dialog box pops up to tell you that an application wants to access something on the keychain and asks whether you want to deny it that right, or to allow it just the once or whenever it's needed. Understanding a little bit more about how this information is stored and accessed means learning about Keychain Access

If you accidentally deny or allow an application unrestricted access to a password, you'll need to open Keychain Access to correct the mistake. It also allows you to tighten up on the security of your passwords, with extra options for automatically locking the keychain and choosing whether it's synchronised to your other Macs.

Just as you might keep separate bunches of keys for work and home, you can move your most sensitive passwords to a second keychain that

has a different password. By doing that, you can keep confidential information on your Mac at home by setting that keychain not to synchronise to your other Macs over MobileMe, while ones for websites that you use daily are still transferred to the one on your desk at the office.

. . . .

◼ NAVIGATE THE KEYCHAIN INTERFACE

[1] Available Keychains
[2] Keychain contents
[3] Search your keychain
[4] Copy a password
[5] Rename items

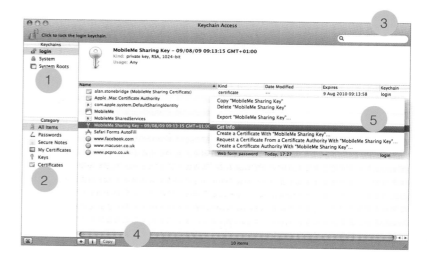

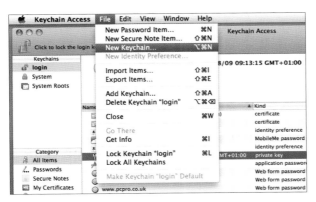

STEP 01 Create a new keychain To create a new keychain that will hold your most sensitive passwords, choose File > New Keychain. Keychains are normally saved to ~/Library/Keychains (the tilde is shorthand for your user folder). Give the keychain a name and save it in that folder.

STEP 02 Give it a strong password You'll be asked to set a password. The bar beneath the Verify box will change colour to indicate its strength. Choose something memorable, but different to the password on your user account. After this, drag existing items in your login keychain to move them to the new one.

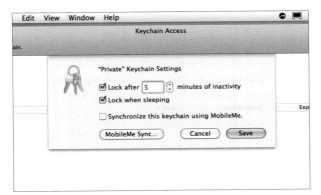

STEP 03 Change the keychain settings Ctrl-click the new keychain and choose Change Settings for Keychain. You can set how soon the keychain locks itself and whether it does so when the Mac is put to sleep. If the keychain holds confidential information you probably don't want it to sync to other Macs, so disable that here.

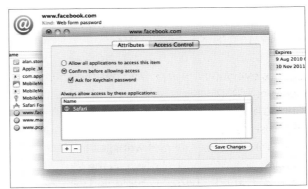

STEP 04 Choose security for individual passwords Double-click a password item and click the Access Control tab to set how freely applications can use it. Ensure relevant apps have to ask for permission by selecting the correct option, but be aware it's just a courtesy by default.

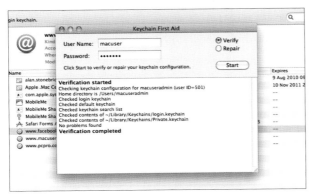

STEP 05 Fixing problems with a keychain Choosing Keychain Access > Keychain First Aid lets you see whether the keychain is damaged. Choose to verify the Keychain and press Start. If the keychain can't be repaired, open preferences and on the General tab, press Reset My Default Keychain. Your existing login keychain is moved aside so you won't lose it for good.

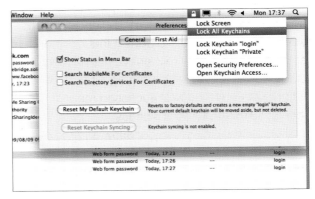

STEP 06 Easier access to your keychains In Keychain Access's General preferences is an option to show its status in the menu bar. Enabling it will show a padlock icon that changes to reflect whether all your keychains are locked or unlocked. Click it and you can immediately lock all of your keychains, as well as your Mac's screen when you're leaving it unattended for a while.

Photo editing tips

No matter how good a photographer you are, it's always possible to improve your photos with bit of tweaking. Here are our tips for top shooting and, when you've got the results on your Mac, edit them.

· ·

It's 180 years since Nicéphore Niépce made the first photographic image; it was exposed onto a pewter plate covered with bitumen of Judea, a petroleum derivative. Until the advent of digital photography, anyone who wanted to improve their photos had to be more chemist than creative, but with software such as Photoshop and iPhoto, it's easy to turn lacklustre snaps into works of art.

That's what we're here to help you do. Over the next six pages, you'll learn how to restore colour to faded photographs, produce stunning black-and- white images that leave the bland results of a quick Desaturate in Photoshop in the dust, create blemish-free skin and much more.

And the best bit is that you don't have to splash out on Photoshop to follow along. This flagship application of Adobe's may give you the most control and best results – and we'll be showing you how tobest harness its power – but we'll also show you how to do the same task in iPhoto, which offers surprisingly sophisticated editing abilities, too.

What's more, it comes free on new Macs, so many of us can use the techniques described in this feature effectively without spending a penny.

Much of what makes a good photograph, though, happens before you press the shutter, not once you've imported it into an editing suite, so we'll also be showcasing essential tips to help you take good, novel, interesting and relevant photographs.

Put it all together, and you have an essential guide to getting the very best photographs possible. No longer will you have to worry about boring your friends and family with holiday snaps,or taking precious memories that don't capture the moment as well as you could.

■ BEFORE YOU SNAP

Your Mac can work wonders in cleaning up and enhancing your shots, but it can only work with the source material you give it. Here's our handy guide to getting the best photograph before you even snap the shutter.

TELL STORIES

In each shot, always have at the back of your mind a little voice asking you what story you want to tell with the photograph. While this sounds a little abstract, it has a real, tangible effect on your pictures. Say you're in a pub with some friends, and you want to take a picture of one of your more 'hilarious' mates doing something characteristically 'hilarious'. Is it more important to capture the party trick specifically – telling the story 'here's what a friend of mine does' – or the reactions of the audience – potentially telling the story 'my friend isn't as funny as he thinks'. The story can be simply aesthetic – 'this is a pretty flower' – but each picture has one, and identifying it will help you take more interesting shots.

Always shoot at full quality
Sure, you'll get more pictures on a memory card if you shoot at low quality, but they're much less flexible. Not only are you limited in the size at which you can print the shots, but if you later decide to crop in on a specific area, the compression or low pixel count will become more obvious and spoil the picture. Ensure that the resolution is set to its highest and compression to its lowest. Ideally, if your camera supports it, shoot in Raw mode for ultimate flexibility. Simply buy more or bigger memory cards if your settings indicate you'll only fit a few on at these settings.

Use macro
Most cameras have a macro function to focus really close on a subject, and it's a great way of recording interesting textures, and to give context. If you're at a historic house, say, try hunkering down and taking a macro shot of some hanging blossom (you may need to hold your hand behind the bloom to give autofocus something to lock on to, then remove it before fully depressing the shutter) with the house blurred in the background. Much more atmospheric than a straight shot of the building at eye level.

Get closer
Asked to take a snap of a group of people, most people will take a few strides back and fit everyone in from head to toe – with a fair bit of background thrown in for good measure. This results in the faces being little more than a few hundred pixels tall. Most pictures – especially group shots – benefit from being taken closer to the subject. Portraits often work well cropped in much more closely than you would normally imagine – force yourself to move the camera closer and you'll be pleasantly surprised.

Change the viewpoint
Stand on chairs and walls, get down on your knees and generally make a fool of yourself to get the best picture. Most people just stand upright and lift the camera to their eye-line, resulting in mediocre pictures that don't tell the story well.

Taking pictures of children? Hunker down to their eye-level; the context this gives tells a better, truer story. By all means take the normal, basic shot, but for each shot you take, force yourself to move slightly and take another.

Background and foreground
The background is as important as the foreground. That's not to say each should be given equal prominence – using shallow depths of field to blur the background and draw the eye to the foreground subject is a time-honoured and useful trick – but one that you shouldn't just ignore.

Turn off flash
Most cameras' flashes just serve to wash out people's faces to blue-ish, pockmarked circles, and many have an effective range of no more than a couple of metres. Add in their ability to spoil photos taken through glass by reflecting back in to the lens, and they're often more trouble than they're worth. See 'Rest and use self-timer' for more.

Rest and use self-timer
Turning off the flash means the camera has to keep the shutter open for longer to take the shot, so things can be blurred. Obviate this by resting the camera on a convenient flat surface (upturned glasses can be readily pressed into service in pubs) and taking the photo with your camera's self-timer activated. Many have a two-second self-timer as well as the more common 10-second variant, and even this provides ample time for the camera to stop rocking on its perch.

The two-shot cheese
Most people, on hearing the command 'say cheese', will freeze their face into a rictus of agonised happiness but relax and share a genuine smile just after the shot has been taken. Use this to your advantage: count down to the 'official' photo, take it, but take another immediately after – everyone will look much more happy and spontaneous in this covert shot.

CONVERT TO MONOCHROME

Many pictures can look much better in black and white. This is partly because we perceive differences in light and dark more readily than differences in colour, and partly because most colour photos actually display a narrow gamut of tonal variation. Converting to monochrome can make pictures dramatic and gives portraits an elegance that's difficult to achieve in any other way.

The first step is to convert your picture to greyscale, so bring up the Effects palette and click the B&W thumbnail. If the result looks insipid, click Boost and click the arrows that appear to the right and left to increade or descrease the intensity of the effect.

CROP YOUR IMAGES

We'd always encourage you to frame a picture properly before pressing the shutter. Occasionally, though, you may need to change format or alter the focus of the shot, or you may decide that your original framing was off, in which case, you can re-frame digitally. Remember that detail will be lost, and, particularly with mobile phone cameras, you may not have enough pixels to allow you to crop in very far while retaining enough resolution to print successfully.

If you want to keep your picture constrained to the dimensions of normal photographic paper, pick one from the Constrain list; snaps are usually 4 x 6in. iPhoto will automatically select the maximum area to fit onto the chosen paper size; the proportions of many digital shots are different from those of traditional photographic paper. Move your cursor inside the selected area to move it around, or drag in the corners to change the size. By default, iPhoto will assume you want to keep the orientation the same, but an option at the bottom of the Constrain menu enables you to change the orientation for cropping. When you're happy, click Crop.

CORRECT RED-EYE EFFECTS

Red-eye is caused by the camera's flash reflecting off the retinas of the photo's subjects, and is at its worst when the flash is positioned close to the lens. Many cameras now have a red-eye reduction feature that fires a pre-flash to contract the subjects' pupils, but even so you might find that some of your evening and night shots seem to be populated by demons.

In theory, this is very simple: just load up the photograph, click the Fix Red-Eye tool. In most cases the automatic setting will be sufficient to solve the problem, with iPhoto detecting red eyes in the image and eliminating them. You can also apply a manual fix by clicking on the eyes and then using the Size slider to make the correction area larger or smaller, as appropriate.

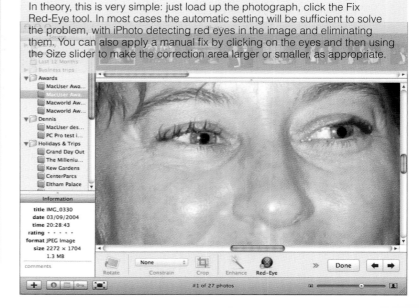

▦ USING PHOTOSHOP

This method is quite labour-intensive, so if you just want a quick-and-dirty mono conversion, convert your working colour space to Lab (Image > Mode > Lab Color) and choose Image > Adjustments > Desaturate. The results are much punchier than the insipid Desaturate command when in RGB. You can then convert back to RGB (or CMYK).

To do it right, convert your colour image to Lab and select the Lightness channel from the Channels palette. Now switch the Mode to Greyscale, which will use the information from the lightness channel to build the mono image. Command-click on the new Grey channel to select it, and then invert the selection. Create a new fill layer (Layer > New Fill Layer > Solid Color) filled with solid black, and adjust the opacity of the fill layer to tinker with its strength.

You may also want to add another adjustments layer to control curves or levels, perhaps to control greyscale performance in shadows.

You can also 'crisp up' contrast to give your images a gallery feel. Duplicate the background by dragging it to the new layer icon at the bottom of the palette, and run the High Pass filter with a radius of about 10. Change this layer's blend mode to Hard Light, and, again, adjust the opacity of the layer to change the strength of the effect.

Adding warmth to a pure monochrome image can make it look a little more human. You could either convert the colour space to duo-, tri- or even quadtone to achieve this, or you could simply convert to RGB and add a Photo Filter adjustment layer with one of the warming filters set to around 15%.

Open the image and choose the regular rectangular marquee tool. If you just want to crop to your proportions, simply select the area you want to crop and choose Image > Crop. To keep pictures cropped to aspect ratios of standard photo paper, simply change the framing style from Normal to Fixed Aspect Ratio, and enter the basic size of the paper onto which you want to print. Units are irrelevant, so you could enter 4 and 6 or 10 and 15 (inches and centimetres respectively, as it happens) for normal photographic paper. Once that's done, select the area you want to keep and choose Image > Crop. Enter the relevant dimensions in Image > Image Size.

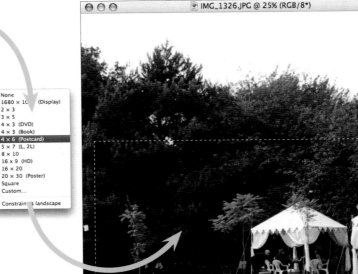

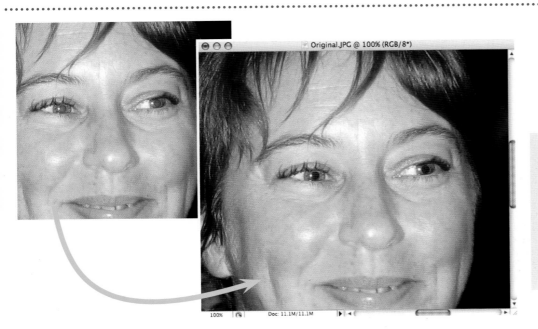

If you have Photoshop CS2 or later, you do have a dedicated red-eye removal tool at your disposal. It's a bit hidden away – look in the fly-out tool menu for the Healing brush – but select it and you'll get a set of cross-hairs for clicking in the centre of the pupils. The default size usually works well for most photos, but the default 50% darken is a little strong and looks artificial in most snaps. Try reducing it to around 30%.

USING iPHOTO

Old, faded photographs do have a charm all of their own, but sometimes you want to restore them to something of their former glory. The techniques we'll discuss here are really only concerned with correcting the colours, not repairing damage – some of the techniques discussed in the Blemish-free skin section would apply here. The trick to this is to spot what colour shifts have taken place and compensate for them.

Most faded photos have a warm, orange cast. Correct this by dragging the Temperature slider towards the blue – not too much, but just enough to neutralise the colours. You may find you need to tint the picture with a little green. Most old photos benefit from quite drastic sharpening, so don't be afraid to really turn it up. Be very sparing with contrast increases – you may find that clipping in the dark slider for the Levels control does a better job. With monochrome images, convert to greyscale, drag the Temperature and Tint sliders to the left, drag exposure to about -40, and bump up the contrast slightly.

It doesn't take much to spruce up humble holiday snaps, and these techniques simply add a little punch to your photos. Whether you've shot landscapes or people, a few seconds spent on each image can pay dividends. They can add drama to the most unassuming shot, but use them with care and print to check that the results aren't too extreme, especially if your system isn't colour calibrated.

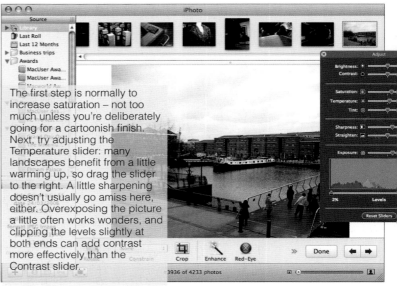

The first step is normally to increase saturation – not too much unless you're deliberately going for a cartoonish finish. Next, try adjusting the Temperature slider: many landscapes benefit from a little warming up, so drag the slider to the right. A little sharpening doesn't usually go amiss here, either. Overexposing the picture a little often works wonders, and clipping the levels slightly at both ends can add contrast more effectively than the Contrast slider.

One of the unpleasant side-effects of taking photos late at night is that people are often a bit sweaty or make-up has smudged, and the use of flash makes these problems worse.

Click the Retouch tool and dab away at the shiny highlights to 'matte them out', using the Size slider to change the diameter of the area to which the adustment applies.

USING PHOTOSHOP

To improve photos, you usually have to do three things: remove a colour cast, increase the saturation and restore some contrast. We'll do all three using adjustment layers, so you don't destroy any detail from the original, and can tinker with all the settings at every step along the way. First, we'll deal with the colour cast, so from the control at the bottom of the layers palette (which looks like a black-and-white circle) pick Color Balance. You'll probably have to drag the top slider towards cyan, and the bottom slider towards blue, but adjust to suit your picture. Keep looking away from and back to your screen, as you can get 'colour fatigue' during this process, which clouds your judgement. Next add a Hue/Saturation adjustment layer and bump up the saturation – a value between 25 and 35 is a good starting place. Now comes the magic – it doesn't make much sense, but your next step should be to add a new Curves adjustment layer; however, don't alter the curve. Instead, simply change the blend mode to Soft Light (or Overlay or Hard Light – experiment to find the one that works best) and adjust the opacity of the layer to alter the strength of the effect. You may at this stage have to make some adjustments to previous layers to ensure the best mix, and grouping all three will allow you easily to show and hide your total adjustments to suit. Remember that these are layer masks, so you can paint onto the mask to have each effect apply only to certain areas, and you can always create more than one of each adjustment mask.

Begin by adding a new Hue/Saturation adjustment layer and bumping up the Master saturation a little. Next, add a Curves adjustment layer. Don't alter the curve at all, but change the blend mode of that layer to Soft Light or Overlay. The image will appear to have much richer shadows than before, and you can adjust the opacity of the layer to change how much this effect is applied. Next, we'll add a Color Balance adjustment layer to correct any colour bias or introduce one to add to the sense of drama. In our picture, we've pushed the yellow a bit further than we would normally advise, but it brings out the colour of the brickwork and looks good. The colour of the sky is now a little insipid, so we've added another Hue/Saturation layer, switched from Master to Blues and increased the saturation. If it's mission-critical, you should mask off different areas using each adjustment layer's mask and apply different settings to each layer to ensure you keep as much detail as possible.

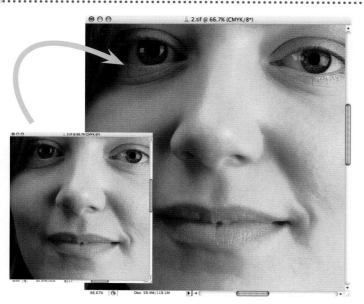

Photoshop's controls are much more sophisticated. You can use the Clone and Healing brushes to remove blemishes, after which you begin to improve overall skin tone. Much of the retouching work depends in part on the quality of the original photograph – particularly the lighting – so ensure a clean shot to begin with. To remove spots, select a relatively soft healing brush, then Alt-click an area to define the source for the repair. You should pick an area with similar texture to the section to be repaired; colour matching will be handled by Photoshop. Once you've defined the source, click on the blemish to remove it. Later editions have a Spot Healing tool, which can further streamline the process. To improve overall skin tone, duplicate the background layer by dragging it to the new layer icon in the layers palette, and apply a fairly gentle Gaussian blur to this layer. Add a new Layer Mask – picking Hide all – and switch to the Brush tool. Ensure your foreground colour is white and then toggle the airbrush on and drop the opacity slider down to about 25%. Use a reasonably big brush for large areas such as cheeks, but keep changing the size and softness to suit where you're working. Next, following the contours of the face and working in broad sweeps, begin to reveal the blurred skin layer by painting onto the layer mask. Less is more – avoid the eyes and mouth completely, and don't push the effect so far that your subject starts to look plastic. Remember that you can simply re-paint the layer mask in black to reduce the effect of the clean-up.

Best Mac Games

Once the poor relation of the console and PC, the Mac is now a leading platform for gamers, with many of the most popular titles now appearing in sync with their Windows equivalents.

ASSASSIN'S CREED: BROTHERHOOD

WWW.UBI.COM

Assassin's Creed has rapidly established itself as a huge franchise. UK mag magazine, MacUser, put this game's predecessor high in the pantheon of Mac games thanks to a well-balanced mix of a great script, stunning graphics and top-notch adventure. Don't worry if you haven't played it yet, because Brotherhood's video prologue explains the centuries-old rivalry of the Assassins and the Templars, which is the main series' primary context.

Most of the action takes place in the past, but those events are being observed, after a fashion, by Desmond Miles and his group of modern-day assassins. Desmond is plugged into a cutting edge device known as an Animus, which taps into genetic memories passed down through his bloodline to build a virtual reconstruction of an ancestor's life.

In this game, that's Enzo Auditore da Firense, who, in the last game, learned of the opposing groups and his familial association with the assassins. The animus plucks places and events

from Enzo's life and puts Desmond in control of the simulation. He can explorer the game's primary setting at will, with more areas becoming available as you fulfil certain objectives advance the story, and by climbing to highpoints in the city, which allows members of the larger landscape to flood into Desmond's mind.

You can walk at street level, deep between rooftops, and go for a swim or gondola ride as you see fit. More purposefully, you'll be hunting thieves, helping harassed strangers and rebuilding the local economy that's been run to ruin by the Borgia. That's achieved by using acquired wealth to reopen local shops, which allows you to upgrade weapons and armour at a blacksmith, grab a horse from a stable and pay a visit to a doctor.

However, you can only rebuild a district once it's been cleared of Borgia influence. That requires infiltrating the high security area surrounding the nearest Borgia tower, assassinating the commanding officer, then working your way to the

top of the tower to burn it to the ground. More thrilling escapades include chasing villains on horseback and sabotaging inventions of Leonardo da Vinci so they would be subverted to the cause. Cause too much of a ruckus and you'll need to blend in and tear down wanted posters to regain your anonymity.

Stealth and combat play a huge role. Precisely picking one enemy to strike when you're surrounded can be tricky with a mouse and keyboard, but it's not impossible. The stunning animation of Enzo's killing rooms is not one for the faint of heart. Sneaking up on an enemy allows him to quietly snap their neck or stab them in the back. Face-to-face brawls offer a variety of takedowns, with no more brutal than when Enzo's sword hacks deep into someone's body.

Which brings us to the titular Brotherhood, a new aspect of gameplay, not just a

subtitle. By rescuing citizens from harassment by soldiers, they join your calls as apprentices and can be sent on missions to other cities in order. The growing experience allows them to take on more lucrative contracts, and when they're not away from home, you can call on them to assist you.

It's enjoyable watching them swooping into bring the first few times, but the Brotherhood is little more than a thin veil to disguise that the gameplay begins to drag. On top, a few missions towards the end seem unfair

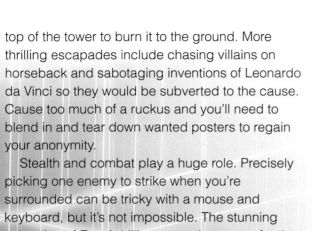

because they lacked clarity on how to achieve your goals.

Through the Animus, Desmond can call on his ancestors acrobatic skills, making him limber enough to do his own bit of exploration in the present. These moments are too scarce, but a direct sequel is already being made, subtitled Revelations. The publisher has confirmed it will conclude Enzo's story and answer some questions about the bigger picture as well. This is both an annoyance and part of the series' brilliance. Once it's under your skin, you feel

compelled to follow the story further, as you would a great TV series.

Brotherhood also introduces a multiplayer component of several moments that put you in the Animus of an Abstergo employee (the corporate face of the Templars) to compete with others. This is a welcome addition, as you'll find little motivation to achieve 100% completion of unfinished tasks in the single player experience once the main story is over.

If you've already enjoyed all Assassin's Creed II has to offer, you'll enjoy the direct continuation of its story. Brotherhood's prologue still leaves a few dots to connect for first timers when it comes to identifying characters. However, like its predecessor, it's one of the finest Mac games around.

PORTAL 2

■ WWW.THINKWITHPORTALS.COM

Portal is the kind of game that gets people who don't play games playing games. This sequel was notable not only for continuing the story of what's become regarded as a classic, but because it was available to Mac users from the first day of release rather than as a belated port. It uses the inventive mechanics of its predecessor with new gameplay elements to deliver an ingenious set of puzzles that push all spatial awareness to its limit.

Last year, portal was retrofitted with an extended ending that showed the heroine, Chell, dragged from the wreckage of Aperture Laboratories to an unknown fate. Here, she wakes up in what appears to be a hotel room. Any sense of comfort derived from her surroundings is washed away when a computer voice chimes in to run through a periodic health check for Aperture's test subjects. So much for escaping. Minutes later, Chell is returned to slumber.

The next time she is roused, it's clear that something has gone wrong. The room is dimly lit and grimy, the computer voice stutters, and the deep indentation where she was lying intimates that a long time has passed. Shortly afterwards, Chell meets Wheatley, an affable artificial intelligence with, bizarrely, a calming Bristolian accent, voiced by Ricky Gervais collaborator Stephen Merchant. The chatty little fellow has a tendency to veer off onto rambling but entertaining tangents as he attempts to guide Chell out of the facility.

Along the way, you'll spot rooms from the first game where the walls and ceilings have collapsed and plant life has grown through the cracks. You are rapidly reacquainted with basic gameplay, but things take an ominous turn when you stumble upon the steely cadaver of GlaDOS, the artificial intelligence you met in the first episode. Even in this state you get the sense that she is best avoided but her inevitable resuscitation leads to a union you'll savour. It's like hooking up with an old friend you haven't seen in ages, and catching up is worth it.

The titular portals are central to the challenges. Portal emphasises thinking your way past problems: rather than a gun that fires bullets, it revolves around a device that links to points in space. As a consequence of being able to open portals in ceilings and floors, as well as walls, you'll spend a lot of time considering a room's layout along all planes and angles. Experimentation is vital, because what seems like a dead-end might set you on the path to enlightenment. Like a toddler gaining understanding of the world from tactile toys, you'll find playing around is conducive to approaching

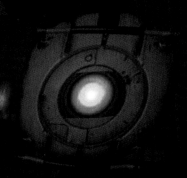

problems in unconventional ways to reach a solution.

That could be as simple as opening a portal on a nearby wall and another on the far side of an impossible pit. However, while light-coloured panels accept portals, dark mottled ones will reject them. Solutions soon require you to string together a sequence of tricks to move forwards. Ultimately, observational skills and mental agility are more important than nimbleness with the mouse and keyboard.

Portal 2 adds a variety of new elements to make you think even harder. Lasers, light bridges and tractor beams can be directed through portals, but perhaps the most fun are the coloured gels that change the physical properties of surfaces. The most challenging puzzles require using several of these in combination, but things are never painfully insurmountable. At worst, you may have to step away a while – a moment of revelation often only demands refreshing yourself from them fatigue.

Each technique since learned is steadily built on, with a challenging yet forgiving learning curve. There's no penalty for dying; instead, you're sent back to the start of an area to try again. The only route to defeat is a lack of self belief. There are several junctures where you will stumble on Easter eggs such as additional dialogue precisely because you've put Chell at risk. At least one such moment, involving a talking gun turret, is bound to raise a smirk.

When you've finished the main adventure, you'll be thirsting for more challenges. The original game didn't have a cooperative mode, so its addition here is a welcome bonus – and an opportunity to lap up a bit more of GlaDOS' sarcasm.

In this mode, you and a friend take on the roles of two robots, Atlas and P-Body. To Valve's credit, you can play with a friend running the PC or PlayStation 3 versions, and you have the option of pairing up with a random person online. The pairing system offers no way to pick a teammate of similar ability, though, so we ended up playing with someone who was understandably eager to carry on from two sets of tests ahead of the point we'd reached. Wherever possible, we'd stick with Valve's advice and play with someone you know so you compose yourselves.

The objective is still to get to each room's exit, but the tests are more gruelling. In part, that's because each player has a portal gun, which doesn't necessarily work to your immediate advantage. Often it's obvious how one of you can pass an obstacle, but an increased presence of force fields that displace your portals will leave you racking your brains for ways in which you can get both players through.

Communicating ideas to remote players is opening a ring of gestures. Among them, one marks the wall or object you're looking at and directs the other players' goes to it with visual and audible prompts. Another initiates a countdown from three so you can flick two switches in unison. It's fun trying to limit yourself to this method, but you can fall back on in-game voice chat or text-based messages if it gets tiresome. Co-op mode's more devious challenges add a lot of value to the game.

The single player portion of Portal 2 alone is longer than the original game. Taken at a steady pace, it took us nine to 10 hours to complete, and co-op mode gives you even more value for money beyond that. Valve has also taken pains to recreate Portal's appeal without rehashing the same old jokes; Portal 2 sparkles with enough wit and intrigue to carry you to the end of the journey without growing weary. Every challenge you overcome rewards you with a sense of accomplishment.

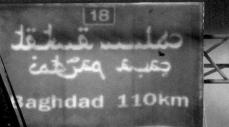

SPLINTER CELL: CONVICTION

■ WWW.UBI.COM

Sam Fisher's only appearance on the Mac until now was his first adventure. We've missed out on his other acclaimed exploits as an agent of the Third Echelon, a US Intelligence agency tasked with protecting the country from terror threats. So, let's get up to speed on where his life is at.

Baciscally, it's all gone to the dogs. His daughter was killed in a hit-and-run incident and his last mission, to infiltrate a terrorist group, didn't go well. Conviction picks up Fisher's trail after years of trying to stay off the political radar. He's tiped off by one of his closest colleagues about a group of hit men closing in on his position. The news stirs Sam's survival instincts, but that's not enough. He wants to know who is out for his blood and why, and he soon stirs up a hornet's nest and uncovers a plot that threatens to rock western civilisation.

Splinter Cell is famed for its stealthy gameplay. Conviction enhances it with a clever shift in palette from mono to full colour when you emerge from cover and risk being spotted by an enemy. When movement catches their attention, a large circle with a protruding arrow indicates their relative position, giving you precious seconds to duck for cover, and to slit the throat of enemies.

There are plenty of skills and tactics at your disposal to scope out enemy positions. Sam uses a mirror to peek through gaps beneath doors, and he's agile enough to enter rooms via crawlspaces and by hanging from pipes mounted on the ceiling.

Although Fisher is trained to do things quietly, Conviction doesn't enforce the silent approach. Explosive barrels dispose of groups with a bang; chandeliers and suspended heavy machinery can crash down on anyone stupid enough to loiter below. The clatter will alert others nearby, and the smart approach is to shoot out the lights and stalk an opponent as he searches for you, then pounce like a panther on your quivering prey.

Even careless gunfire can be used to your advantage. When the bullets pepper nearby walls, enemies are alerted to your general location. Once pinpointed, that's your chance to flank them as they bring arms to bear on the silhouette that marks your last known position, buying you time to sink one of their number from elsewhere.

Enemies can be taken out with a rapid volley of shots, but aiming for their skull is brutally effective and there's something disturbingly satisfactory about seeing their bodies crumpling to the floor. Aside from the violence, there's a sprinkling of colourful language, so it's best to send the kids off to bed before you start playing this one.

The game is littered with cruel but cool moments. Fisher can hang from narrow ledges and climb with a grace that's surpassed only by Spider-man. An enemy standing close to an open window can be quietly pulled out. We didn't tire of toying with enemies throughout the story's eight or nine hours of action, even though the final two levels are less inspired in their design. There's a co-op mode that adds a prologue to the story.

Our Core 2 Duo-powered iMac's Radeon HD 4850 struggled until we lowered the resolution to 1280 x 720, and we had to knock the effects down a notch for a couple of later, smoke-heavy scenes.

Splinter Cell: Conviction's storyline is full of cliches, but that's balanced with some neat touches that add some humanity to Fisher's character to illustrate the enormous weight bearing down on his mind. For example, there's a playable flashback from his service in the first Gulf War, which reinforces the strength of a key relationship.

It's a high-calibre action adventure of the kind that's rarely seen on the Mac.

BACK TO THE FUTURE: THE GAME EPISODE 1

■ WWW.TELLTALEGAMES.COM

Great Scott! One of the most cherished films of the 1980s is back. Time travelling teenager Marty McFly and inventor Doc Brown return in a five-part graphic adventure that picks up shortly after the third film. Doc's absence from 1986 has left him presumed dead and his estate being sold off. Marty knows better, but he doesn't know where – or when – the kooky scientist might be. Six months is an entirety when you've got time machine to play with.

Out of the blue, a souped up DeLorean appears, but the only passenger is Doc's pet dog, Einstein, and a mysterious shoe, so your first task is to work out when in time he's stranded and go to his aid. Investigative work is a perfect fit for the point-and-click adventure genre and Telltale is adept with it. The mouse pointer is your means to check out Marty's surroundings and interact with other characters, and you can explore more widely using keyboard controls.

The time travelling duo's antics mess up the timeline, leaving them with a tangle of altered destinies to unravel by talking to the inhabitants of Prohibition-era Hill Valley to work out what's different from the correct timeline, then fix it.

The game is heavy on dialogue, with multiple threads to conversations. That's fitting, because you'll draw insight into how to solve dilemmas from tangential clues in what people say, as in the films. That demands your attention, but you can fall back on an adjustable hints system if you really get stuck. There's also the option of having new objectives pop up on screen in case you missed the significance of something said.

By the time you reach Hill Valley's town square, you'll see streets in the distance that you can't explore. One side of the square is even out of bounds, thanks to invisible walls that block your path to prevent deviation from focused progression of the story.

This instalment is riddled with gangster cliches, but it's hard to fault the game on originality when it's so well strung together. The story was drawn up with input from series cocreator Bob Gale and the characters are brought to life with top-notch voice acting. AJ LoCascio puts in an excellent turn recreating the wimpish tones that Michael J Fox committed to film, and Christopher Lloyd returns as Doc Brown.

However, the game isn't without troubles. We encountered a showstopping glitch in the first episode that left us checking all available locations and conversations in case we'd missed something. Searching online revealed that some players have encountered the same problem, leaving them unable to progress without going back to an earlier save point.

We primarily played the Mac version. The iPad version suffers from a noticeably lower resolution, occasional but big skips in the frame rate and some iffy graphical effects. The game is framed by black borders; as with Sam & Max, Telltale hasn't moved the on-screen buttons to this area to exploit the aspect ratio. The virtual joystick is flexible enough to pop up wherever you place your thumb, and you can reveal points of interaction by typing with two fingers.

Only the first episode is available at the time of writing and Telltale couldn't tell is when the rest would hit the App Store. It's a shame there isn't a release schedule, because the game is well suited to the touchscreen and casual play. Since you can only buy the Mac version as a complete five episode season, you're better off sticking with that. The full set should be available by the time you read this.

BORDERLANDS

■ WWW.GEARBOXSOFTWARE.COM

Borderlands is set on the world called Pandora, but it's nothing like the one in James Cameron's Avatar. This nasty little backwater reeks of post-apocalyptic mad Max and the wild West. Cue plenty of gunfights and skirmishes with the local wildlife. No sooner have you arrived than a mysterious woman relays local legend of an artefact called the vault and tips you off that it is the real McCoy. As with any story involving treasure, you set out to find it.

That's your ultimate objective, but this isn't a straight first person shooter. Borderlands stirs RPG elements into the mix for a more involved experience that starts with you choosing to play as a soldier, hunter, siren or berserker.

Advancing the story requires taking on objective-based missions. Every kill and completed mission gains you experience, but some are too difficult without first investing time to increase your character level, as we found out when we came up against the first major named opponent. That scuffle forced us towards other missions until we gained strength to face him.

As you play more, you gain points that can be assigned to three different branches of the skill tree. Each is divided into three levels and you need to assign five points to one branch to access the next level abilities.

Even weapons need to be compared when dropped by enemies or found in storage lockers. If the recoil, accuracy or magnifications scope isn't on a par with what you are using, you can scrape together some cash by selling them.

Thankfully, borderlands masks the practice of grinding by re-spawning enemies after a short time. Dally long enough and opponents who slaughtered on the way into a cave or encampment will be waiting for you on your way out. The good part is that this minimises how much you need to go out of your way to find trouble. The artificial intelligence is generally good. Opponents soon start to aim ahead of your movement if it's too predictable, although it seems implausibly clever when widely dispersed enemies pinpoint you as soon as you fire.

There is a sense of excitement when enemy types start to diversify into stronger and fiercer variants. Taking on skags, Pandora's equivalent of dogs, requires you aim carefully at the underbelly or, if you're quick on the trigger, fire a few shells into their mouth when the leap forward to bite.

Missions are made up of typical RPG tasks: collecting items for someone, fixing machinery and killing a quantity of a particular enemy. Many scenarios flesh out your background knowledge of Pandora, even when they're not directly tied to the story. They also offer an opportunity to explore the landscape, which you can do even faster when vehicles become available, although these add nothing else significant to the gameplay.

The biggest disappointment is the poor adaptation to the Magic Mouse. Instructions say to right click to aim down the gun barrel before firing, but you can't then left click with a Magic Mouse. Binding the control to a key still prevented us firing until we switched the mouse.

We can't talk about borderlands without praising its striking graphic novel-esque art style. The game ran well on our 3.06GHz Core 2 Duo iMac with a Radeon HD 4850 graphics processor even at 2560 x 1440, as long as we left dynamic shadows off. That option impacts on the frame rate too much, even at more common resolutions.

Borderlands gets repetitive if played solo for long bursts but the world is interesting enough to draw you back for more later. It's better savoured in corporative mode with up to three other players. Either way, there's weeks of gameplay to soak up in this edition, which supports all four add-on packs.

Everything Mac

History of the Mac

The Mac has a long and varied history, but exactly how did we get where we are today, where there's not a patch of beige to be seen in Apple's current line-up – only glass, plastic and brushed aluminium? This is the story of the Mac...

. . . .

" Apple may now be best-known for its portable devices – the iPhone, iPod and iPad – but it built its fortune on computers and continues to derive a large proportion of its income from its various Mac models and the software they run.

It hasn't always been sweetness and light, though. Apple's history is a story of peaks and troughs, with the company being wildly successful in its earlier and latter days, but struggling through doldrums in the interim.

This is the story of how the computer on your desk – or your lap – came to be there, and of the company that invented it. "

Apple, the company behind the Mac, was founded in California on 1 April 1976. Though it's never been confirmed, many believe it was named after Apple Corps, the Beatles' publisher; a poor choice of name that led to much legal wranglings over the years. Apple Corps dragged Apple Computer through the courts, made expensive financial settlements, and was assured by Apple Computer that it would keep out of the music business – a promise that was called into question with the arrival of the iPod, iTunes and online music store.

In retrospect, in a world where you can barely ride a train or bus without seeing a pair of distinctive white iPod headphones, it may have seemed a rash move to choose that name, but in 1976 the world was a very different place. Computers were primitive, the Internet was non-existent, and music came not on hard drives but flexible vinyl discs. That was the world into which Apple was born.

The two men we must thank for bringing us, over 30 years later, such masterpieces as the iMac, iPad and iPhone are Steve Jobs, the company's current CEO, and Steve Wozniak.

They met at the Homebrew Computer Club, a gathering of wannabe geeks in Silicon Valley. Despite the differences in their ages (Wozniak is almost five years older) the two men struck up a friendship, and started working on projects together. Jobs had spent some time as a

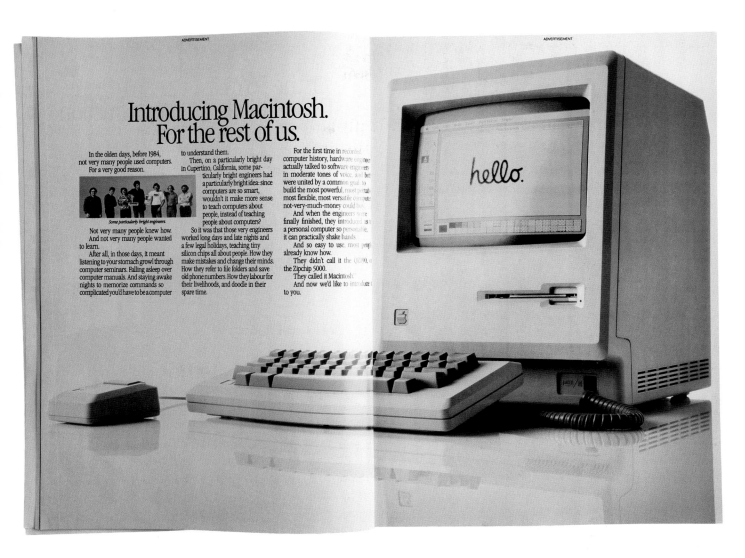

programmer for Atari, then a leading light in video games production, while Wozniak had written a programming language and designed a circuit board for a brand new computer microprocessor. It was almost inevitable that the two men should found a computer company, along with friend Ronald Wayne, who we can thank for drawing the original Apple logo, which depicted Newton sitting beneath his famed apple tree.

The story of how they funded their first product – the circuit board Wozniak had designed and which they christened the Apple I – is well-known. Jobs had sold his camper van; Wozniak his programmable calculator. Finally they had start-up funding, but neither of them could have known that those few dollars they raised would be the foundations of a multi-billion dollar corporation.

If you look at the Apple I today, it doesn't look much like what any of us would consider to be a computer. It was quite literally a bare bones system that you had to put together yourself. Many of the photos that you can find of it on the Internet show it in a wooden case with the word Apple crudely sawn into the top, but this was a mere stopgap, and as such every Apple I would be unique.

The Apple II arrived the following year, and proved to be a revolutionary machine. For starters, it boasted colour graphics, and after initially shipping with a tape recorder for storage that was soon swapped out for a floppy disk drive. Despite this, it wasn't until VisiCalc arrived on the platform, allowing businesses to do their spreadsheeting tasks on a computer rather than squared paper, that it became a must-have machine.

By now, Ronald Wayne had already bailed out of Apple Computer and had sold his 10% stake in the company to Steve Jobs for a paltry $800; a move he should now be regretting, with its stock having accelerated to sky-high prices. Jobs had brought in a third partner, Mark Markkula, a one-time employee of Intel, who helped the company to secure funding to the tune of $250,000.

Perhaps inevitably, the Apple II was followed by the Apple III at the start of the 1980s, and then the III+.

By then, though, Jobs had paid a visit to Xerox' research facilities at Palo Alto, the so-called Parc, where he saw the Alto Computer. This was a radical departure from the accepted norms of computing, as it eschewed screens full of text for a graphical interface, in which the three-button mouse was king. Jobs, and colleague Jef Raskin, were impressed by what they saw, and when they returned to Apple they started working on integrating a similar interface into two computers in its labs at that time: the high-end Lisa business machine, and the low-end consumer Macintosh, named in honour of Jef Raskin's favourite variety of apple.

Although the Lisa came out first, and was the first commercial computer to support a graphical user interface (GUI), it was hugely expensive, and didn't have the staying power of the Macintosh, which is the direct predecessor of the ultra-modern Macs we know and love today.

The Macintosh was finally sent to the shops in January 1984, and promoted with a memorable advert that aired in a break of the televised Superbowl that year. The ad, which cost a reported $1.5 million, portrayed a world not unlike that in George Orwell's book 1984, which was brought crashing down by the appearance of an athletic saviour with a hammer, which she hurled through one of the iconic telescreens that are a central focus of the novel.

'On January 24th, Apple Computer will introduce Macintosh. And you'll see why 1984 won't be like "1984",' said the voiceover and on-screen legend. How true it was.

The advert itself was almost as revolutionary as the computer it promoted. Directed by Ridley Scott, who had just finished directing Blade Runner, it is held up as an icon of good

advertising. Advertising Industry publication Advertising Age called it the best commercial of the 1980s and TV Guide names it the greatest commercial of all time, according to reports on CNN. It is much-quoted, reproduced in still photos and, at the time, received free replays by stations discussing its content, which would have gone a long way towards recouping the original cost of the slot in which it aired.

The advert was a dig at the growing influence of IBM – the largest computer company at the time – and the standards it had set with its PC, which still form the basis of all PCs sold to this day. Apple's advert portrayed IBM as Big Brother in Orwell's dystopian future, while it saw itself as the bright light that would free the world from IBM's domination.

Although Jobs loved the ad, and had even travelled to Shepperton Studios in the UK to oversee its week-long, $750,000 shoot in a studio filled with 200 British skinheads – not actors – the board was less keen and tried to offload the slots

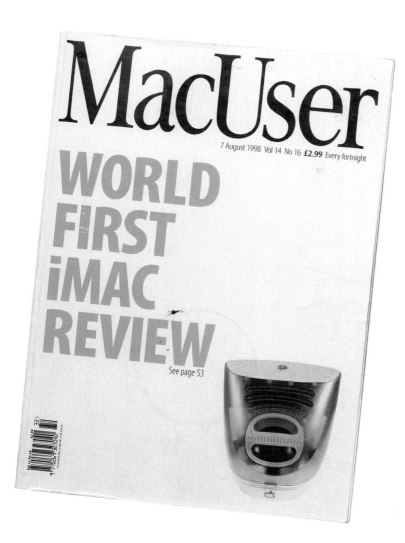

MacUser

7 August 1998 Vol 14 No 16 £2.99 *Every fortnight*

WORLD FIRST iMAC REVIEW

See page 53

Those specs may sound very conservative today – as indeed they are – but at the time they were enough to bring this machine to the interest of desktop publishing professionals. At $2495, it massively undercut comparative products, and the introduction of an affordable laser printer, and PageMaker layout software should perhaps be given credit for the Mac's continued success – to this day – in the field of design and print.

The Macintosh was revamped several times, but despite its success it was to be the ultimate author of Jobs' downfall at the company.

He had recruited John Sculley, one-time president of Pepsi, to act as Apple's CEO. He was a solid businessman, and found himself overseeing a company virtually split in two. The Macintosh team was proclaiming itself to be custodians of the company's future, while the Lisa team, selling its computers at $10,000 a pop, claimed it was the source of the company's income. Inevitably, the two didn't get on. Jobs' Macintosh team almost became a separate entity inside Apple, which was clearly something no CEO or board could condone.

Sculley and the board took the only course of action open to them; they stripped Jobs of his responsibilities. Jobs sold all but one of his shares in Apple and left to found NeXT Computer, a firm that developed extremely high-end machines, and a revolutionary operating system called NeXTstep.

Skip forward 10 years, and NeXT is doing well. Apple, though, less so. It had had a good few years, releasing a string of successful products, like the PowerBook (see a later version below). However, it had steadily lost market share to PCs

they had already bought in which to air it. Ad agency Chiat-Day, which had orchestrated the whole campaign claimed it was impossible at such a late stage, so the ad ran nonetheless.

Andy Herzfeld, a member of the original Macintosh team, recounts the board's reaction after the airing, and subsequent media interest on his site *folklore.org*: 'A week after the Macintosh launch, Apple held its January board meeting. The Macintosh executive staff was invited to attend, not knowing what to expect. When the Mac people entered the room, everyone on the board rose and gave them a standing ovation, acknowledging that they were wrong about the commercial and congratulating the team for pulling off a fantastic launch.'

And so the 'affordable' Mac was born. It had a 9in monochrome screen, an 8MHz processor and 128KB of memory. Storage was limited to a 3.5in floppy drive. A hard drive would have been unimaginably expensive at the time. The machine came bundled with MacPaint and MacWrite.

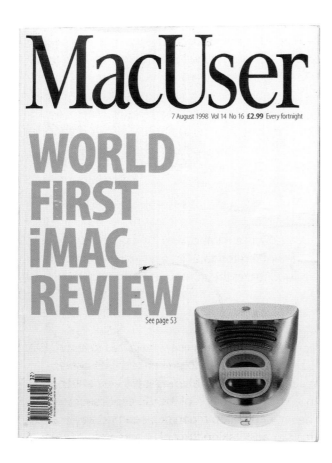

See page 53

running Windows, and was trying to keep up the battle by licensing its own operating system to third-party hardware developers while simultaneously running abortive projects to develop ever better versions that never saw the light of day.

Nonetheless, it had the reserves to buy Jobs' new company, and in doing so bring him back into the fold, as a consultant. Now it was Jobs' turn to start bossing around the board. He ousted the current CEO of the time – Gil Amelio – and started to make immediate changes. He canned the failing operating system projects, terminated the Newton and cancelled the contracts with third-party developers to make Macintosh-compatible computers of their own. Apple was set to resume its role as the sole arbiter of both the hardware and software sides of its business.

Work started on porting the NeXTstep operating system from NeXT's own machines to the Mac, and it is that push that brought us to the Mac OS X environment that runs our Macs to this very day.

Almost straight away, Apple's fortunes were revived. Microsoft invested $150 million in the company and pledged to continue producing Microsoft Office for the platform, guaranteeing its continued viability in the business world. The following year, in May 1998, the most revolutionary product since the original Macintosh was unveiled by then interim CEO Jobs to an assembled crowd in San Francisco. It was the iMac.

This machine was both a nod to the past and a pointer to the future. It was an all-in-one device, where the guts of the computer were built into the back of the monitor, and it sported a design like nothing that had gone before it. Out went boring beige boxes, in came translucent plastics in funky colours. Jobs had teamed up with young British designer Jonathan Ive to breathe new life into the computer world, and it had worked.

Suddenly Apple was back in the spotlight. It was the new darling of the computer world, and countless peripheral manufacturers jumped onboard. Printers, scanners, mice, keyboards… seemingly everything now incorporated a flash of colourful plastic in an effort to make PCs look as trendy and desirable as the iMac, but none of them quite pulled it off.

That original iMac went through several iterations, which saw it evolve from a simple home business/web browsing/emailing machine into a fully-fledged multimedia device with video editing tools. It was eventually joined by the iBook, which took its cues from the iMac, being moulded from similar translucent plastics (in tangerine and blueberry colours), and integrating a carry handle by the hinge (the iMac had a carry handle in the top). It was a love-it or hate-it product, which bore a striking resemblance to a plastic toilet seat. Fortunately this wasn't sufficient a problem to put off the countless users who bought one and it was particularly popular in the education market.

2001 and 2002 saw radical redesigns of these two product lines. In 2001, the iBook was given a more sober white casing, and lost its bulging curves. In 2002, the iMac swapped its TV-style monitor for a flat screen, with the workings of the computer now housed in a dome below, rather than behind the screen. Sales continued to rise. It seemed that the 'i' badged range of products was just what the world had been waiting for.

By now Jobs was officially back in control. He

The computer that revived Apple's fortunes was the semi-transparent iMac, which has been through four redesigns. iMacs are now feature flat-screen monitors that stretch to 27in. Many are as powerful as the Mac Pro, with only reduced expansion options – and, of course, the screen – separating the two.

was no longer the interim CEO; he had the confidence of the board and he was breathing life back into a company that many, including Dell CEO Michael Dell, had pretty much written off. They had never dreamed how things might change.

New products followed, each one better than the last, and although not all seemed like logical additions to the range, such as the Mac mini, which looked good but was considered by some to be under-powered and over-priced in comparison to PC equivalents, it seemed that Jobs and Ive, between them, had an almost faultless understanding of their customers' wants and desires.

But then Apple hit something of a wall. It had put all of its eggs in one basket where processors were concerned. While most PC manufacturers split their ranges between chips from Intel and AMD, Apple was tied in to deals that saw it centre its designs on PowerPC processors from IBM and Motorola. They had served the company well for many years, but suddenly they seemed to top out. While customers clamoured for ever faster chips, the factories struggled to produce them. In a desperate attempt to sate public cries of frustration, it rigged up a Power Mac, one of its professional desktop computers, with a liquid-based cooling system that allowed the processor to be run at a faster speed than that for which it was designed. In true Apple style, it was an elegant implementation, but still it was something

of a get around.

Next the notebook line-up started to suffer. PC competitors started to pull ahead with cooler, faster chips from Intel and Apple was starting to lag. A mobile edition of the G5 processor used in the latest desktop machines seemed as far away as ever and, taking the only course of action open to it, Apple announced in 2005 that it was to move away from the PowerPC processor, and standardise on the Intel platform, making its machines more like regular PCs than ever before.

This sent shock waves through the community. For customers it was great news; they'd finally have the speedy machines they were after, and perhaps at lower prices. For developers it was potentially terrible news. They had written their software to work with the PowerPC processor, and now they'd have to re-code it for an entirely new architecture.

Apple calmed their nerves somewhat by explaining that it would initially build in a compatibility layer into the operating systems on its new Intel machines. Called Rosetta, this would translate the instructions coming from the older software into the language understood by the new processors. It also demonstrated how easy it was to make the old PowerPC software natively compatible with the Intel chips.

However, the ease at which applications could be ported across depended entirely on their complexity. Simple tools like text editors could often be automatically re-encoded by the tools that translated the code from something humans would understand to the kind of low-level binary numbers understood by processors and memory. Other, more ambitious applications like Microsoft's Office suite, or Adobe's Photoshop, required more serious surgery, and a lot of work and investment from their publishers.

Fortunately very few headline applications failed to make the move, so that by January 2008 order had been restored with every major Mac application, including Word, Excel, PowerPoint, Photoshop, InDesign, Dreamweaver, QuarkXPress and a host of other staples now running more happily and more efficiently on Apple's new Intel processors.

But of course the story of the Mac isn't just about products starting with 'i'. Over the years Apple has worked on first consolidating and later diversifying its product line up to include servers, ultra-light notebooks, consumer and professional desktop machines and media boxes that sit underneath a television to stream movies and music direct to the living room.

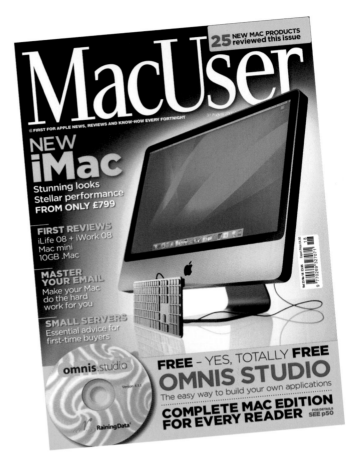

■ FUTURE OF THE MAC

So where does it go from here? That question could be answered in any number of ways, but it's almost certain that the correct answer won't involve the company licensing its operating system for use by third-party developers again. It tried that for a while, and it wasn't a success. Now, with Microsoft Windows in an even more dominant position, it can't afford to try it again.

Apple's financial outlook has never looked better than it does right now, thanks to a close-to-perfect fusion of hardware and software that couldn't possibly be maintained if it allowed others a modicum of control over the products on which its operating system is used.

Almost all of those products are based on various editions of its operating system. That means, beside its closely-integrated music and movie download businesses, Mac OS X has become the key to the company's future existence. It is one of the world's most advanced operating systems, and finally increased sales are starting to do it justice. It has won plaudits from

old hands and new arrivals alike, and it's getting rave reviews in the traditionally Windows-focused computer press. Meanwhile, the company is working hard to build it into an ever-increasing range of products, as it forms the basis of the iPhone, iPad and all recent iPods, apart from the shuffle. That's no mean feat, considering the system requirements of its competitors.

While brands like iTunes, iPhone, iPad and iPod remain the company's most visible icons, the word 'Mac' will live on for the foreseeable future for as long as Apple keeps on building computers, despite the fact that in the most recent release it has been dropped from the operating system name. Microsoft is seeing its market share being slowly eroded and the best-placed company to benefit from this is Apple. That's not to say it will become the dominant player – it won't – but it offers great potential.

At the moment we are seeing more and more software applications move off computers' local hard drives and onto the web. Google is stealing

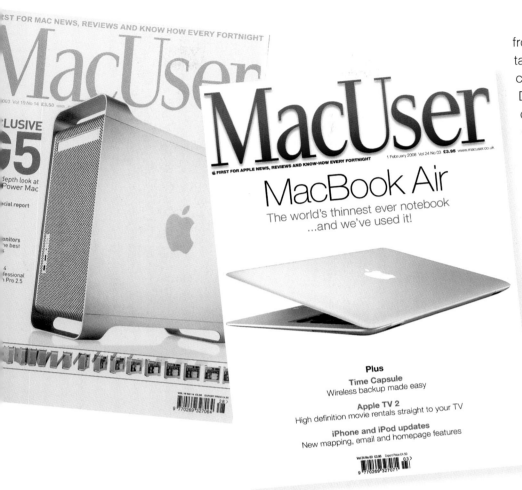

from some quarters that Apple had taken its eye off the ball where its computers were concerned. Developers were taken away from coding a previous release of Mac OS X and reassigned to the iPhone, much to the distress of faithful Apple computer users who saw the release date of their next software upgrade slipping back at a terrifying rate. When it arrived, though, Mac OS X 10.5 was better than most had dared hope – a few grumbles aside – and it was clear that the delay was nothing more serious than a minor blip.

Apple is now making more money from selling computers than at any point in its history. It's gaining ground as one of the world's biggest manufacturers of mobile computers, trouncing the one-time big names of the industry. Investing in a Mac today gets you in at the ground floor, and if you have previously bought an iPad or iPhone you'll already be familiar with a lot of the concepts at the heart of OS X – particularly now that Lion integrates many iOS-style features, such as the Launchpad and reverse-direction scrolling.

However, there remains one major sticking point for the Apple watcher, and that's what will happen to the company – and the Mac – once Steve Jobs moves on. He can't stay at the helm forever, and there is still no obvious successor in place. Internal plans may be in place to handle this eventuality, but whatever happens and whenever it happens, Jobs' departure is sure to rock the company, its stock and its customers.

Right now Jobs seems as important to the company as its operating system and the Mac brand. Following continued interest in his health, the question of Apple in the post-Jobs world remains pressing. Jobs is Apple, and Apple is Jobs as much as it is the Mac.

a march with its highly competent online office suite, which gets better every day. Adobe is following its lead with Buzzword, an online word processor, and it now has a very successful online edition of Photoshop, used exclusively through the browser.

You might think that this is bad news for the Mac, but that couldn't be further from the truth. Once we're all running our software online, it won't matter what kind of computer we have or what operating system it runs, so nobody will be asking whether it will work with their computer – all they'll be interested in is how easy it is to get their Mac or PC online so they can use it. Here, the Mac has a trump card. It's supremely easy to get online, and it's just as happy running its own browser, Safari, as it is with the cross-platform Firefox, which you'll find on as many PCs as Macs.

Apple, then, will continue to develop, improve and sell the Mac. That's a relief to many. With the arrival of the iPhone and iPad there was concern

Glossary

The Mac may be wonderfully easy to use, but the world of computing remains littered with technical terminology and acronyms, some of which is specific to the Mac, and some of which is in more general everyday use.

. . . .

"Over time the terms in use in the Mac industry have evolved slowly. Apple's marketeers come up with such memorable and enduring product names that they remain in use for years. 'Mac' is over 25 years old, but still it is being used in other derived product names, such as Mac Pro, iMac and MacBook Air.

Other terms, such as AirPort and Dock, describe key features of Apple's software offerings that would be given far less impressive terms on other platforms.

Over the next seven pages we'll define all of the key terms you'll need to keep in mind when reading about or discussing the Mac. Have them handy and convince your friends you're a Mac expert."

■ .MAC

Online service owned and run by Apple, that was replaced by MobileMe. MobileMe has itself since been replace by iCloud.

■ APPLE TV

Small box-like device used to download TV shows and movies from the iTunes Store and play back the media on an HD television. It can also share music and video libraries stored on a Mac. First introduced in January 2007, it received a significant free software upgrade in January 2008, indicating that Apple sees media downloads as an increasingly important part of its future. A further update – this time to the hardware, which was reduced in size and re-dressed in black, rather than white plastic – arrived in 2011.

■ BOOT CAMP

Application shipped as part of Mac OS X that allows you to run Microsoft Windows on Apple computers with Intel processors. It gives Windows full access to all of the Mac's internal hardware so that it can work directly with the processor, memory and storage. This delivers excellent performance making the Mac – surprisingly – one of the best computers on which to run Windows - better, even, than many PCs. Alternative methods of running Windows rely on poking a hole in OS X to access the underlying hardware through virtualisation.

CLICK WHEEL

The circular controller on the front of an iPod classic and nano, into which four buttons arranged at the points of a compass are incorporates to allow you to skip backwards and forwards through tracks and navigate the menus.

COVER FLOW

Feature found in iTunes and the latest generation of iPods, the iPad and the iPhone, which allows you to flick through the covers of the albums in your music collection. With the iPhone, iPad and iPod touch, you can also tap the albums to access their tracks. A similar feature in Mac OS X allows you to flick through files in the Finder and pages in your browser history in the same way.

CREATIVE SUITE

Series of bundles from Adobe, comprising its most popular programs, including Photoshop, InDesign, Dreamweaver and Flash. Currently at version 5.5 it is an effective way to buy more than one app at a time, as most bundles cost little more than two of the component programs.

CURSOR

Vertical bar used in word processors to indicate the point at which your typing will appear. Sometimes also used to describe the mouse pointer.

DASHBOARD

A hidden layer of Mac OS X 10.4 Tiger and later on which you can run mini applications called Widgets. These run like sections of web pages to perform specific tasks, such as tracking stock prices, reporting the weather or translating phrases.

DESKTOP

This is the graphical main area of the screen on top of which windows open and applications run. Its background can be customised to show an image of your choice, and it can also be used as a temporary storage area for files, although this is not to be recommended as it shows poor file management and can impact on your Mac's performance.

DOCK

Translucent bar running along the bottom of the screen housing icons that are shortcuts to your most regularly-used applications. By right-clicking or Ctrl-clicking on the dividing bar in the right half of the Dock you can access its customisation menu, and from there move it to one side of the screen, change its size or have it automatically hide itself when not in use.

DOUBLE-CLICK

To click twice in quick succession on the button of a mouse, the button in front of a trackpad, or the trackpad itself. This action when executed, rather than just selecting the item clicked on, will open a file in its associated application or launch a piece of software.

DTP

Acronym for desktop publishing that describes the process of designing pages on a screen rather than using molten metal, as was once the case with all printed matter. All magazines and newspapers, fliers and brochures are now designed using DTP software, which is a mainstay of the Mac platform. The two leading DTP applications are Adobe InDesign and QuarkXPress, although Apple Pages (part of iWork) and Microsoft Word offer similar tools tailored to home and small business users.

EXPOSÉ

Utility that reorganises your open windows to help you work more efficiently with your files. It is activated through the keyboard and can either display all active applications, split up active windows in the current application or clear the screen to give you access to the Desktop.

FINDER

The part of the Mac's operating system that handles navigation through files and folders, as well as connecting to servers, mounting and unmounting external drives and burning CDs and DVDs. When you have no applications open, and are viewing the Desktop background you are in a pure Finder environment, as indicated by the word Finder at the left of the Menubar.

FONT

Term usually taken to describe the visual look of a set of characters (letters, numbers and symbols). However, it can also be taken to mean more than just the style of the characters but also their dimensions, weight and other attributes.

FRONT ROW

Media playback software found on Apple TV and Macs with Mac OS X 10.5 or later, retired in 10.7 Lion. It comprises large menus optimised for viewing on a regular TV screen, and is controlled by the Apple Remote, which can be bought separately from the Apple Store and retailers.

GARAGEBAND

Home-user music creation application found in iLife in which songs can be constructed by dragging pre-recorded musical clips, called Loops, into the working area.

GB

Abbreviation for gigabyte, which is 1 million kilobytes of data. A single gigabyte is enough to store about 250 music tracks on an iPod.

IBOOK

Consumer notebook that appealed to students and less demanding home users. It was introduced shortly after the original iMac and after several iterations Apple finally retired the product line in 2006. Not to be confused with the iBooks ereading software that ships on iOS devices.

ICAL

Calendaring application bundled with Mac OS X that lets you set reminders for upcoming appointments and track tasks that need to be completed. It uses industry-standard formats, allowing you to share appointments with people through a range of applications and operating systems, as well as publish your diary online.

ICLOUD

Online synchronisation and apps service provided by Apple as a replacement for MobileMe. Can be used to synchronise photos between connected devices, such as iPads and iPhones, and as a backup device for important documents created in iWork and other compatible suites. Also features a calendar, address book and webmail service that uses old MobileMe email addresses, each of which is suffixed with the @me.com domain. The basic service is free for all users.

IDISK

Web storage space that was included with a MobileMe subscription. It could be made to work in exactly the same way as a local hard drive in Mac OS X, and would even show up in the list of drives in a Finder window. Certain applications such as iPhoto and iWeb could also use it as a place to publish photo galleries and websites.

IDVD

This is an application that is used to burn movies to DVD, complete with chapters and menus for use on a consumer DVD player and TV, or another computer. iDVD is found in the iLife suite.

ILIFE

Lifestyle suite produced by Apple, which comprises iTunes, iPhoto, iMovie, iDVD, iWeb and GarageBand. It receives an update roughly every 12 to 18 months, and can be seen as a creative companion to a regular office suite. It is included free with every new Mac.

IMAC

An all-in-one computer, in which its inner workings are hidden behind the screen. The keyboard and mouse are the only external components. The current metal and glass iMac is the fourth generation of the machine, which started out as a semi-transparent computer in a curvy round case in a choice of colours, and is credited by many as being the computer that revived the ailing Apple's fortunes following its debut in 1998.

INSPECTOR

A panel that is used in many software applications to examine the current attributes of an element. It is also used as a way of altering them. Examples include controllers for fonts and text sizes in a word processor, or the colour of objects in a graphics application.

■ INTERFACE

The collection of menus, buttons, text, graphics and panels that make up an application. In Mac OS X, this includes the menubar at the top of the screen, the Dock at the bottom, the windows containing files and applications and the icons.

■ IPAD / IPAD 2

Hand-held computer that looks like a large iPhone with a 9.7in screen and software keyboard. Compatible with the iPhone and iPod touch.

■ IPHONE

Part pocket computer, part media player, part communications device, this is Apple's play for the mobile phone market. It sells itself on its cool looks and excellent software. It attracts a high contract cost, which is somewhat offset by the bundled unlimited use of the Internet and a generous allocation of calls and texts.

■ IPOD

The world's best-selling music player. Made by Apple. There are four distinct varieties of iPod: shuffle, nano, classic and touch. In the past there has also been the iPod mini, but this was phased out when the nano arrived. All work with iTunes on either the Mac or PC.

■ ITUNES

Free application for PCs and the Mac used for downloading and organising music and podcasts, as well as listening to Internet radio streams and uploading music to an iPod. It is also the home of the iTunes Store through which Apple sells music, movies, TV shows and applications.

■ ITUNES MATCH

Online service that is part of iCloud, which reproduces your iTunes library on Apple's servers so that you can listen to your music wherever you happen to be. Costs $25 per year to join.

■ IWEB

Web design software included with iLife. It can publish to regular web hosting space, but was designed to work primarily with the webspace included as part of Apple's MobileMe service. It takes advantage of server-specific features that are not available as a part of third-party hosting packages.

■ IWORK

Apple's own office suite, comprising Pages (word processor), Numbers (spreadsheet) and Keynote (presentation package). Each application uses its own file format, but it can also import and export Microsoft Office files for compatibility. Each application prides itself on the quality of its output, boasting many low-level desktop publishing-style tools.

■ KEYNOTE

Presentation application used for creating slides, comprising text, images, sound, movies and transitions. It is not directly compatible with PowerPoint, although it can read and write PowerPoint files.

■ LAUNCHPAD

New feature in Mac OS X 10.7 Lion that gives you a screen-wide view of the apps installed on your Mac. Closely redembles the home screen of an iPad, with spring-open folders.

■ MACBOOK

The family name for Apple's range of notebook computers. It comprises three different lines; the consumer MacBook, the high-end MacBook Pro and the highly desirable, ultra-slim MacBook Air. Together their screens range in size from 13in to 17in. Each has a built-in web camera housed in the bezel of the lid and ships with the latest version of the Mac operating system, although as they feature the same Intel processors as you'd find in a PC notebook, they are also capable of running Microsoft Windows, either natively through Boot Camp or under the Mac OS X operating system.

■ MAC MINI

Small, consumer computer, about the size of a box of biscuits. Seen by many as the ideal media computer because of its integrated DVD drive and HDMI port, combined with a compact chassis that makes it perfect for slipping under the TV;

likely found in more living rooms more than any other.

Apple also ships a second edition of the Mac mini that runs OS X Server for use in business environments and home offices.

■ Mac OS X

Apple's native operating system. The current edition is version 10.7, with each new release incrementing the number after the dot. Each one is given a wildcat-related codename in development, with the latest one being Lion. This was preceded by Snow Leopard, Leopard, Tiger, Panther, Jaguar and Cheetah. It was developed out of work done by NeXT, a company founded by Apple co-founder Steve Jobs, and later bought by Apple, in the process bringing Jobs back into the company fold. It is based on a business operating environment called Unix, which makes it very secure and robust and less prone to infection from viruses and spyware than Microsoft Windows.

■ Mac Pro

Apple's professional-level computer. It ships without a monitor, in a drilled aluminium case. It is more powerful than an iMac or any portable computer Apple produces, but the primary reason for buying it is the expansion options it offers, with room for more memory and hard drives than Apple's consumer computers. It also ships with up to two processors, rather than just one, to crunch through intensive tasks more quickly.

■ MB

Short for megabyte, which is 1000 kilobytes. Old-style 3.5in floppy disks used to hold about 1MB of data, but these days even a simple Microsoft Excel spreadsheet can be many times this size. As such, fewer and fewer measurements in computing are expressed in terms of megabytes, with gigabyte measurements becoming more common usage to describe file sizes.

■ Menubar

Strip of drop-down menus found at the top of the screen. It performs the same function as the bar

of menus attached to the top of every individual application in Windows, but as it's not attached to the application window itself it instead tailors itself to feature only those options relevant to whichever application is foremost on the screen at any one time.

■ Mission Control

Handy feature in Mac OS X 10.7 Lion that lets you see all of the apps and Widgets currently active on your Mac just by swiping the trackpad with four fingers. It builds on the success of the existing Spaces and Exposé features.

■ MobileMe

Online service owned and formerly run by Apple. It offered remote storage of files, Hotmail-style webmail, photo galleries and web publishing. It was a paid-for extra, but as it was so well integrated into the Mac operating system and many of Apple's applications – in particular those in the iLife suite – it was a worthwhile investment for many users.

■ Multi-touch

Term used to describe hardware devices employed by Apple in the iPhone and various MacBooks that allow you to manipulate on-screen elements by sliding, twisting, flicking and pinching your fingers on a screen or trackpad.

■ Numbers

Apple's spreadsheet application, forming part of the iWork suite. It was introduced in 2008 and has its own file format, although it can import and export Microsoft Excel-compatible files. It has excellent design tools, which go a long way to making your spreadsheets look attractive and engaging, but its ability is to include more than one table on a page.

■ Office

Generic term used to describe Microsoft's business applications suite comprising Word (word processor), Excel (spreadsheet), PowerPoint (presentation), and various email and database applications, depending on the year of release and whether it is a PC or Mac edition. Its native file formats have become something of a business standard adhered to by many rival applications.

◼ OPERATING SYSTEM

Software that controls the most fundamental hardware of a computer and passes instructions to it from the applications that they run. Mac OS X and Windows are both operating systems, but other popular alternatives include Linux and Unix, on which Mac OS X itself is based.

◼ PAGES

Apple's own word processing application, found in the iWork suite. It boasts good home-user desktop publishing features, which were once to the detriment of its tools for regular plain text writing, although in later editions this imbalance has been redressed, making Pages a first-class text creation and editing tool.

◼ POINTER

The on-screen arrow moved using the mouse or trackpad. In a spreadsheet such as Excel or Numbers, it is usually replaced by a cross when moving over the grid of cells in a table.

◼ POWER MAC

The predecessor of the Mac Pro, once forming the upper echelons of Apple's desktop computer line and favoured by professional users, particularly in creative and design environments.

◼ PREFERENCES

Each application has a section dedicated to adjustable settings, called Preferences. You'll find it by clicking on the application's name in the menubar at the top of the screen, and then clicking on Preferences in the menu that drops down. More extensive settings used to control how the Mac works in general are found in System Preferences. Find this by clicking on the Apple icon in the top left-hand corner of the screen. Its contents vary according to application.

◼ PROCESSOR

The brain of your computer, the processor is the chip that does all of the calculations that make it work. There are several processors in every machine, covering general system tasks and graphics. All recent Macs use the same kind of main processor as a PC, made by Intel, but older Macs use the so-called PowerPC processor line, and may be unable to run some of the latest software releases, including Adobe Premiere (professional video editing application), FileMaker Bento (database for home-users) and Mac OS X.

◼ RAM

Acronym for Random Access Memory; a series of fast chips used by the processor to temporarily store information while it is being worked on. All data stored in the Ram is lost when the Mac is turned off or rebooted. Files should therefore be saved at regular intervals.

◼ RIGHT-CLICK

Clicking with the right-hand button of a mouse to bring up a menu of options relevant to the item on which you have clicked. The mice that Apple used to ship came with only one button, so right-clicking was could be performed by holding down the Ctrl key while clicking to call up the same menu. Apple's current mouse offering, the Apple Mighty Mouse, can be configured for two-button use in System Preferences.

◼ SOFTWARE UPDATE

Small application found by clicking on the Apple icon in the top-left corner of the screen, which checks with Apple's servers for new and updated versions of the software on your Mac. It will automatically run every so often on its own, but if you notice it has not run in the last couple of weeks, it's worth invoking manually. This is the Mac equivalent of Windows Update and Office Update on the PC.

◼ SPACES

Feature of Mac OS X 10.5 and later that allows you to have up to 16 virtual screens running on your Mac at the same time. This allows you to organise your active applications according to function, or run 16 of them in full-screen mode, instead of windows.

THUNDERBOLT

Interface now being integrated into new Macs that allows for high speed data transfer to a wide range of devices, including connected drives and monitors.

TIME CAPSULE

Hard drive with wireless features, allowing Macs and PCs to connect and use it for storage. It was designed specifically to work hand-in-hand with Time Machine. Time Capsule replaced a feature called AirDisk that was included in pre-release versions of Mac OS X 10.5 Leopard that allowed Time Machine back ups to be made over a wireless network.

TIME MACHINE

Automatic backup system built in to Mac OS X 10.5 and later. Once you have plugged in an external hard drive and given Time Machine permission to use it, the application will copy changes made to your system every hour. Should you lose an important file or make changes that you should not have done you can then roll back through each hour of changes to find the file and return the data to its previous state.

TRACKPAD

Touch-sensitive area on a notebook computer, between the user and the keyboard. Sliding your finger across its surface will move an on-screen cursor, while tapping it will cause the pointer to select the item over which it sits. Usually accompanied by one or two selection buttons just beneath it to perform a similar task. Using two fingers on the trackpad of any MacBook-based notebook scrolls the contents of the current open window.

TRASH

Found on the Dock, the Trash is where you drag files and applications when you want to delete them from your system. Other applications, such as iTunes, may also send files here when you delete them from within their own environment. Items sent to the Trash are not immediately deleted, allowing them to be recovered at a later date if deleted in error. Once emptied, however,

the files are lost forever. The direct equivalent in Windows is the Recycle Bin. Options for securely emptying the Trash write over its contents using blank data to reduce the chance of the original underlying data being recovered using specialist tools, and so are useful to use when selling on your Mac.

USB

Universal Serial Bus; a port and cable combination that lets you transfer data to and from your Mac. It is used to connect almost every kind of device (hence the Universal part of its name) including printers, scanners, iPods, iPads and cameras.

WIFI

Colloquial term used to describe a wide range of wireless networking technologies. It can usually be taken to mean any kind of wireless connection over which you might browse the web or send and receive email.

WINDOW

The container holding an application or an open file on the screen in any graphical operating system, such as Mac OS X. OS X Lion allows for the expansion of all applications to full screen, if their developers support it, thus doing away with their window boundaries, subject to developers including the necessary lines of code to make this possible.

WINDOWS

Microsoft's operating system. The current edition is Windows 7, but its predecessors, Windows Vista and XP, both remain in widespread use. Windows will only run on the Mac with the help of Boot Camp software, which comes as a part of Mac OS X 10.5 Leopard and later, or virtualisation software from third-party developers.

WWDC

Worldwide Developers' Conference held every summer at which Apple outlines its future strategy for Mac OS X, its mobile products and other key technologies, and usually announces a high-end product or two.